How To Be An Agnostic

Also by Mark Vernon

THE GOOD LIFE

THE MEANING OF FRIENDSHIP

PHILOSOPHY FOR THE CURIOUS

ETHICS FOR THE CURIOUS

PLATO'S PODCASTS: The Ancients' Guide to Modern Living

CHAMBERS DICTIONARY OF BELIEFS AND RELIGIONS (editor-in-chief)

UNDERSTAND HUMANISM

WELLBEING (Art of Living Series)

42: DEEP THOUGHT ON LIFE, THE UNIVERSE AND EVERYTHING

WHAT NOT TO SAY: Finding The Right Words At Difficult Moments

BUSINESS: The Key Concepts

How To Be An Agnostic

Mark Vernon

First published in paperback 2008 as *After Atheism: Science, Religion, and the
Meaning of Life* by PALGRAVE MACMILLAN

This revised edition published 2011 by
PALGRAVE MACMILLAN

Palgrave Macmillan in the UK is an imprint of Macmillan Publishers Limited,
registered in England, company number 785998, of Houndmills, Basingstoke,
Hampshire RG21 6XS.

Palgrave Macmillan in the US is a division of St Martin's Press LLC,
175 Fifth Avenue, New York, NY 10010.

Palgrave Macmillan is the global academic imprint of the above companies
and has companies and representatives throughout the world.

Palgrave® and Macmillan® are registered trademarks in the United States,
the United Kingdom, Europe and other countries.

ISBN 978–0–230–29321–2   paperback

This book is printed on paper suitable for recycling and made from fully
managed and sustained forest sources. Logging, pulping and manufacturing
processes are expected to conform to the environmental regulations of the
country of origin.

A catalogue record for this book is available from the British Library.

A catalog record for this book is available from the Library of Congress.

10   9   8   7   6   5   4   3   2   1
20   19   18   17   16   15   14   13   12   11

Printed and bound in Great Britain by
CPI Antony Rowe, Chippenham and Eastbourne

For Nicholas George

Contents

List of Illustrations

Acknowledgements

A book like this is the product of many conversations and encounters, of many experiences and parts of life shared. Thank you and I look forward to more. In terms of producing the text in particular, I want fulsomely to thank Jeremy Carrette, Paul Fletcher and Piers Benn who have read drafts and made suggestions. Needless to say, all faults remaining are mine. Great thanks are also due to my sometime editor Dan Bunyard. For this new edition of the book formerly published as *After Atheism* – here thoroughly revised and added to throughout, including two chapters that are almost completely new and a third entirely new – thanks too to my copyeditor, Sally Daniell, to Laura Conn, Abby Coften and Melanie Blair at Palgrave Macmillan and to Pri Gibbons also at Palgrave Macmillan for championing my cause.

Introduction: There's Something, Not Nothing

> Our doubt is our passion.
>
> Henry James

Imagine that Stephen Hawking, the famous theoretical physicist, is reincarnated. In his last life, in a book called *The Grand Design*, he had declared that philosophy is dead. So, this time round karmic law decrees that his father is a philosopher.

One day, when little Stephen is about five years old, they're sitting in the summer house with Fido, the pet dog. And Stephen asks one of those questions children love to repeat.

Daddy. Yes Stephen? *Why is Fido?* Well, Stephen, Fido had a mummy and daddy like you.

Yeah but, why is Fido? Err, you mean why is he a dog? That's because his parents were dogs, and his parents' parents were dogs too. They belong to what we call the same species. [Stephen is precocious in this life too.]

But why is Fido? Well, we know that Fido's parents' parents' parents' parents – a long way back – were not dogs, but were wolves. That was before human beings made them pets.

Oh. Why is Fido? Before there were wolves there was another species out of which wolves grew. We call it evolution, Stephen, and it's a very important process in the natural world.

Ev-o-lu-tion. [Stephen likes the feel of that word.] *But why is Fido?* Before that species, there was another, and another, and another, all the way back to tiny animals we call cells.

Why IS Fido? I think you're asking about biochemistry now. Err, roughly you can say that when the stuff of which everything is made is put together in a very complicated way – like a fantastic lego puzzle – then it takes on this very special property we call life.

WHY IS FIDO? Before life? There was just stuff – matter. It hung around for many billions of years on planet earth.

But why is FIDO? Before the earth, there were stars, and galaxies, subatomic particles and strange things like black holes. [Stephen has the odd feeling that he knows all about black holes, though he's only five.]

Yeah but, why is Fido? Scientists have thought it all started with a big bang, Stephen, a kind of spontaneous eruption out of which everything came. Or if not that, then a sudden inflation or spot springing from a brane.

Wow! Why is Fido? Well, whatever the scientists decide, it'll be according to the laws of physics.

BUT WHY IS FIDO?

At this point Stephen's father pauses. Being a philosopher, he realises that Stephen is now asking a very different question to all the ones he's asked before. You see, before, his questions could be answered with reference to some preceding state of affairs, out of which Fido can be said to have come. Now, though, he is asking about where everything came from, and being everything, there is no antecedent reality to refer to. To start to talk of nothing, not even abstract laws of nature, let alone wildly compressed energy, is to try to put everything in the context of nothing. But nothing is precisely that: not a quantum field fluctuating in the vacuum, not one universe springing out of a multiverse. Nothing is more radical than that. It is nothing. It's impossible to conceive of, in fact. No wonder Stephen's father pauses.

I'm not sure we can ask that question, Stephen. It makes no sense.
But I want to know: why is Fido?
Well, some say the universe just is. There's a famous philosopher from about 100 years ago, Bertrand Russell, and he thought that.

[Stephen harrumphs.] *But why is Fido?*
There is another answer.
Yes? [Stephen sits up.]
It's not exactly an answer.
Oh?
More like a mystery.
I like mysteries.
I'm not sure you're going to like this one.
Tell me!
Well, there was another philosopher who was a friend of
Bertrand Russell, in fact. He was called Ludwig Wittgenstein,
and he said, 'Not how the world is, but that it is, is the
mystery.'
Wow!
There's something else.
What?
The mystery is sometimes given a name.
What's the name?
It's called God.

If this dialogue sparks even a scintilla of curiosity in you, this
book should be of interest. It could be said to hang on that small,
nagging and momentous question: why is there something, not
nothing? It's been called the secular miracle – though it's one
that some dismiss, particularly when the asking leads, in its final
stages, to the mystery signified by the word 'God'. Not that you
or I necessarily find belief in God straightforward or immediately
compelling, a hesitancy that doubles when it comes to trusting
any particular religion and its systems. This book is for agnostics. Neither, though, are you a wannabe atheist, as some of the
committed godless are wont to describe us (which treats us like
some gay men treat bisexuals: gay really, if only we'd properly
come out.) You have a sense of the spiritual in life too, by which
I mean that thread of transcendence that runs through being
human and eludes the best descriptions of biologists, psychologists and sociologists. It's often hidden though shared, perhaps in

music. It's only glimpsed, though is as undeniable as a medieval spire. It takes us beyond that which can be conveyed by the laws of nature – though wonder at those laws will also suggest it.

The spiritual can be likened to light, according to the medieval writer Bonaventure. We don't actually see light, he reasoned, but rather we see what light reveals – things, colours, shadows. More remarkably, if we did see light, then we presumably wouldn't see anything else at all: to see light would be like staring into a luminescent fog. Rather, light is like the carrier wave of a radio signal. It must be present to see, but must be invisible in order to allow seeing. The spiritual too is a way of seeing the world, in the colours and shadows of meaning.

In other words, the agnosticism that stirs me is not a sterile kind of uncertainty, which sits on the fence, or worse, can't be bothered to articulate what it breezily doubts. The position I want to flesh out is engaged. It senses that what we don't know is as thrilling as what we do know. And nowhere is this encounter with the deepest aspects of the human condition clearer than when raising the question of God. What I'll attempt to ask is not just how to be an agnostic, but why it matters too. I think it matters much because to be an agnostic is to be at the vanguard of the attempt to revivify the symbols and reasons, myths and rituals that have long conveyed the spiritual to our forebears, though they have been losing their lustre, emptying out, in the centuries of the modern period.

It's an important task because the spiritual is so crucial a part of what it is to be human. It's like love: deny it, and it will distort you. You'd expect religious writers to assert as much, as they do. Augustine talked about individuals having restless hearts that seek rest in the divine. But secular writers can convey the same sensibility. Socrates is one, and a particular inspiration for me. He realised that, for us humans, our own life is too small for us. We are not like other creatures who appear to be content with their lot. We yearn for more. And yet, neither are we like the gods, who have it all. This in-between status is a tremendous blessing, because it fires our creativity, innovation and passion. However, it can also be a curse, because the desire for more will be frustrated, at least on occasion. We must learn to live within our nature, Socrates realised. It's an art and for this insight, and the life in which he worked it out, we remember him. That he wrote nothing, and yet remains iconic over 2000 years on, is evidence to me that this wise ignorance is of profound significance.

Priestly formation

Our spiritual predicament became pressing for me at a personal level because I used to be a priest. I trained for three years at an Anglican theological college. It was a dysfunctional institution that inspired and dismayed in turn. We excused it by saying that at least it was never lukewarm. Then, I worked as a clergyman in a high Church of England parish in the North East of England. It was a role with a clear sense of purpose being situated in a working-class community where, if much else had departed, the church remained.

But mostly it was not a sense of social justice that made me don a dog-collar. Nor was I like those Christians who have a passion for conversion coupled to a certainty that belief is as clear as the summer sky. I was ordained because I was gripped by a religious imagination; the human spirit that cannot put meaning, beauty and transcendence – the very fact of existence – down. I loved the big questions. Friedrich Schleiermacher, the theologian, had stressed that religious feeling is primary, dogmatics secondary: 'True religion is sense and taste for the Infinite,' he wrote. That made eminent sense to me. I felt drawn to another theologian, Paul Tillich, when he wrote that God is not a being, nor the monarch of monotheism, but is being-itself, the ground or power of being. Or there's the philosopher Ludwig Wittgenstein's celebrated intuition that beyond the world of the senses, that can be captured in propositions, there are things that can only be shown or intuited, and so might be best passed over in silence. The weightiness of such theology and the resonances of catholic liturgy mattered to me because I longed to glimpse these mysteries. I took it that questing and doubts were more energising of an authentically religious outlook than any confessional formulations, which were, at best, pointers. And at the time of my ordination, buoyed up by the massive pillars and ancient sanctity of Durham cathedral, I found a certainty: God is love, love of the good, beautiful and true. And we in his Church are called to be lovers – I say that advisedly – too.

This, I was to realise, is a sensibility that is profoundly felt and easily perturbed. The problem was that I could not say for certain how it all added up: how could it, when its object is God who is not an object or even ultimately a 'who'. So, in retrospect it is not surprising that disillusionment with God's earthly work set in too fast. The presenting symptoms for my crisis were loneliness in the job and frustration with the church. Underneath that a number of neither coherent nor attractive objections raged. It depressed me that some clergy spent so much time policing their version of orthodoxy – monitoring who believed what about the Bible, the resurrection, homosexuality or women priests. It annoyed me that people wanted security from churchgoing more than challenge. The 'hatch, match and dispatch' routine that filled the week in between Sundays felt more like an industrial process than rites of passage. I was uncomfortable being an ambassador for a national organisation that often seemed at least as hypocritical as it was helpful.

Against this background, the voices of theologians and philosophers came to seem irrelevant. They implied that dogmatics should be derivative of the religious quest, whereas the church, in practice, seemed to do the reverse. So, I turned increasingly to humanist thinkers. 'Ah!', I began to think. Here is an account of things on the ground that is better than the double-talk of theology. Here is a discourse with edge. The threads of my faith thinned. And then snapped. Seeking succumbed to a new certainty. Doubts became a refusal of God. And now how I suspected that love-talk. It seemed like an excuse, like an opiate

Illus. I.1: Durham Cathedral has stood for over 900 years, 'half church of God, half castle 'gainst the Scot', as Sir Walter Scott put it.

to cover harsh realities: in truth, there is no 'more'. For spiritual read superstition. For transcendent yearnings read The God Delusion. After a little less than three years in the church, I quit. I had become a conviction atheist, a lover of the freedom and reason of the deicidal age.

It felt like growing up, like the history of humanity's conception of divinity played out in my own life. For centuries, people believed in many gods. Then, in a gradual process that began before Christ, tribal cultures mingled with each other and realised that their gods were like other gods: polytheism gave way to monotheism. And after that – and this, I now reckoned, was the genius of Christianity – God became a man, which also meant that Man had become God. Paradoxical though it may seem, with the birth of Christ, the death of God was only a matter of time. How lucky we are that this has been made manifest in our own age.

Cultures of certainty

It was exhilarating. Living waters of Enlightenment thought were mine for the imbibing in a new phase of life. So it surprised me, 18 months or so after leaving the church, that I had a breakdown. The presenting symptoms of my collapse were not unusual: a love affair that did not work out. That I could not stop weeping for days after its denouement, so much so that I had to hide away in a friend's house, was a sign that something more substantial was wrong. I had precipitous dreams in which I fell down dark tunnels and woke up conscious of living in a godless world.

Once I managed to gather myself again, I interpreted this flood of feeling as my emotions catching up with what had been an almost wholly mental decision to doff the clerical collar. This, I reckoned, must be what it is like to stare emptiness in the face. The question was whether I had the courage to continue in what I then took to be an ultimately meaningless life. I envisaged the experience as a kind of rite of passage: my whole person had now been born into atheism.

When Nietzsche announced the death of God, he told a story, and it seemed to reflect something of my experience. A madman entered a marketplace where atheists were about their secular business. 'I seek God! I seek God!', he yelled – and they laughed. 'Is he hiding or on holiday?', they suggested in contempt.

For a while, after I left, I scoffed at believers too – until, that is, I noticed how Nietzsche continued. The crowd had the smirks wiped off their faces, for this madman was also a prophet. 'We are murderers,' he shouted, before proceeding to tell them what their killing had done. We think that we are now masters of the world, but we have actually unchained the sun, made our home cold, and strayed unawares into infinite space. 'Is not the greatness of this deed too great for us?', Nietzsche concluded. 'Must we ourselves not become gods simply to appear worthy of it?' Man as the new God: how frightening a thought is that.

His point is that the death of God is not a triumph, it is a tragedy. And a while after my atheistic turn, I began to sense it. My newfound certainty crumbled because atheism, as much as religious conservatism, seemed to entail a poverty of spirit. Militant non-believers began to look as unappealing as the fundamentalists who do not do doubt. Then, when I thought back to the breakdown, it told me something different. The emotional trauma was to do with emptiness for sure, and the way that my mind had forced my spirit to run before it could walk. But it also told me of the need to give voice to the restless heart's reasons, which reason does not always understand.

Again, Nietzsche understood as much. If all can be explained by science, as is this man-made-god's belief and hope, why have values or spirit at all, he asked? If nature and history can be understood as mechanisms, rules and laws, then is not purpose, imagination and freedom inevitably sidelined and slowly squeezed out? If we are not something, are we not in fact nothing? Of course, in practice, even the fiercest atheist adopts some set of values to light up the world with meaning. They might even say that inventing, not inheriting, morality is part of the liberation from God. Nietzsche tried to make himself something through sheer force of will. Other atheists invoke human sympathy as the basis for morality, so that our home does not seem so cold. Only human sympathy is never simple, and is often quite vile – and their evolutionist friends whisper to them that it could be a delusion too, a mere adaptation that's good for survival.

Part of the trouble is that we are not divine: we can't pull something out of nothing. So this humanism can easily be made to look flimsy and challenged. It is why, I suspect, contemporary ethical discourse so often sounds like a repeat record. 'Freedom of speech, human rights, equality for all!' 'Freedom of speech, human rights, equality for all!' 'Freedom of speech, human rights, equality for all!' Yes, yes and yes! But to what end? On what basis? And why? The same thought exposes the emptiness of what often seems like modern life's sole goal, namely, the pursuit of consumptive growth and technological progress. Many great goods have arisen with the spread of wealth and the appliance of science. The trouble is that this way of life only nourishes us in certain ways. It can entertain us, but not make us happy. It can heal us, but not make us whole. It can feed us, but only in body. It offers defences, but does not leave us grounded. The double trouble is that this material approach to life is so good at the entertaining, healing, feeding and defending that it is easy to believe, or hope, that it can, or one day will, solve all other human ills too; that it's enough. Some say it might even make us immortal – another deification of humanity.

What is missing is meaning. A materialistic humanism finds it hard to address the questions of morality, values and spirit. Following the scientific rationalism it holds in high regard, it tends to boil it all down to a discussion of mechanisms, rules and laws. This may create an illusion of understanding and a sense of purpose. But meaninglessness keeps rearing its head because, well, mechanisms, rules and laws are actually not very meaningful. This is why atheism felt like a poverty of spirit to me. This is why 'Why?' is the cry of our age and we are no longer quite sure who we are. Sisyphus is our hero: forcing the boulder of his humanity to the top of a mountain, hoping to lend it the authority of a high place, only to see it roll down again. In truth, it's absurd, as Camus realised – and only a few can honestly stomach that thought. 'Thus wisdom wishes to appear most bright when it doth tax itself,' says Angelo in Shakespeare's *Measure for Measure*.

What is doubly distressing is that contemporary Christian discourse often sounds the same way too. It readily loses its humanity and resorts to the same discussion of mechanisms (being saved), rules (being good) and laws (being right). In so doing, it empties itself out.

It was with the Copernican revolution that things began to change. The new science seemed to render many Christian conceptions of the universe unlikely or invalid. The Victorian age that followed was one in which belief struggled with disbelief and science seemed to be winning out. Hence Nietzsche's announcement. What is overlooked, as I did at first, is that he also exposed science as bad religion – because it unchains the sun and leaves people floating unguided among the stars. Science did not win conclusively. But it has been successful to the extent that it has profoundly affected the terms of debate. It has stolen for itself the crown of authority which was once worn by the so-called Queen of Sciences, namely theology. The imprimatur today comes not from Rome but the lab.

Thus, having been challenged to justify itself, Christian orthodoxy seeks evidence too, of a transcendental kind. It used to be faith seeking understanding, now it is surety seeking proof; it was a search, it is now a statement. As one of the founders of American fundamentalism, A.C. Dixon, declared: 'I am a Christian because I am a Thinker, a Rationalist, a Scientist.' The most successful examples of contemporary churchgoing are conservative and often reactionary. Even liberal churches have not escaped unscathed. They are increasingly defined by what they are not against – be that being not against homosexuality, women priests, contraception or divorce. What they struggle to do is to articulate a vision on their own account. They too sense that the

11

great myths which inform their traditions have lost weight. Can they speak to us still, my nervous Christian friends will ask.

For a while, after atheism, I thought I should keep a Wittgensteinian silence about these things; to 'pass over in silence'. If my journey had taught me anything, I reasoned, it was that sometimes to speak is only to reduce, possibly to ruin. But that did not last for long. For there's also the attempt to catch a glimpse. It has also been said that some people are not musical when it comes to religion. Well it became apparent to me that I was. My imagination was rekindled and I began to enjoy the big questions again. I could not pretend that centuries of spirituality should be discounted as the flotsam and jetsam of more primitive and superstitious times. I figured that while I didn't have a priestly vocation, I was 'called' – by circumstance, temperament and curiosity at least – to engage with the perennial human quest.

That said, I could not simply become a Christian again. My scoffing at belief stopped but so had the appeal of belonging to a church. This was partly a matter of being sensible: I grew to value Christianity again, to value my links with it, but warily. I need a certain distance. It was also a matter of being honest. The modern Church requires you to adhere to a creed that is more substantial than God is love: one should really be able to make a good stab at believing that God is Father, God is incarnate in Christ, God is in his Church and God is revealed in the Bible. Hand on heart, straightforwardly, I could not and cannot. I can no longer do the apologetics for the Christian tradition that the priest must be able to do, though I do want to encounter the tradition they conserve and represent. I remember hearing a comment made by the British politician Tony Benn, on how he sides with the prophets in the Hebrew Bible – the ones who say that God is in the desert and the wandering – rather than the priests, who build splendid but defensive temples. No doubt, prophets and priests are both needed: we humans must dialogue with those who see things differently to us because no single view will do. But I felt clearer about my place in this discourse now.

I was neither a believer nor a non-believer – a doubting Thomas, doubting Richard Dawkins combo. My suspicion is that this predicament, at least in outline, is a common one. Not only am I a product, as it were, of the development of Western ideas over the last few hundred years, since the Enlightenment that precipitated Nietzsche's death of God; but I feel this kind of story must resonate with the many who are as dissatisfied with conservative belief as they are with militant disbelief. Around 40 per cent of Americans are not members of a church, though say they do not simply not believe in God. And about the same number of Britons frankly admit they don't really know what to think.

On being agnostic

We are what is called agnostics, or to be more precise Christian agnostics. I think it is important to emphasise the 'Christian' for two reasons. First, it is in a Christian context that agnosticism as a question of assent typically comes about – not least because of the modern history of Christianity and science. In Eastern religions, being agnostic makes little sense since the form of these religions is so different. And in Judaism and Islam, religious systems that are in some ways close to Christianity, it seems more natural to talk of degrees of practice than belief. Second, it is better to talk of Christian agnosticism because the idea of God with which agnostics struggle (and which atheists deny) is Christian. It is monotheistic and shaped by the Christian tradition.

Agnostic – meaning 'not known' – was a word first coined by T.H. Huxley in 1869. As a Victorian populariser of science, he found himself at the centre of the religious crisis sparked by the rise of evolutionary science. The agnostic, Huxley said, is not an atheist but is someone who tries everything, and holds only to 'that which is good'. In an essay, entitled Agnosticism, he wrote:

Positively the principle may be expressed: In matters of the intellect, follow your reason as far as it will take you, without regard to any other consideration. And negatively: In matters

13

of the intellect do not pretend that conclusions are certain which are not demonstrated or demonstrable.

Huxley and others like him were passionate men. They brought their whole person – reason and feeling, learning and experience – to debates with dogmatists of science and religion alike. Today, though, the word agnostic has come to mean something both less engaged and more passive. Its strong sense – the considered

Illus. I.2: T.H. Huxley coined the word agnosticism, and it's one that has stuck for describing a mid-position between the certainties of atheism and theism.

conviction that nothing of ultimate things can be known with certainty – has been subsumed in the weak sense of someone who is simply non-committal or indifferent. This must partly have happened because times have changed. In Huxley's day evolution was setting a new agenda, and Christianity often felt under threat. Eminent Victorians had to struggle with what they might believe and what they should doubt, and with that struggle came their convictions – for or against or deliberately unsure. Today, though, someone can be agnostic with little more than a shrug of the shoulders. Like flat-pack goods, agnosticism can just click into place, part of the drab mental furniture of the theologically uninspired. I remember a flyer we were given at the start of the Oxford lecture course on the historical Jesus. It contained a list of what he can be known to have said for sure. It was not long. However, the real sadness was not that so little is known about Jesus, but that it takes so little effort to arrive at that conclusion today. This is inevitable given the settled results of biblical criticism. But before it had established these results there was something to be fought over, something to be passionate about. Similarly, the introduction to analytical philosophy course I attended had me doubting I was sitting on a chair in less than five minutes. It was an uncertainty that was so easy it was boring.

Victorian agnosticism has been likened to God's funeral, though it was a way of seeing the world and a framework with which to approach life. The weak form of agnosticism of today can often be no such practice, or barely a principle, but merely a tacit non-belief. This presents two challenges to someone who senses that agnosticism has more to offer than that. First, it is necessary to show that agnosticism still matters at an intellectual level. If it had work to do in the Victorian period – to challenge the excesses of religion and science – then we must identify what work it has to do today, and why that matters. Second, if agnosticism is to be an alternative to dogmatic scientific and religious worldviews, and not just a critique of them, it needs to move beyond being an intellectual exercise to become an ethos. To what can the agnostic turn to satisfy the spiritual side of ourselves? How are we to talk about transcendence? Can we fill the God-shaped hole? More broadly, our question is not just what is agnosticism, but what is what can be called the agnostic spirit? How can it live?

In fact, I believe, the agnostic spirit is vital in science, for believers, and lies at the heart of what it is to be human – which is to say that our humanity is reduced without it. Properly understood it has a quality that everyone, bar the tyrant, would cultivate.

The writings of the philosopher Kierkegaard suggest why it should matter to the unquestioning believer. For him, faith was a problem not because it was disproved but because it seemed so impossible. He develops this in his book *Fear and Trembling* around the quintessential figure of faith, Abraham. Why Abraham? Because when God asked him to sacrifice his son Isaac, as a test of faith, Abraham said yes. On every conceivable level, this 'yes' of faith was impossible for Kierkegaard:

> [W]hen I have to think about Abraham I am virtually annihilated. I am all the time aware of that monstrous paradox that is the constant of Abraham's life. I am constantly repulsed, and my thought, for all its passion, is unable to enter into it, cannot come one hairbreadth further. I strain every muscle to catch sight of it, but the same instant I become paralysed.

Agnosticism is the position from which Kierkegaard struggles with faith. The paradox is that it is his agnosticism that gives faith its meaning: he argued that doubt underpins faith, since it ensures that the believer really has faith and faith alone. He calls this the leap of faith. He knows that it would be the most remarkable, refined and extraordinary thing. That is why it is agonisingly out of reach. He therefore despises those who say they have it or, for that matter, simply dismiss it: if faith can turn water into wine, he quips, they would turn wine into water; they make a 'clearance sale' out of theological convictions.

Kierkegaard is not the only modern prophet who challenges Christianity in such a way. Another is Simone Weil. She too talked of not being able to become a Christian, out of a kind of faithful humility. She wrote: 'For it seemed to me certain, and I still think so today, that one cannot wrestle enough with God if one does it out of pure regard for Truth.' So if modern belief judges itself according to the standards set by a fact-testing, relevancy-seeking scientific humanism, the challenge is to recover the spirituality of the religious imagination. There is a negative and positive aspect to this. Negatively, I want to argue that being beholden to the scientific worldview distorts Christianity, and arguably other religions too. Positively, by exploring the apophatic tradition, as well as revisiting the so-called proofs of God along with issues like the problem of evil, I want to make the case that not knowing who God is, and even that God is – being radically agnostic – is essential to theology. It is more fundamental than anything positive that can be said about God. The general point is that the agnostic spirit and a spiritual way of life are one and the same thing. To lose the former is to lose the latter.

When it comes to science, agnosticism is crucial too: it is for those who are neither utopian about a technological future, nor Luddite about the achievements of the present. Negatively, the technological age needs a vivid view of the limits of science, so that it does not put too much faith in it, and an agnostic attitude can provide that. Positively, agnosticism takes these limits as pointing beyond what science can comprehend, to the persistent mysteries of life – aspects of existence that carry value and meaning because they are bigger than us, and are best captured and expressed in non-scientific ways because they are glimpsed not grasped. The hope is that these ways of talking can regain some of the authority that the scientific worldview tends otherwise to monopolise. Moreover it seems to me that the reinvigoration of these other visions of reality is an increasing pressing need. In a society that faces what has been called an epidemic of ennui, and is on the verge of environmental crisis, it is not just more technology we need but more than technology.

Remarkably, science actually quite spontaneously inspires new kinds of spiritual response, from the flamboyant New Age to a

17

quiet sense of wonder. The metaphor of warfare, to characterise the relationship between science and religion, is at best only partially accurate. It's as if human beings cannot but help detect more than meets the eye, which might be called the spiritual – and not just because to do so serves some obscure, deluded evolutionary instinct. Rather, the success of science is linked to the modesty of its ambition. For, by strictly affirming only what is empirically verifiable, it highlights the fuller panoply of human experience that is no less real, just beyond its scope. This partly becomes clear when posing the biggest scientific questions: what is consciousness, how do we perceive things as good or beautiful, whence the laws of nature, why is there something not nothing? But it also springs quite naturally from discussions of science itself. It's present in Darwin's famous last sentence from *On The Origin of Species*:

> There is grandeur in this view of life, with its several powers, having been originally breathed into a few forms or into one; and that, whilst this planet has gone cycling on according to the fixed law of gravity, from so simple a beginning endless forms most beautiful and most wonderful have been, and are being, evolved.

If science has affected the terms of debate, it has also given new impetus to natural theology, or what we'll explore here as 'cosmic religion'. Can it satisfy the yearnings Socrates identified? Interestingly, other philosophers of his time thought so. So the loss of confidence in traditional religious practices – church-going and the like – does not mean that *homo religiosus* has become an endangered species. The evidence is that many regard themselves as 'spiritual but not religious', another facet of the agnostic landscape we'll critique.

Wisdom's lovers

In Plato's dialogue the *Phaedrus*, the eponymous friend of Socrates asks the founder of Western philosophy a question.

Where and how can he find truth? Phaedrus admires the orator Lysias, thinking him a great speech-maker and writer. He presumes that he is also, therefore, wise. Socrates replies that this is not right: 'To call him wise, Phaedrus, seems to me too much, and proper only for a god. To call him wisdom's lover – a philosopher – or something similar would fit him better.' This is someone who does not possess but lacks the wisdom they desire.

Socrates is talking about himself. He is a lover of limits, of being thrown onto the unknown. He is also someone who turned to philosophy having become disillusioned with the overreaching science of his times. And he is a man with a religious imagination. He is fascinated by the big questions of life. He understands the limits of being human, of standing in between the mostly ignorant animals and the wise gods. The seminal moment in his career came with a message from an oracle. It told him that uncertainty is characteristic of the human condition, but that human beings need not be pig ignorant. They can understand their predicament by becoming conscious of what they do and don't know – by being wise agnostics. This is why Socrates calls himself a lover of wisdom, a philosopher. Moreover, being a philosopher added up not just to a legacy of thought but to a life that informed a civilisation. It mattered. Socrates is, if you like, the patron saint of religiously-inclined agnostics.

In that same spirit, we start with a life – the life of Socrates.

Socrates' Quest: The Agnostic Spirit

I am very conscious that I am not wise at all.

Socrates

If you had to choose a site for the greatest oracle in the ancient world you would be hard pushed to beat Delphi. Sitting both confidently and precipitously on a ledge below the Phaedraides – the 'Shining Cliffs' – in central Greece, it looks like the vertiginous utterances must have felt to the people who sought Apollo's word there for over 1000 years. Today, a wide road, built for coaches, brings visitors up from the plain of Thebes. Its sleepy meander seems oblivious to the calamitous events that took place beneath the tarmac: 'there is no road away from Delphi', said Seneca, reflecting on Oedipus' attempt to flee the oracle's curse by the same route, only to kill his father on the way. But after an hour or so, you turn one final bend, and suddenly the telltale signs of broken pillars and a ticket office emerge from the cypress trees.

All that remains of the Temple of Apollo itself are the foundations and a handful of resurrected columns that tantalisingly indicate where the portico and its famous inscriptions – 'Know Thyself' and 'Nothing in Excess' – once stood. The most recurrent feature on the site is that of the treasury building, mini-strongholds built by Greece's competing city-states to show off their wealth and strength. These may be thought of as spoilers, unromantic reminders that religion and politics merged with one another for the ancients, or that most of what so moved them has been lost. But a visit to Delphi will not disappoint.

Go at the end of the day, as the sun sets behind Mount Parnassos and throws yellow light onto the stones. Below is a

Illus. 1.1: The ruins of Delphi, high on the slopes of the 'Shining Cliffs'.

valley flooded with olive trees that appear to flow westward onto the lowlands and, in the distance, the sparkling Gulf of Corinth. The hubbub of modern tourism lessens and the hubbub of past pilgrims re-emerges: it is easy to imagine tawdry trinkets being bought in the stoa as personal mementos of a blessing, alongside the machinations of the Hellenic heavyweights who came to what was a veritable United Nations in order to curry favour and win control.

It was to this place that Socrates' childhood friend, Chaerephon, came in the 430s BCE. First, he purified himself in the Castalian spring and paid a fee. Then, he bought a goat for sacrifice, over which was thrown a jug of cold water. The goat shuddered, for this was the sign that the oracle would respond to a question. Next, he had to wait for his lot to be drawn. And finally he was ushered into the holy chamber to speak with the Pythia. Sitting on a tripod, wearing a bay leaf crown, and, some say, sniffing the hallucinogenic vapours that drifted up from a cleft in the rock, she uttered the words that launched a quest that would shape a civilisation. 'Is anyone wiser than Socrates?' Chaerephon asked impulsively. 'No one is wiser,' she said.

Solving the riddle

Chaerephon returned to Athens, told his friend what the oracle had said, and awaited his response. Socrates was only in his mid-30s and yet he already had a considerable reputation as a man of significance. Chaerephon must have thought that the endorsement of the oracle would not only be a huge confidence boost but, as the word got around, would propel him to his rightful place among the greats.

He could not have been more wrong. Socrates was profoundly disturbed. He could not accept what Chaerephon reported. The reason was that although his career had taken off, he already knew that human knowledge was strictly earthbound. His wisdom, such as it was, consisted in a growing sense that he was not wise. Like an observer of the night sky humbled by the immensity of the universe, his idea of philosophy was not of inevitable progress towards the bright stars of certainty and illumination, but was a dawning awareness that the forces that shape the world stem from dark masses and unknown energies. He resisted the accolade because it smacked of hubris, the very thing that he suspected was going wrong with the discourse and politics of the still newly democratic Athens.

But what then should he make of the oracle? The Pythia could be lying. Argument in Athens was a competitive business, with fortunes made or lost as reputations waxed and waned. It was not beyond the bounds of possibility that a rival Sophist had taken the opportunity to speak with an attendant priest. A suitably compliant chap might have 'interpreted' the oracle for Chaerephon. The rival's hope might have been that a divine declaration of Socrates' supremacy would make the young upstart look ridiculous.

More likely, though, the oracle was a puzzle. It must be put to the test. So Socrates decided he would search Athens to see if he could find someone who was wiser than he.

He went first to speak to Anytus, a well-known Athenian and rising political star. He was thought to be talented, and indeed thought himself very able. If Anytus proved wiser than Socrates, then the oracle would be refuted. He asked the politician questions about what was just and pious, and beautiful and good – standard fare for someone whose business was inspiring the masses in this democratic city. But Socrates discovered that Anytus' wisdom was flaky. Worse, he believed the myth of his own brilliance. This man was not wiser than Socrates because he was not wise at all.

The first test had failed. But it did give Socrates a clue as to the meaning of the riddle. Anytus knew nothing worthwhile but thought he did. This differed from Socrates who knew he knew nothing. 'So I am likely to be wiser than he is to this small extent, that I do not think I know what I do not know.'

One fool does not condemn an entire class, so Socrates went to speak with another politician, and another, systematically working his way through the leaders of the Assembly. No one passed the test: 'I found that those who had the highest reputation were nearly the most deficient.' Moreover, mixed in with a growing distaste for the self-righteousness of politicians and mounting alarm at what it meant for the city, he noticed that he was becoming unpopular. The gadfly was emerging from his chrysalis and another dimension to the oracle's words was becoming clear. His search was starting to feel like a mission, to bring down the mighty from their Assembly seats.

Ancient Greek religion was unlike our own in many respects. In particular, it had no canonical texts, like the Bible, or magisterium of priests to enforce doctrine. But one group of thinkers was particularly important in defining the limits of pious behaviour and what counted as orthodoxy, namely, the poets. The works of Homer and Hesiod were especially venerated. Their stories of courage and sayings on the virtues provided the canon-like texts of the day. Phrases like, 'Of all things, change is sweet', or, 'Friends have everything in common', littered debate as proof texts and reference points, much like public figures today cite truisms such as, 'People love freedom', or, 'Treat others as you would be treated'.

The poets were, in other words, another group of people one or more of whom might be wiser than Socrates. He certainly had some great comic and tragic writers as contemporaries, including Sophocles, Euripides and Aristophanes. So, having found politicians lacking, Socrates took to questioning these individuals. Again, he wanted to 'catch himself more ignorant'. He identified what he thought were the most meaningful and considered examples of their work and asked them about it. He was disappointed. And further, he noticed that bystanders who happened to overhear them as they talked, often offered better interpretations of the poems than the poets themselves. This led Socrates to think that their poetry was not bad *per se*; he was not a Philistine. Rather, poets confused their ability to use words with wisdom. 'I soon realised that the poets do not compose their poems with real knowledge, but by some inborn talent and inspiration, like seers and prophets who also say many fine things without any understanding of what they say...'

The wisdom of politicians and poets was found wanting. Socrates next wondered whether the oracle was referring to a different kind of knowledge, that of artisans and professionals. After all, he reasoned, they know how to make things like shoes and how to do things like heal someone, matters about which he knew nothing. Surely, they would be wiser than he. He spoke to them too.

It turned out that Athenian craftsman were certainly good at their craft. But like the London taxi driver who has the Knowledge and an opinion on everything else, they made the mistake of thinking that an ability in one area meant they were knowledgeable about everything else too. A third group of people had been questioned and shown up for their ignorance.

But at last Socrates was getting it. 'Would I prefer to be as I am with neither their wisdom nor their ignorance, or to have both?' he asked himself. He would prefer to be as he was, not wise, but not ignorant of his lack of wisdom either. And with this realisation the riddle from the oracle was solved. He understood what it meant. 'This man among you, mortals, is wisest who, like Socrates, understands that his wisdom is worthless.'

Man the measure?

Today it is easy to think of Socrates as a champion of rationalism – a critical mind who was not truly appreciated for centuries, when the clouds of religious superstition cleared, as it's sometimes put. However, what can be gleaned of the historical Socrates, through Plato's appropriation of him, suggests that he was no such atheistic figure at all. Rather, he was a conviction agnostic.

Agnosticism about gods, that sometimes became or was interpreted as atheism, was one of the features of developments in fifth-century BCE Greece of which Socrates was part. Protagoras' book *On Gods* captured the mood. Its first sentence reads:

About the gods I cannot say either that they are or that they are not, nor how they are constituted in shape; for there is much which prevents knowledge, the unclarity of the subject and the shortness of human life.

Protagoras veiled the gods with uncertainty. He also raised the prospect that human knowledge is relative: 'The measure of all things is man, for things that are that they are, for things that are not that they are not.'

Plato seems to have taken a more conservative view of what we would now call religious beliefs. In the *Laws*, he writes:

> Nowadays some people don't trust in gods at all, while others believe they are not concerned about mankind; and there are others – the worst and most numerous category – who hold that in return for a miserable sacrifice here and a little flattery there, the gods will help them to steal enormous sums of money and rescue them from all sorts of heavy penalties.

He objects to the wilful derision and self-centred trivialisation of religious practices because of the arrogance associated with both. He basically thought that respect for spiritual matters was good. At worst, it encouraged an attitude conducive to the virtue of humility. That said, he struggles at many points in his dialogues with what a proper conception of the gods might be. 'It is difficult to find out the father and creator of the universe, and to explain him once found to the multitude is an impossibility,' Timeaus says to Socrates in the dialogue called *Timaeus*, continuing: 'If, then, Socrates, we find ourselves in many points unable to make our discourse of the generation of the gods and the universe in every way wholly consistent and exact, you must not be surprised. Nay, we must be well content if we can provide an account not less likely than another's; we must remember that I who speak, and you who are my audience, are but men and should be satisfied to ask for not more than the likely story.'

Socrates too is presented as being in between the extremes of methodological atheism and superstitious belief, though in a different way to Protagoras again. It seems he thought that a regard for religious practice was a good thing for human beings because of the way it focused on his central interest: how we might understand the nature of human ignorance – our status in between animals and gods. This agnosticism leaves open questions about the nature and existence of divinities, because nothing much can be said about either matter. (Xenophon puts an apparently positive argument about the existence of gods into Socrates' mouth in his Memoirs of Socrates but its purpose – in Xenophon's slightly clumsy way – is negative; to distance Socrates from the accusation of atheism. It clearly does not work as a proof, and Socrates in life would have seen straight through it.) So, Socrates' theology – his God-talk – would have been almost wholly conducted at the human level, around human limits. The value of the divine was to remind us of what lies beyond us. It's a spiritual stance that coincides with his understanding of himself as a philosopher.

Beautiful people

The story of Socrates questioning the people of Athens is the story of his full emergence onto the public stage. It is told in the *Apology*, probably Plato's earliest dialogue and also closest to the historical Socrates. The dialogue is a reconstruction of the speech Socrates made to defend himself at his trial. In it he also rehearses what was, in effect, his philosophical creed:

1. The human condition is one of uncertainty.
2. Reason, coupled to an agnostic attitude, can help us understand that condition.
3. Human wisdom, such as it is, is found in a deep appreciation of the limits of our understanding.
4. Such self-knowledge is best gained with others and seeking it is to care for the soul.
5. The 'ignorant wise', those who lack or refuse this self-knowledge, ought to be challenged for everyone's sake.

The creed caused him great difficulties for he was very good at undermining the security and wounding the vanity of his fellow over-confident citizens. We read that people thought talking to Socrates was like being stung by a ray. Others rapidly made themselves scarce when they saw him coming. If he was hard to tolerate, they were hard on Socrates too. His new philosophical vocation rapidly became a source of danger to his person. The men he tended to upset the most were also the most powerful, and therefore the most ambitious and most prone to violence. They slandered him in ways that were hard for him to refute. At his trial, Socrates complains that they accused him of things that he himself despised. For example, they said that in debate he made 'the worse argument the stronger'. This was something the Sophists did, those professional know-it-alls who could be bought and who turned philosophy into a cockfight. To accuse Socrates of doing the same thing was to misunderstand him completely: he plumbed ignorance. They also said he sought meaning in the clouds. One of the surviving plays of Aristophanes is *The Clouds*, a harsh satire caricaturing Socrates as a nebulous philosophiser. This was dangerous because it carried the implication of atheism, not so much not believing in gods, as questioning the gods people did believe in – a position that while not unknown or overly shocking could become politically charged, should someone choose to use it against you. Protagoras had only just escaped being executed when his agnosticism was misinterpreted in this way.

However, there was a silver lining to these dark clouds of unpopularity. Young men, especially rich, well-turned-out young men, with time on their hands, started to follow Socrates around Athens. For them, it was like knowing Mark Twain or Oscar Wilde: they hoped he would bump into someone of significance and make a mockery of them. And they loved him for it. Better yet, these youths began to realise that Socrates was serious. They sought him out not just for entertainment but because they thought they might learn something. At his trial he was also accused of corrupting youth, meaning turning them against their elders and betters. That too was a serious charge in a city that hoped for so much from the next generation.

This can be seen happening in the so-called Socratic dialogues of Plato, ones that Plato probably wrote early in his career, so reflecting what he had learnt from his teacher and not yet wholly shaped as his own. With them we can drill down a little more into what this philosophy of wise ignorance meant in practice.

Take the *Lysis*. It begins with Socrates out and about in Athens. He is walking between the Academy and the Lyceum, and, at the invitation of two young men, Hippothales and Ctesippus, he stops just outside the city walls – perhaps near the present-day dusty excavations of Kerameikos. They want him to join them in their discussions by a newly built gymnasium. Gymnasia were a favourite haunt of Athenian youths. In this one the statuesque Lysis was exercising, someone on whom Hippothales had a massive crush. In the dialogue, Socrates spots it immediately, albeit no great feat since Hippothales blushed at the merest thought of his beloved. What is interesting for us, though, is that Socrates tells Hippothales that he has a remarkable ability to spot when someone is in love, as well as identify the person with whom the lover is smitten.

What did Socrates mean by this? It is, in fact, directly related to what he discovered about himself after grappling with the words of the oracle. He is a lover of wisdom, like Hippothales is a lover of Lysis; both lack what they desire. The comment, which is repeated in other dialogues too, provides an insight into how Socrates must have felt, not just thought, about his calling as a philosopher. At times it ached. Hence the reason Socrates can spot lovers: he has an immediate sympathy with them. This seems likely to have been another reason why he got on so well with young men. It also shows that although Socrates was convinced the human lot was riven through and through with uncertainty, it did not mean he lacked passion. He was not like the agnostic who shrugs their shoulders with indifference. Rather, the lack of wisdom made his heart grow all the fonder of it. Like Romeo who gasps, 'Did my heart love 'till now?', at the merest thought of Juliet, Socrates longed for what he lacked. His ignorance, and knowledge of his ignorance, powered a relentless desire for the truth about himself, his fellows, and the verisimilitudes of the world around him.

There is a second dimension to this philosophical love that comes out in the encounter too. Socrates is drawn to others, not only because of his sympathy, but also because it is with others that he gains the best understanding of himself, and they of themselves. This is again implicit in his reaction to the oracle. He did not test himself on his own, as a modern recipient of such words might do, perhaps by experiment, perhaps by trying to write a book. Rather he went out onto the streets. As Plutarch later put it:

> Socrates did not set up grandstands for his audience and did not sit upon a professorial chair; he had no fixed time-table for talking or walking with his friends. Rather he did philosophy sometimes by joking with them, or by drinking or by going to war or to the market with them...

This meant that Socrates got to know people, and the better he got to know them, and they him, the better the philosophy. It was, for Socrates, not just about exploring ideas but was about understanding how people are the way they are. He believed the key to wisdom was self-understanding as well as defining abstractions. He had to get to know others to see if they were wiser than he was, a test that puts character as well as clever-ness under the spotlight. In addition, it is an approach that recognises that intuition and emotion are on a continuum with reason. How we implicitly react to things should count along-side how we explicitly rationalise them. As Wordsworth realised, thoughts are 'representatives of our past feelings'.

When it really worked, this was a process of befriending: 'I think that someone who is to test adequately the soul which lives aright and the soul which does not, needs to have three qualities: knowledge, goodwill and willingness to speak freely,' Socrates once said to one of his interlocutors. Alternatively, in the *Lysis*, he later confesses that he would rather have a friend more than anything else in the world, even more than all the gold of the Great King. With such a friend he would understand himself: they would be perfect mirrors to each other and, in that mutual trust, would know each other as well as they knew themselves.

Living uncertainty

This picture of Socrates' philosophy can be developed some more by considering further his engagement with the Delphic oracle. Ancient oracles are much misunderstood today. It is easy to think of them as a kind of cryptic fortune-teller or sophisticated roller of dice. But they are more fascinating than that. While no doubt they could be corrupted and ridiculed, at heart they were a system for decision making in a world very conscious that nothing could be predicted, much was up to luck, and everything was uncertain. Consulting the oracle, and receiving equivocal replies, did three things. It dramatised the experience of not knowing. It impelled the work of interpretation. It called all possibilities into question.

Consider two of the most famous consultations at Delphi. A first was when Croesus, the king of Lydia, sought the oracle's blessing on his proposed war against Persia. The Pythia uttered the words: 'A great empire will be destroyed.' In his hubris, Croesus took the empire to be that of his enemy. It was, in fact, that of his own. The cynic would respond to this by saying that the oracle always has the last laugh: it speaks in ways that can be re-interpreted after the event. But that, I think, would be a misunderstanding. Ancient people too knew that oracles must be doubted. Croesus himself had previously tested all the major oracles of the ancient world by asking them what he would be doing at a certain time on a future day. Only Delphi got it right (cooking lamb and tortoise in a bronze pot, as it happens). It is as if the very triviality of that prediction emphasised the effort you should go to when considering what the oracle says on matters as serious as going to war. Had Croesus seen through his pride, and heard not endorsement but different possibilities implicit in the oracle's words, he would have stared the unpredictability of war in the face, and perhaps saved the lives of his people.

A similar lesson was missed by the Roman Appius. As civil war was looming, at what we now know to be the end of the Roman republic, he asked the oracle about his future. The Pythia said he will 'escape the awful threats of war' and 'stay at peace in Euboea'. Appius took this to be consoling; he would not die and so need not fear the horrors that internecine carnage brings. But, again, had he allowed the words to sink in properly, he would have detected an ambivalence. It might mean he avoided the war. But it might also mean that he would die before war broke out – which is exactly what happened. He thought he had cheated death, but death cheated him, and brought him eternal peace in Euboea.

Every part of the oracle experience, then, gave cause to pause and reconsider. It represented not the sleep of reason but the opposite, the call to wake reason up and discern. It began with the effort of the journey to the shrine. Delphi was high in the hills. Siwa, the oracle Alexander the Great consulted about his parentage, was several days ride into the middle of the western Egyptian desert. Then, there was the preparation and ritual, coupled to the risk that the oracle might not speak. Finally, if the oracle did oblige, what had been said had then to be resolved, for the proper way to hear it was to dwell on its ambiguity and generate its meaning. As was the case with Socrates, being ambivalent about an oracle was not to question its truth so much as to struggle with its significance. To take the oracle seriously was to know yourself a little better. The experience was like a therapy that could transform blind action – deluded or devoid of self-knowledge – into wise action.

In some ways it did not even matter what the oracle said. Oracles were not designed to issue laws or edicts. They gave signs that showed, which the wise pondered greatly. Like paying an expert today, the real benefit might not be in the advice itself so much as in the commitment to the consultation process. The oracle/therapist says 'x' and 'not x', and thereby sets an agenda. The advice provides an authoritative, unsettling point of reference that can then be talked around.

Even to those who would say it is folly, the oracle might reply, 'well, yes'. It instantiates the folly of seeking certainty in life. Its unknown unknowns put human credulity centre stage. Instead, it suggests a path in between a believer's certainty and an unbeliever's cynicism that simultaneously mirrors the in-between reality of the human condition. Little wonder that Socrates should come to appreciate the fullness of his vocation through the voice of an oracle. Experientially, an oracle is not unlike his philosophy.

Know thyself

The oracle can tell us more still about Socrates. Consider the two inscriptions on the temple at Delphi. They were said to encapsulate the wisdom of the Seven Wise Men, a traditional if variable list of the most outstanding intellects of ancient Greece, usually including Thales, the first philosopher. 'Nothing in excess' is generally taken as advocating moderation. 'Know thyself' meant 'know you are not a god before you enter this temple'. What Socrates does is internalise these commands and transform them from warnings into a quest. 'Nothing in excess' comes to commend a moderate regard for oneself. 'Know thyself' becomes the imperative to understand yourself. In these two maxims one finds another summary of his philosophy. They pose the question of how one can know oneself and highlight how hard it is to understand and accept the uncertainty of the human condition. For if the human condition is one of uncertainty, then the question, 'who am I?', is frightening. It is elusive and will never, finally, be settled.

The ancients, it seems, were fascinated by such questions. Evidence of popular tips, perhaps not entirely unlike those that can be found in glossy magazines, survive for us to inspect. One papyrus found in the ash-covered town of Herculaneum, neighbour to Pompeii, records a 'four-part cure' from anxiety: (1) Don't fear god; (2) Don't worry about death; (3) What is good is easy to get; (4) What is terrible is easy to endure. This is a summary of Epicureanism, one of the ancient philosophies to develop a genuinely popular following. But notice how the four-part cure begs a question: 'how should one live?' will never be fully answered unless the prior question of 'who am I?' is.

Socrates suspected that it was not only glossy magazines, as it were, that could fail to address the real question. He thought that any form of written philosophy risked doing so too. That is presumably why he did not write anything in his own hand. Wisdom cannot be read off the page, or, as Plato put it, it is not like water that can be poured from one vessel into another. The point is that reading philosophy can be as much of a distraction as following four-part cures and the like: it can pose as philosophy without touching on the crucial matter of self-understanding.

> I have no time for such things; and the reason, my friend, is this. I am still unable, as the Delphic inscription orders, to know myself; and it really seems to me to be ridiculous to look into other things before I have understood that. This is why I do not concern myself with them. I accept what is generally believed, and, as I was just saying, I look not into them but into my own self.

Am I a beast, Socrates continues in this section of the *Phaedrus*, or do I have a divine nature? – again recalling the in-between status of what it is to be human. This, then, is how Socrates tries to ask the question. Knowing oneself becomes a matter of developing the right attitude to oneself and the world around one. This care for oneself too becomes part of his philosophy.

All in all, Socrates' agnostic enquiry became a committed way of life. What had started as a puzzle from the oracle was now a vocation. It was a quest that deployed reason as a tool, to test the limits of what people really knew: scholars today talk of Socrates' method, the so-called elenchus – meaning the drawing out of the consequences of a position or belief to see whether they are contradictory or inconsistent. But Socrates was also conscious that reason has limits. Like a pianist who quickly learns that technique is only the start of making music, Socrates learnt that reason is far from the whole of life. Reason can do much work – notably alerting you to your ignorance. But the development of matters as diverse as your character and intuitions, your circle of friends and the cultivation of what you love, and the challenge of the Delphic imperatives, must also play their part.

Are gods good?

But even all these elements do not capture the whole of it. There is a theological dimension to incorporate too. His references to the gods were a pervasive and subtle part of his make-up, made all the difference to his philosophy, and are as important as the personal and political aspects of his life. If questioning is the beginning of wisdom, it seems that he thought a religious sense is what draws it out.

Consider one of Socrates' most famous theological arguments, found in another dialogue, the *Euthyphro*. It tells the story of another of Socrates' conversations with a young man, after whom the dialogue is named, and takes place in front of the magistrates' courts in the marketplace. Euthyphro had come there to prosecute a charge of murder, and no ordinary murder, but one allegedly committed by his father. What is even more startling about the case is that the person whom his father had supposedly killed was only a slave. What had happened was that this slave had himself killed another slave in a drunken rage. Euthyphro's father had bound the offender and dumped him in a ditch. However, he had then forgotten about him and, left there, the slave died of exposure. Euthyphro is a puritanical young man who feels his father must be brought to justice to cleanse what he considers to be a stain on his family. And this is what interests Socrates. Socrates thinks that for Euthyphro to pursue such a headline-grabbing case, he must be very sure that the moral benefit he would gain from the prosecution would not be outweighed by the offence of dishonouring his father. In short, Euthyphro is acting dogmatically – as if he has very certain knowledge of what it means to be pious.

Euthyphro argues that he is right to prosecute his father because he believes that the gods denounce murderous acts. This is what makes the crime so bad. Socrates is fascinated by this assumption. In it, he sees a more general thesis: what is good is what the gods love. And, conversely, what is wrong is what the gods hate. Moreover, thinks Socrates, this thesis raises a wider question still. Is what is good loved by the gods because it is good, or is it good because it is loved by the gods?

Euthyphro is slightly confused by this point. So Socrates helps him out. Consider, he says, whether saying something is good is like saying something is seen. Something that is seen depends on someone seeing it. So is something being good dependent upon someone, like a god, saying it is good? Euthyphro thinks this cannot be right, since the good is good because it is good, not because of any feelings someone, even a god, might have for it. Socrates tends to agree.

The reason this debate is remembered is that many modern philosophers have taken it as profoundly undermining of theistic belief. It suggests that what is good is prior to anything a deity may say about it, which not only implies that the deity is subject to something over which it has no options, but that morally speaking we do not need theism to tell us what is good. The standard, theistic reply to this conclusion is that God is goodness itself. The atheist's argument is flawed, theists say, because it suggests that there is some kind of separation between the virtue and the divinity which in the case of God there is not. But, replies the atheist, you cannot escape the fact that you say God is good because God has the properties of goodness. In which case, you should be able to list the properties of goodness without reference to God. And so the argument goes round and round.

What is salient in Plato's account of it in the *Euthyphro*, though, is that Socrates does not pose any arguments like this at all. It apparently never occurs to him, or Euthyphro, that the dilemma is a challenge to the gods. This could be put down to a number of things. Perhaps the pressing matter in the dialogue is not whether the gods exist but whether Euthyphro should prosecute his father. Though the conversation broadens out in other ways, so why not in this direction? Alternatively, it might be thought that Socrates lived in a society in which the existence of the gods was basically beyond question; ancient Athenians did not experience the world as disenchanted as we, it is said, do today. But, as already described, agnostic and atheistic ideas did circulate in ancient Athens, so it is significant that Plato does not choose to make something of them here.

Personally, I think that Socrates does not see the dilemma as troubling vis-à-vis the gods because of his conviction about the uncertainty of the human condition. This implies, first, that he thinks that no one, with any seriousness, can presume to know what may or may not cause a divinity a sleepless night. And, second, it implies that what is far more obvious to him is that the dilemma should be troubling to human beings. Whatever it may be to be a god, it is human beings who must grapple with what it means to be good, not them.

The dialogue ends inconclusively, as they usually do. Euthyphro is troubled by Socrates' line of thought, but rather than trying to come to terms with what it might mean for his dogmatism, he hurries off, stung. Whether he continued with the prosecution of his father we do not know. We can, though, ponder some more of what it suggests about Socrates' approach to theology and how that connects with his way of life.

First, it implies that Socrates was not very interested in debates about whether gods exist or not. Perhaps he suspected that when conducted as a knock-out between a theist and an atheist they go nowhere fast. Having said that, he was interested in theological debate: if God-talk can avoid getting hung up on 'proofs', then it can become a way of critiquing human knowledge, of reflecting on the human condition. Examining what people take to be divine is valuable because it reminds them that they are made lower than gods and that aspirations to god-like knowledge will remain just that – aspirations. Then, if this can be stomached, the attitude it nurtures itself becomes a valuable source of insight. With such humility, the vain attempt to 'overcome' is ditched, and the challenge to understand is taken on. And this, in turn, is what makes life worthwhile. It produces the best kind of human beings, people who are not merely ignorant, but recognise the ways in which they are. To this extent, they become wise and lovers of wisdom. To put it another way, the unexamined life is not worth living, negatively because it would be deluded, and positively because examining all those other things in life – character, intuition, friendships, loves and fundamentally 'who am I?' – gives life shape and meaning.

Marginal belief

To the extent that he reframed theology as an anthropocentric activity Socrates was heterodox for his times. Consider the issue of the gods and goodness again. It was common to regard the gods as somewhat arbitrary when it came to the goodness of their deeds. When Zeus and his wife Hera argued on Mount Olympus, Zeus would do a monstrous thing one day and Hera some good, and then, after an argument the next day, Zeus would do the good thing and Hera some horror. Who could tell how it might turn out? Similarly, when a city-state sought the assistance of its divinities in times of war, the plea was not the modern-day sentiment 'our cause is right', with the implication that God must be on our side. Rather it was 'you owe it to us', because of all the sacrifices your citizens have performed for you.

Socrates rejects these ideas. Quite reasonably he thought that if we can see that the actions of Zeus and Hera are arbitrary and unjust, then they as gods must be able to see that too. So they cannot be like that to start with. That they are popularly taken to be so smacks of human mistake. Similarly, on the matter of bargaining with the gods, Socrates thought that whatever the heavenly realm might be like it must be one of moral consistency and divine harmony. So, whatever it might be to communicate with the gods, it is ridiculous of people to think that they can be bargained with. This was actually a far more dangerous idea than straightforward atheism. It implied that one city-state, like Athens, might not have the gods on its side when pitted against an enemy, like Sparta, which did.

Having said that, Socrates is depicted in Plato's dialogues as being quite conventional in his religious practice. He makes sacrifices, attends feasts, pours libations, offers prayers and pursues oracles. Partly, he seems to have believed that religious practice should be respected since it opens the mind and cultivates the agnostic spirit; it is an exercise in intellectual humility. Partly, he is acknowledging that reason alone is limited and that for all someone might be influenced by rational argument, the care of the soul – the holistic aim of his philosophy – clearly takes more than sound logic.

Inner daemons

There is another aspect of Socrates' spiritual sensibility that we cannot pass over – simply because of the number of times that Plato and others refer to it. This is what Socrates calls his *daimonion* or daemon. 'It's a voice that, when it comes, always signals me to turn away from what I'm about to do, but never prescribes anything.' Although the voice is intimate and only ever heard by Socrates, he was well known for it: the charge of introducing new gods that he faced at his trial probably referred to this suspiciously private apparent access to the divine.

What the daemon tells Socrates not to do ranges from the trivial to the life-threatening. Most often, it tells him simply to sit down when he is about to stand up, usually so as not to miss an encounter with others who are about to pass by. Sometimes it offers similarly negative advice for others: it once told Socrates to tell Charmides, Plato's handsome but tyrannical uncle, not to train for a race at Nemea, an ancient Olympic contest that involved running 200 km in just over a day. Much more seriously, Socrates believed he was obeying his daemon when he stayed in Athens to drink the hemlock. He could have easily got away.

What are we to make of Socrates' daemon? There is a medical theory that Socrates suffered from a form of epilepsy, but whatever the truth of that, it does not explain the significance the experiences had for the sage: if it was an affliction, it was one he valued. It is probably wrong to think of it as a voice too, as if it were a guardian angel or some kind of internal conversation with himself. Rather, the *daimonion* experience itself expresses uncertainty – Socrates does not know whence it comes or whither it goes – and strangeness, as if it were a force or urge that, if familiar, he fails to understand.

In the *Symposium*, there are two incidents that enlarge on this. The first occurs when Socrates meets a priestess, called Diotima. They had a conversation in which Diotima explained who or what Eros (Love) is. Socrates had assumed up to that point that Eros was divine. But no, says Diotima. Eros is a daemon, an entity that exists in between the heavenly realms and human society. The gods 'mingle and converse' with humans by these daemons, she says, mostly when people sleep, or for some when they are awake – a process that Plato elsewhere alludes to as 'yearning after and perceiving something, it knows not what'.

Eros is a particularly interesting daemon because of his origins. When Aphrodite was born, the gods held a party. Poros (meaning 'way'), son of Metis (meaning 'cunning') was there, got drunk and fell asleep in the garden. Meanwhile, Penia (meaning 'poverty') passed by, and discerning a cunning way out of her poverty, slept with Poros and became pregnant. Eros was the result.

Diotima continues her story by describing Eros in more detail, and she does so in ways that exactly match Socrates. Both are poor, ugly and shoeless. Both long for something they lack, but are endlessly cunning in the pursuit of what they love – divine wisdom. Thus, concludes Diotima: 'He is in between wisdom and ignorance as well.' The message is clear. Socrates' daemon is like Eros: it is a go-between for an in-between, and is another manifestation of the way his philosophy drives him like love.

The second incident comes after Socrates and Diotima have finished speaking, when Socrates' sometime pupil Alcibiades, now an Athenian leading light, comes in. He proceeds to give a speech in praise of Socrates, though as it turns out it is as much a rant – not least when describing the disturbing, daemonic effect Socrates has on him:

> I swear to you the moment he starts to speak, I am beside myself: my heart starts leaping in my chest, the tears come streaming down my face, even the frenzied Corybantes seem sane compared to me – and I tell you, I am not alone. I have heard Pericles and many other great orators, and I have admired their speeches. But nothing like this ever happened to me: they never upset me so deeply that my very own soul started protesting that my life – my life! – was no better than the most miserable slave's. He always traps me, you see, and makes me admit that my political career is a waste of time, while all that matters is just what I most neglect: my personal shortcomings that cry out for my closest attention. So I refuse to listen to him; I stop my ears and tear myself away from him, for, like the Sirens, he could make me stay by his side till I die.

Notice how it is not just Socrates' rational challenges that causes Alcibiades to doubt everything. It is a psychological force that he wields and that causes so much distress. This force brings Alcibiades' political aspirations into question and his deepest, darkest motivations. What he describes is a complete collapse

Illus. 1.2: Socrates' ugly appearance accentuated the inner beauty of his unsettling wisdom.

of self-confidence – 'my heart, or my soul, or whatever you want to call it, has been struck and bitten by philosophy', he continues. Again, a clear message about Socrates is being given. Socrates' daemon calls into question every part of life. In this, it is intimately connected to his philosophy.

Socrates in conversation

Bertrand Russell called himself an agnostic, though one who was 'atheistically inclined'. This is different from the agnosticism of Socrates. If Russell's agnosticism made him tend towards atheism, on the assumption that not knowing is a comment about the probable non-existence of gods not the nature of humankind, Socrates' agnosticism made him want to hold onto God-talk and religious practice, as he took it to be mostly a reflection of his conviction of the in-between status of human beings, and helps summarise some of the characteristics of Socrates' approach that we have been examining.

In a magazine called *Look*, published in 1953, Russell clarified what agnosticism meant for him. He was asked a series of questions. There is, perhaps, some benefit in juxtaposing excerpts from some of the actual answers he gave with ones Socrates might have given, had he been asked too. A virtual conversation defines, as it were, two poles on the continuum of agnostic belief.

What is an agnostic?

RUSSELL: An agnostic is a man who thinks that it is impossible to know the truth in the matters such as God and a future life with which the Christian religion and other religions are concerned. Or, if not for ever impossible, at any rate impossible at present.

SOCRATES: I too have never found anything but uncertainty in divine matters, but that is a bad reason for unbelief. The same could be said about most matters we enquire into. My agnostic is someone who is religiously minded, as you might put it, but who, unlike the believer who speaks of his gods with confidence, lives so as to examine what he feels about these things.

Are agnostics atheists?

RUSSELL: No. An agnostic suspends judgement ... At the same time, an agnostic may hold that the existence of God, though not impossible, is very improbable; he may even hold it so improbable that it is not worth considering in practice.

SOCRATES: No – but not because it is not worth considering in practice. I do find many of the things people say about gods unlikely, but I am very drawn to what you call theology no less; at the very least, examining someone's God-talk, for or against, often exposes the assumptions they make not about God, but about what it is to be human.

Since you deny 'God's law', what authority do you accept as a guide to conduct?

RUSSELL: An agnostic does not accept any 'authority' in the sense in which religious people do. He holds that a man should think out questions of conduct for himself.

SOCRATES: We should certainly try to think out questions of conduct for ourselves, or perhaps a better way of putting it is to say we should cultivate those virtues within us that align us with what is good. But that does not exclude respecting any higher authority – the resources of what wise people have discovered before. Sometimes we must accept on authority, for we cannot decide everything afresh for ourselves.

Does an agnostic deny that man has a soul?

RUSSELL: The question has no precise meaning unless we are given a definition of the word 'soul'. I suppose what is meant is, roughly, something non-material which persists throughout a person's life and even, for those who believe in immortality, throughout all future time. An agnostic is not likely to believe that a man has a soul.

SOCRATES: I do not understand this objection to the idea of a soul – though it is no doubt hard to pin down. My pupil Plato, and his pupil Aristotle, used to argue endlessly about it. But that only goes to show it's worth talking about, for must we not take care of ourselves as souls – as persons, with purposes and desires? And nothing is more beautiful than a soul growing wings and flying high.

Are you ever afraid of God's judgement in denying him?

RUSSELL: Most certainly not. I observe that a very large portion of the human race does not believe in God and suffers no visible punishment in consequence. And, if there was such a God, I think it very unlikely that he would have such an uneasy vanity as to be offended by those who doubt his existence.

SOCRATES: I understand Professor Russell's concern with divine vanity; Homer is full of it. But, then, we should be more careful of the way we talk about the gods, not blame the gods. Divine judgement must be what we strive for in justice. And, since justice is so difficult to define, we can only gain from submitting our own ideas to what a god's judgement might be. So, yes, I am afraid of divine judgement.

How do agnostics explain the beauty and harmony of nature?

RUSSELL: I do not understand where this 'beauty' and 'harmony' are supposed to be found. Throughout the animal kingdom, animals ruthlessly prey upon each other … I suppose the questioner is thinking of such things as the beauty of the starry heavens. But one should remember that stars every now and then explode … Beauty, in any case, is subjective and exists only in the eye of the beholder.

SOCRATES: Beauty is certainly in the eye of the beholder. But then the eye can lead you to lovely things. And if I may say so, professor, although I know nothing, there is one thing I am good at: spotting people's problems with love. Your agnosticism seems to make you very wary about what you should love. Does it not close you down? Love should open you up, for love, even mad love, is needed to find those things that are truly beautiful.

What is the meaning of life to the agnostic?

RUSSELL: I feel inclined to answer by another question: what is the meaning of 'the meaning of life'? I suppose what is intended is some general purpose. I do not think that life in general has any purpose. It just happened. But individual human beings have purposes, and there is nothing in agnosticism to cause them to abandon these purposes.

SOCRATES: When death hangs over your head, the meaning of life is not academic, believe me. What is important is not life but a good life. But even that takes us only so far. For myself, I have the blessing of a keen sensibility that strives to understand how we are ignorant. If we can get that right, I think we might get lots of other things more right too.

Is faith in reason alone a dangerous creed?

RUSSELL: No sensible man, however agnostic, has 'faith in reason alone'.

SOCRATES: We can agree on that.

Unlike the orthodox believer, Socrates' uncertain attitude undermines any certain beliefs. Unlike the committed atheist (or near atheist), his questioning sensibility remains open to what God-talk might reveal about the in-between human condition. Socrates is religious because he is a committed passionate agnostic.

Last words

He achieved something that only a handful of thinkers in history achieve; he changed the consciousness of a civilisation. 'We cannot fail to see in Socrates the one turning point and vortex of so-called world history,' said Nietzsche, who, as frequently, wished he could fail to see Socrates at the vortex of history. The purpose of putting the figure of Socrates at the beginning of this book is that the subtle inspiration behind his philosophy is often forgotten today. The rich ambiguities that characterised his way of life are belittled by the hard-and-fast demands of the rationalist outlook. Its subtle colours are lost amid the blacks and whites of thought abstracted from life.

In 399 BCE, Socrates was found guilty of not recognising the city gods, introducing new deities and corrupting the young. He was sentenced to death. Scholars have debated ever since whether Socrates was guilty of these things or whether an amalgam of unfortunate political associations, presumed atheism, and stinging his enemies one too many times were the real causes. Probably it was a mixture of all three and Socrates' agnosticism was right there at the heart of it, disquieting his opponents.

A month or so later he drank the hemlock and died. His last words were: 'Crito, we owe a cock to Asclepius; pay it and don't forget' – not, at first glance, overly inspiring, though, as is the way with last words, they have been much reflected upon. Asclepius was one of the gods of healing; the sacrifice of a cock was a thanksgiving for overcoming illness. Socrates' last concern was, likely, religious, and once again he turns conventional piety around: he was not going to live but was about to die. Was Plato's point merely rhetorical, saying he was pious to the last, for all that his accusers said otherwise? Nietzsche interpreted the last words as Socrates' giving thanks for the final escape from the sickness which is life itself, an idea he hated since it was the opposite of his 'will to power'. Alternatively, they might make sense if Socrates hoped he was about to leave this in-between life and be cured of its ignorance. We cannot say for sure, not least because elsewhere Socrates says he is not sure whether there is an afterlife, let alone whether he is sure what that after-life might be like. His agnosticism is echoed in his last words too – giving thanks, as his humility would, though exactly to whom and for what he knew not.

Cosmic Religion: How Science Does God

> Follow knowledge like a sinking star, beyond the utmost bounds of human thought, beyond the sunset, and the baths of all the western stars.
>
> Alfred, Lord Tennyson

If you think of Isaac Newton, what image comes to mind? Is it an upright man with Restoration curls who, prism in hand, calmly explains the splitting of light to an attentive audience? Is it a dishevelled sage with tatty cuffs who, lost in thought under a tree, is hit by a falling apple and – eureka!? Is it a desiccated don who, prowling the cloisters like a wild beast, has reduced everything to an equation in his masterpiece, the *Principia?* Or is it a sulphur-soiled alchemist who, half mad with mercury poisoning, distills reason as a mere by-product of the true search for the elixir of life?

The empiricist philosopher, David Hume, preferred something like the first: 'In Newton this island may boast of having produced the greatest and rarest genius that ever rose for the ornament and instruction of the species,' he wrote in his *History of England.* The romantic idea of genius is represented by the second image. It sees the apple as emblematic of the sudden moment of radical breakthrough: 'A ripe fruit fall from some immortal tree/ Of knowledge ... ', wrote the poet Alfred Noyes. The third, more ambivalent image is perhaps more like Keats', when he sighed, 'Do not all charms fly/ At the mere touch of cold philosophy?'

And finally, there is Newton the alchemist, the man who worried more about crucibles and symbols than calculus and science. 'Newton was not the first of the age of reason. He was the last of the magicians, the last of the Babylonians and Sumerians, the last great mind which looked out on the visible and intellectual world with the same eyes as those who began to build our intellectual inheritance rather less than 10,000 years ago,' declared John Maynard Keynes, who saved many of Newton's alchemic manuscripts from destruction.

The evolution of the iconography of Newton, which Patricia Fara charts in her book *Newton: the Making of Genius*, is simultaneously a reflection of changing attitudes to science. That Newton's image varies so much, and on occasion is so fiercely contested, is indicative of the way the meaning of science has itself been contested in the 300 years since his death. Not unlike the figure of Socrates, there are, on the one hand, the rational materialists for whom any rehearsal of Newton's hermetic 'superstitions' is broadly irrelevant and vaguely offensive. Then, on the other hand, there are the romantic New Ageists in whose mouths the same rehearsal is meant as a condemnation of science as it has become.

But why, specifically, was Newton so interested in alchemy? What purpose did it serve in relation to his undoubted astonishing achievements? Why did one of the greats of mathematics think of himself in 'the noble Companie of true Students in holy Alchimie'?

The dark glass

There are those who would say it was extraneous. Perhaps like Schopenhauer's long walks, Glenn Gould's tuneless humming, or Van Gogh's self-mutilation, alchemy was for Newton the excess of genius, a forgivable indulgence, a means of relaxation. There are others who say it was instrumental. For them, Newton's alchemy was in the service of his work at the Royal Mint. It was the way that research into metallurgy was done in those days; for 'alchemy' one should really read 'coin milling technology'.

However, the most recent scholarship demonstrates substantial links between Newton's alchemic experiments and theoretical

Illus. 2.1: Sir Isaac Newton – gentleman, sage, rationalist or alchemist?

achievements. A good example is provided by his fascination with comets. Today, this is usually remembered in relation to Newton's friend, Edmond Halley. He was the first to use the new laws of gravity to predict when the eponymous comet, and 23 others, would return – which they did. However, for Newton, comets were fascinating not just because they appeared in the sky but because the intermittency of their appearing resonated with his view of God. His was a deity who intermittently intervened in the universe. So, he conjectured, might the impact of a comet on earth have been the cause of divine interventions like Noah's flood?

Another example of his interplay of religion and science is found in the way Newton thought about the mysterious action of gravity at a distance. He postulated that the universe was filled with a tenuous ether. This ether served two purposes. First, being made of tiny particles, it could provide a vehicle for the transmission of the gravitational force. And second, it might also be the medium for the spiritual forces necessary to animate an otherwise inert universe.

Newton's natural theology did go to extremes that seem simply weird to us now. He turned his science to such matters as the dimensions of Solomon's temple, the number of the Beast, and the recovery of lost knowledge from ancient times. One of his close followers identified over 300 occasions in which biblical prophecy was supported by mathematics (though he made the fatal mistake of predicting the end of the world just 30 years ahead of his own time: it didn't happen). Scientific luminaries such as Joseph Priestley and David Hartley valued Newton's alchemy too. They routinely and favourably cited him for his expertise in esoteric matters. But one should hesitate to mock. Think instead what speculations of today will seem outlandish to scientists 300 years hence. The multiverse theory? Eleven dimensional space? Memes?

Not that such considerations humbled others. Leibniz, a contemporary rival of Newton once joked thus: 'According to their doctrine [Newton and followers], God Almighty wants to wind up his watch from time to time: otherwise it would cease to move. He had not, it seems, sufficient foresight to make it a perpetual motion.' But Leibniz misunderstood Newton's premise. Science could not explain God away. Quite the opposite: science was a way of glimpsing the majesty of the divine. The very regularity of the world he was unveiling originates in 'the counsel and dominion of an intelligent and powerful Being', Newton wrote. This was evidence for, not against, faith: 'the Supreme God exists necessarily, and by the same necessity he exists always and everywhere'. Newton was not orthodox. He went to great lengths to conceal his disbelief in the Trinity, not least because it was against the law. However, the pressing question for him was not, does God exist, but how does God intervene in the world, and how does the new science resonate with, and reinvigorate, his theological beliefs?

His scientific work was part of a broader vocation to seek a deeper truth. At one level, the new science provided possible answers to the pressing religious questions of the day, like the wherewithal for miracles, in the form of events like cometary appearances or immaterial substances like ether. These issues seem anachronistic now, of course. But at another, more durable level, his scientific concerns were an expression of an immensely energetic and engaged sense of wonder. They were a kind of spiritual practice.

It is hard to be certain exactly how the intensely private Newton would have described this feeling himself but it is reasonable to suppose it is captured in a quotation he took from Milton's *Paradise Regained*:

> I don't know what I may seem to the world, but, as to myself, I seem to have been only like a boy playing on the sea shore, and diverting myself in now and then finding a smoother pebble or prettier shell than ordinary, whilst the great ocean of truth lay all undiscovered before me.

There is a wondering humanity there – that the pebbles and shells of mathematical equations are mere reflections of a full understanding. There is the consciousness that, for all the successes of thought and experiment, human beings see only through a glass darkly. This humility before nature, shaping the desire to understand it better, might be thought of as the high-minded benefit of ancient alchemy.

Spirituality of science

It was hardly alchemy, but for me, a sense of such wonder became a part of my appreciation of science as a result of an undergraduate astronomy project. The aim of the exercise was to estimate the heights of mountains on the moon. This involved taking photographs of the lunar surface and measuring the lengths of the shadows that fell across its cliffs, peaks, valleys and plains. Calculating the height of the sun above the horizon, from the position of the mountain in question and the time of the photo, revealed something of our natural satellite's geography. My efforts were, of course, utterly trivial in the grand scheme of things. Today, lasers and radio waves are bounced off these grey peaks and can determine their elevation within meters. However, the exercise was worthwhile, even seminal, for me inasmuch as the thing I remember most was the experience itself.

The photos had to be taken in the early hours of winter mornings, when the sky was clear, the moon was high and light pollution was low. Arising at 3 a.m. on dark, frosty mornings clothed the project with a sense of expectation: it reminded me of monks who say the office of Matins at similar hours as the people around sleep. Then there was the business of staring onto another world. The moon is a high-contrast place: with no obscuring atmosphere and pitted like pumice, it feels close through even a relatively low-powered telescope. Thomas Traherne imaged a 'celestial stranger' coming to earth and being amazed at its beauty: 'Verily this star is a nest of angels!,' he has his visitor muse. 'This little star so wide and so full of mysteries! So capacious and full of territories, containing innumerable repositories of delight when we draw near!' The same sentiments occurred to me during my lunar observations. Not that we were simply gawping at it. The project cultivated a methodological precision in our observations, partly to gain as high-quality pictures as we could, and partly then to examine those images closely and select the best representative features for study.

Many of Newton's contemporaries were into alchemy for reasons of money, not faith. They were paid to research and hoped to reap the rewards of the Midas touch. However, Newton was part of a long tradition that was critical of the merits and even the possibility of such base alchemic aims. In 1627, Francis Bacon wrote about the 'making of gold' in his *Naturall Historie in ten Centuries*, lamenting how alchemy too often nurtures 'vanities', 'superstitions' and 'forgeries'. He preferred a more altruistic alchemy that valued experimentation for the benefits it brought to the world at large, not for its profits. A similar attitude was adopted a generation before Newton by Robert Boyle, often called the father of modern chemistry. In his book, *The Sceptical Chymist*, he laid out his loathing of the grasping obscurantism often associated with alchemy. He shows great appreciation for 'adepts' and later thought that he was close to turning quicksilver into gold. However, his call was for discipline, clarity and the full reporting of investigations.

In these more moral assessments of alchemy can be seen a concern for its spiritual, not material, significance. This higher tradition saw alchemy as a framework in which the transformation of the alchemist was as significant an aim as the transmutation of matter. The Philosopher's Stone – the mysterious substance that is the common ingredient to all alchemic concerns – was aligned with love, a love that searched creation. The quest for the perfect metal, gold, was taken as an allegory of the perfection of humanity. Rather like the search for the holy grail, that presumably many knew would and could never be actually found even as they committed themselves to it, these pursuits were valued for the way they took the devotee to the limits of knowledge, in a synthesis of the scientific and the spiritual. It nurtured a sense of integration by underlining the fact that there was always more to explain. It nurtured a sense of wonder by emphasising the tremendousness of the cosmos. It was expressed in esoteric terms not so much because of inherited superstitions (Newton and his fellows were not fools) but because it strove to describe what was taken as being essentially indescribable. To believe that the alchemic efforts of Newton and others were futile is to miss the point. Like the ancient oracle, whose wisdom derived from equivocal words that forced a struggle of interpretation, alchemy's allure was not to dissolve but to enter into its very mysteriousness.

Alchemy's inheritors

Alchemy as an explicitly acknowledged goal of science died out as the scientific worldview became mainstream. Lead can now be turned into gold by bombarding the metal with high energy particles – though the expense of the process far outweighs any profit from the gold. But I suspect that contemporary cosmology embodies something of the old alchemic spirit still.

Today, many individuals – physicists and laypeople alike – are interested in phenomena like quantum entanglement, possible links between consciousness and reality, and the fine-tuning of the universe. The interest stems not just from the wonder that is the natural response to scientific discovery. They also feel tempted, and sometimes compelled, to draw what might be called sacred conclusions from it. This is more than a powerful sense of wonder. The suggestion is that there are uncanny resonances between what science unveils and older spiritual convictions. The implication is that science might be a welcome source of new insights, which could revivify old myths that have grown cold to the agnostic mind. It's what Einstein called 'cosmic religion'. Cosmology might even be thought of as the new metaphysics – the way we now ask the big questions of where we come from, what we are, whence we're headed. If the scholastic theologians of the Middle Ages liked to speculate about the number of angels on pin heads, we today like to speculate about the number of dimensions wrapped up in string theory.

An obvious example of such contemporary 'theo-physics' concerns the so-called God particle. This is the Higgs boson, required by the standard model in particle physics to account for the observation that many particles have mass. But why should an esoteric entity to do with mass gain such a weighty theological ascription?

It was named by Leon Lederman, a former director of Fermilab. He thought the divine reference was suitable because the particle is so crucial to contemporary physics, and yet simultaneously so elusive. And is that not a bit like God? If God does exist, then God would be the ground of everything, and also never quite seen – only detected in the after effects of the divine wake, like traces in a particle collider. Ponder the Higgs boson and you ponder something of the concept of God.

Physicists profess to hate the title. But the media love it. And that surely reflects a wider public consciousness, sparked by physicists like Stephen Hawking, that to have a 'theory of everything' would be to know the 'mind of God'. Again, there's metaphysics in that dream, because a theory of everything would have many divine properties. It would be a unity – one entity from which flows the diversity of all that exists. It would be flawless – a complete and beautiful truth that could not be added to in any way. It would be necessary, which is to say it could not be otherwise and is entirely self-sufficient. God, if God is, is like that. Again, science is reviving, not throttling, belief.

The links between cosmology and metaphysics can be drawn in other ways. Consider speculations about extra-terrestrial life. The interesting feature of this subject is that we constantly and regularly return to it – in books and newspaper articles – although precisely nothing of ET has been discovered. SETI has been operational for 50 years with no positive results. But we never cease to be bored by the search, not just because we're fascinated by the possibility of ET, but because we are fascinated by ourselves.

Thinking about what intelligence might be like elsewhere is a way of musing on our own nature. Again, it's metaphysics. Is extraterrestrial life (are we) massively rare, and that's why the vast cosmos is apparently so silent? Is it (are we) violently destructive, so that intelligence wipes itself out before it gains the technology required to span the distance between the stars? Is intelligence so extraordinary that once it emerges it evolves startlingly rapidly – and that's our destination too? We don't detect alien intelligence because it outstrips our own, just as the cognitive powers of bacteria are outstripped by us. Or is the universe too enormous, and we'll never know whether there is intelligent life out there, which is to say that our cosmic state mirrors our existential loneliness? Whatever scenario you prefer, there'll be a reflection on what it is to be human implicit in it.

But if science prompts existential and metaphysical questions, can it deliver any answers in this domain? It is the dominant discourse in the modern world when it comes to considering what counts as true. So it's no surprise that individuals with spiritual concerns should, like Newton, turn to it – doubly so if they are of the agnostic type, having a God-shaped hole that seeks fulfilment. But as the alchemical dream proved elusive, might science fall short too, if we turn to it as a new source of the sacred?

Part of the problem is that no two physicists will agree about what their science implies – whether they believe physics has any metaphysic import. They vary on just about every question you may ask. And many don't bother to ask at all, or at least they keep their thoughts quiet. But, as a rough guide, and reflecting on the conclusions of those who do speak out, I reckon there are five different conclusions that physicists reach. Considering them may help decide.

The vastness of emptiness

The first is strictly atheistic and materialist. There is no need to hypothesise a quantum spirituality or cosmological divinity – and a lot of misunderstanding arises when you do. In fact, science does not only not spark theological beliefs or spiritual feeling, it is really rather against them. Steven Weinberg is one physicist who has come to this conclusion. 'The more the universe seems comprehensible, the more it seems pointless,' he's written, adding: 'We ourselves could invent a point for our lives, including trying to understand the universe.' Indeed, a key source of his commitment to science is found in replacing supernatural explanations with naturalistic ones. The maps of old used to feature dragons at the edge of the world. Now, though, we have maps that show no dragons on the boundaries of the unknown. There's no cosmic religion. Any meaning must come from us humans ourselves. It's up to us.

Weinberg feels this is self-evidently true. The story of twentieth century physics is the story of convergence. Theories that once seemed separate have been combined: it was for his work on the integration of two of the fundamental forces in nature, the weak and the electromagnetic, that he won a Nobel prize. He believes that this trend points towards the possibility of arriving at a theory of everything. 'Our deepest principles, although not yet final, have become steadily more simple and economical,' he reflects. They've achieved that convergence as a result of the materialist assumptions physicists have made.

There is a humility in this view. It's demonstrated well in the writings of another physicist who falls into this camp, the Astronomer Royal and President of the Royal Society, Martin Rees. He is highly conscious of the millennia that stretch ahead of us human beings, disaster notwithstanding. Given that humankind only has 8000 years of intellectual history to its credit, and that we only know of a tiny patch of the possible universe – which may elsewhere be inhabited by minds immeasurably superior to ours – this should instil two attitudes. First, a modesty about our achievements. Second, a consciousness of the possibility that our minds may ultimately not be up to grasping much about meaning and reality. As Montaigne warned: 'Man is quite insane. He wouldn't know how to create a maggot, and he creates gods by the dozen.' Cosmic caution, rather than cosmic religion, is the response natural to this mindset.

Rees is happy talking about the mystery of things too, though he means it in a natural sense: science can articulate questions and attempt to find some answers, though answers may not be forthcoming and even when they do arrive they are likely to pose deeper questions again. Why should the universe be transparent to our probing and not just strange to us? The risk is that into these wells of mystery can be thrown all sorts of speculations, some scientific, some spiritual. The difficulty is in discerning the useful conjectures from the bad, the reasonable from the mad. And for this reason, Rees prefers to stick with those mysteries that can be tried by scientific means: define theories and test for empirical evidence.

All in all he's concluded that religion probably has nothing to offer science; he affirms Stephen Jay Gould's notion of 'non-overlapping magisteria', which is to say that the two enterprises are about entirely different things. The hydrogen atom, the simplest structure in the universe, is hard enough to understand. It just seems wildly extravagant to believe we can understand things that are far more complicated, let alone anything that might be associated with the idea of God. He prefers to contemplate the vastness of space and time than the concerns associated with traditional spirituality.

This can feel rather empty, for all that many physicists, perhaps most, do reach a conclusion something like it. They stand in awe of the universe and know that understanding comes slowly and may never finally arrive in its entirety. However, some venture further.

Orderly, beautiful, wise

They may do so because they ask themselves a question that I think all physicists whisper from time to time. It was famously posed by Eugene Wigner in 1960, when he wrote an essay entitled: 'The Unreasonable Effectiveness of Mathematics in the Natural Sciences.'

That mathematics is the language of the natural sciences has been long celebrated. Galileo wrote as much in the seventeenth century: 'The universe cannot be read until we have learned the

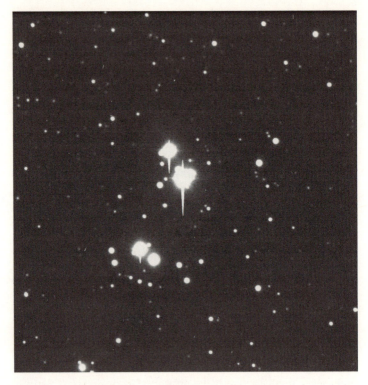

Illus. 2.2: Cosmologists have always been humbled by the vastness of the universe they study.

language and become familiar with the characters in which it is written.' That language is maths and geometry, he continues, 'without which means it is humanly impossible to comprehend a single word.' From this arises a further observation commonly felt among physicists, the sense that mathematics is not created, it is discovered. In his essay, Wigner ponders what that might mean, and in particular the meaning that might be drawn from the fact that human beings can discover laws of nature, and that nature appears to obey mathematical laws. It seems like a miracle. Wigner writes:

> It is... a miracle that in spite of the baffling complexity of the world, certain regularities in the events could be discovered... It is hard to believe that our reasoning power was brought, by Darwin's process of natural selection, to the perfection which it seems to possess.

It's this notion of perfection that precipitates our second option for the meaning of physics. It can be called Platonic. Roger Penrose is a physicist who has worked out this position quite explicitly. He is quite clear that the physical laws of nature are mathematical, and that the laws seem to be accurate to a quite extraordinary degree. They also clearly existed before any human being had a mathematical thought; indeed, they existed before there were human beings. Moreover, as Gödel has demonstrated in his incompleteness theorem, there are axioms within any sophisticated system of mathematics that cannot be proven: they are true and that truth value has to be intuited. Mathematics provides a very remarkable model of the physical world and it's hard to resist the conclusion that it's written into the world in some way.

Now, it is entirely possible that we may never grasp why mathematics is so effective, and what the origins of its perfections might be. But we can say something about its effectiveness, namely that it is routinely described by qualities like 'order' and 'beauty' and 'wisdom'. The notion that mathematics is ordered and beautiful is perhaps relatively familiar. So let me pick up on the idea it is wise.

Consider the case of Einstein who found that the equations of General Relativity implied things about the universe that he refused to believe, like its expansion. He added a 'cosmological constant' to the equations to cancel the effect. Later, though, he had to accept expansion when it was empirically verified by Hubble. This famously led Einstein to calling the cosmological constant 'the biggest blunder of my life': it turns out that the cosmological constant is in fact meaningful, standing for what is now called the vacuum energy. In this sense, you could say that the equations Einstein discovered were wiser even than he.

The implication is that without understanding why and how the mathematics works, we may be justified in concluding that qualities like order, beauty and wisdom are written through the fabric of the universe. Moreover, if mathematics is discovered, to do mathematics is to discover these things as well. Could that not lead to a cosmic spirituality? Mightn't it say something about the existence of transcendence?

Such aesthetic and epistemological aspects do indeed lead theists – as opposed to Platonists – to call on mathematics as evidence for the existence of God or, to put it in a more nuanced way, they say that the power of mathematics is exactly the kind of thing you would expect in a universe created by an ordered, beautiful and wise deity. As the philosopher Leibniz put it, 'When God calculates and thinks things through, the world is made.'

For the theist, the belief is that human beings can apprehend God's 'thinking through' by doing science. Religion and science are, in fact, part of the same enterprise. As the physicist and priest Michel Heller writes in his book, *The Comprehensible Universe*:

> In the human brain, the world's structure has reached its focal point: the structure of the world has acquired the ability to reflect upon itself... In this conceptual setting, science appears as a collective effort of the Human Mind to reach the Mind of God... The Mind of Man and the Mind of God are strangely interwoven.

There is something profound in this line of thought and its deployment of the metaphor of the mind of God. To conclude the converse – that the natural world is determined by mathematics and that mathematics is itself formed from within the natural world, without reference to any transcendent reality – seems to bury the issue of the effectiveness of mathematics, not deal with it. Mathematics has an a priori and necessary nature. Implicit in the notion of a law of nature is the idea that they are fundamental too. So, if these are the laws, then what meta-law fixed them? Given all this, the theistic explanation might start to look irresistible. Science recharging the spirit once more.

But it is a big leap to go from the metaphysics of mathematics to the God of Abraham, Isaac and Jacob. For one thing, mathematics is not personal. No one would suggest you worship an equation, for all that it may inspire awe. It is this that leads to the Platonist conclusion: maths does seem to have an existence that is not dependent upon human thought, but that doesn't imply a full blown theological cosmology.

Penrose makes another very good point. You can live your whole life with a very minimal knowledge of mathematics, and live it very well. So while Plato required his pupils to have a thorough knowledge of geometry before they entered his Academy, the school of life does not require proficiency in maths: meaning is not dependent upon calculus, nor spirituality on algebra. His preferred view is to say that the Platonic nature of mathematics is a mystery but that it doesn't actually say much about cosmic religion. That can be understood by comparison with the argument made by Plato from the *Euthyphro*. Recall that Socrates asks whether something is good because a deity says it is good, or whether it is good anyway, and concludes that such debates say more about our difficulties grappling with what is good than they do about the existence of gods. Penrose concludes:

> I don't take that view [that God created the universe]... I'm not going to argue against that view. I'm not going to take a religious view in this at all. I would say it's neutral with respect to the existence of God.

He is not a militant atheist. In fact, he is quite happy to talk of his Platonic view of mathematics as 'God-given' in his books.

But for him it is but a suggestive metaphor, one that points to what we don't know as much as what we do. Further, he recognises that Platonism is not a conclusive answer to the effectiveness of mathematics. It raises all sorts of problems about how the Platonic world interacts with the natural world, for example.

Consciousness and emergence

A third looks at things differently again, and it has to do with a newer concept in modern physics, that of emergence. Paul Davies is the cosmologist I associate with this option and for him the key issue is not the success of mathematics, but the existence of self-consciousness in the cosmos. It is, after all, what makes it possible to talk about meaningfulness in physics at all. At least one structure has arisen within the universe, namely the human brain, which can observe the universe, and attempt to understand it and itself. Moreover, that structure has a self-conscious purpose. 'It seems to me that there is a genuine scheme of things – the universe is "about" something,' he concludes in his book, *The Goldilocks Enigma: Why is the Universe Just Right for Life?* 'So we are perhaps not after all such nobodies. We are not for nothing,' concurs the playwright Michael Frayn in his book, significantly entitled *The Human Touch*.

Let me say a little more about how Davies arrives at such a conclusion. He first notes how striking what is commonly known as the fine-tuning of the universe is, that is, how it's right for life. The most dramatic example of this is the apparent fine-tuning of the dark energy. This is something that even atheistic physicists like Weinberg find extraordinary. What it boils down to is the notion that this stuff called dark energy appears right to about one part in 10 to the power of 123 or 124. This is phenomenally unlikely. It represents the equivalent chance of tossing a coin and getting 400 heads in a row. Or, if all the atoms in the known universe were coins, and each flipped billions of times a second, the age of the universe might just about allow one atom to have produced 360 in a row by now. It's a tuning that needs explaining.

One possibility is to say it means nothing. We inevitably view this lottery of life from the position of winners, and if we weren't winners and so here, ideas about fine-tuning wouldn't arise. The advocates of a massive multiverse occupy this position: it just happens that we live in the one that works for life. Davies doesn't like this since it seems to dodge the central question by invoking endless, absurd infinities.

Another possibility is to say that a universe with life in it is itself inevitable. That is, physics should derive a theory which cuts out the chance and makes the emergence of self-conscious observers more or less inevitable from the very beginning. This can be the position of two apparently opposing views. On the one hand, it can be the view of atheist physicists who seek a theory of everything: roughly, a successful theory of everything would be a theory that included necessary first conditions that would lead to us. On the other hand, it can be the view of those who believe in a creator God: roughly, a necessary divinity would in some way build in consciousness and us.

Davies objects to both these options since they imply that the Goldilocks enigma rests on conditions that fall outside the realm of science – be that necessary first conditions or a creator God. Both beg the question of why those conditions or why God. The fine-tuning remains unanswered.

The third possibility – and the position Davies likes the most – is to posit a theory of the universe that contains its own emergent explanation. This might now be possible given two results of quantum cosmology. First, at the quantum level, mathematics can be interpreted as lumpy, which would suggest that the laws of nature do not in fact exist in some Platonic realm. Instead they'd be part of the contingent fabric of the universe. As Davies explains:

> The universe on a mega-scale would resemble a cosmic United States of America, with different shaped 'states' separated by sharp boundaries. What we have hitherto taken to be universal laws of physics... would be more akin to local

by-laws, or state laws, rather than national or federal laws. And of this pot-pourri of cosmic regions, very few indeed would be suitable for life.

The second result of quantum cosmology that chimes with the emergence view is the possibility that observers are required to settle the laws which exist in one particular form or another, in one particular part of the universe or another. As the ever provocative Eugene Wigner put it: 'The very study of the external world led to the conclusion that the content of the consciousness is an ultimate reality.' From this, Davies sets up a causal loop: observers are necessary for the universe, as the universe does in fact obey laws, even if they vary. In short, the existence of the universe, the laws of nature and conscious observers are all interconnected. They emerge together.

Another cosmologist, John Wheeler, called this law without law, or order from disorder. Of the co-emergence of the universe, law and observers, he wrote: '[The cosmos] has not really happened, it is not a phenomenon, until it has been observed to happen.' The Buddhist astronomer Trinh Xuan Thuan warms to such ideas. He explains the concept of emergence as the organisation of elementary particles into ever more complex states, until the building blocks of life appear, and then life itself – capable of reproducing itself. 'This form of organization doesn't require outside intervention or mysterious forces,' he continues. 'Rather, order 'emerges' as soon as the complexity reaches a critical threshold.' In terms of meaning, Thuan believes this makes sense within a Buddhist framework that stresses interdependence – which Matthieu Ricard, in a conversation with Thuan, put like this:

Consciousness fashions reality and reality fashions consciousness, like the blades of two knives sharpening each other. A proper understanding of interdependence thus implies transcending the conventional notions of levels of existence or of dualism between 'self' and 'the world', or between 'conscious' and 'inanimate'.

There is much that is appealing in this picture of things for the agnostic or spiritually inclined. However, there are questions to raise about it too. For example, remember Godel's incompleteness theorem. It says that no mathematical system of a certain complexity can fully explain itself: you need some ingredients from outside. That would seem to preclude the self-causing system that Davies' quantum cosmology requires, since the universe could never completely 'understand' itself. The causal loop would be broken.

Alternatively, reflect again on Wheeler's observation, that something has not really happened, it is not a phenomenon, until it has been observed to happen. Does this imply that the universe did not existence before human eyes turned to gaze upon it, or at least the eyes of some other intelligent awareness? That seems bogglingly counterintuitive. Some of that vertigo might be lessened if you ask what counts as an observation: can a machine observe or a bacterium or an interacting particle? But if observation requires some kind of self-conscious entities, with the implication that the universe did not really exist until human beings or some other self-conscious animal evolved, then it seems fair to ask what did we or they evolve from: a shadowy, half-existing universe?

Another response to these conundrums is to develop notions of backward causation, which in the strange world of quantum physics may not be so strange. However, there is a feeling of the blind leading the blind here: quantum physics can be interpreted in a number of ways. How are we to decide which way is right? And there is also the fact that so much in this option rests on the nature of consciousness, about which science basically has no idea. So we come to a fourth option for the meaning of physics.

New age physics

It's the most overtly spiritual, and can be associated with the New Age. Fritjof Capra is a seminal figure here. He begins his book, *The Tao of Physics*, by describing a vision he had in the summer of 1969 looking out to sea from the beach of Santa Cruz.

> I was sitting by the ocean one late summer afternoon, watching the waves rolling in and feeling the rhythm of my breathing, when I suddenly became aware of my whole environment as being engaged in a gigantic cosmic dance.

Capra develops the idea that the language of physics has come up against the limitations of language when describing reality, as has long been recognised by the great Eastern mystics. Just as it is impossible to say what a photon is, only that it is sometimes like a particle, sometimes a wave, so the mystics understood that truly seeing reality is beyond human words and must be intuited in enlightenment. He believes that science has developed a new way of probing reality that complements the older ways of probing reality developed by the mystics.

> Physicists explore levels of matter, mystics levels of mind. What their explorations have in common is that these levels, in both cases, lie beyond ordinary sense perception. And, as Heisenberg has taught us, if the perception is nonordinary, then the reality is not ordinary.

Capra's ideas were and are influential. In its latest guise, it is often referred to as the Universe Story, after the title of a book by the cosmologist Brian Swimme and theologian Thomas Berry, *The Universe Story*. It tells the scientific story of the universe, from the Big Bang to the emergence of human consciousness, and does so as a new sacred myth. Swimme believes that, as he puts it, 'The universe is attempting to be felt.' Appreciating this insight leads to an experience of the numinous which Swimme defines as, 'being shocked by the splendour of existence'.

The Universe Story commands an increasingly large following and manifests what Gordon Lynch, the sociologist of religion, has called 'progressive spirituality'. The progressive element refers to the ethics and politics that it inspires: followers of the Universe Story are, say, highly ecologically aware and politically inclusive. They explain that this springs directly from what the new physics tells us about our place in the universe, that being defined by its relationality. We are literally linked to the stars in that we are made of stardust. We are entangled like quantum particles. We are creatures with all sorts of possible tomorrows, like the non-determined states of quantum mechanics. The difference is that we must take responsibility for those tomorrows, since we have emerged into self-consciousness.

Lynch believes that in much the same way as the charismatic movement of the 1980s started out as a marginal movement in the church and is now mainstream, so the Universe Story, and related new scientific sacred myths, will become mainstream over the next decade or so. For example, his research shows that already hundreds of women's Roman Catholic religious communities are following something like its ecological view of life.

Brian Swimme himself describes the Universe Story as a sacred myth that can orientate anyone in life. He is what might be called a pantheist, and develops the idea into a politico-spiritual programme. The origins of the myth go back to the Copernican revolution, when it was proposed, first, that the sun was the centre of things, before it was realised that even the sun was sailing unanchored through space. This insight had a massive impact on western civilisation. The medieval sense of self melted away, and the modern sense of self emerged – which like the sun enjoys the liberty of mobility, though also the loneliness of not being quite sure where it belongs in the cosmos.

Today, Swimme continues, we're at a similar moment of breakdown and creativity. Physics is now able to tell a story that reaches back 13.7 billion years, when the universe came into existence. Since then, the tale is of growing complexity. Undifferentiated energy became the web of forces and condensations we call atoms; atoms formed into molecules; molecules dust; dust stars and planets; planets provided an incubator for life; life led to that extraordinary phenomenon we know as intelligence, and even more surprisingly, self-awareness. The modern sense of self is, therefore, now changing into what might be called an ecological self. We're developing a sense of being part of the Earth's systems, and thereby connected to the cosmos as a whole.

If this kind of talk is not your thing, it is tempting to write it off – to call it 'New Age' pejoratively. Alternatively, it could be said that it is too tied to the new physics: as the physics changes, as it will, these New Agers risk having the scientific rug pulled out from under their metaphysical feet. Although Capra anticipated the problem.

> Many concepts we hold today will be replaced by a different set of concepts tomorrow. But this replacement will occur in an orderly way, and the basic themes that I use in my comparison with mystical traditions will be enforced, I believe, rather than invalidated.

Further, it is part and parcel of the spirituality of the Universe Story that we are only beginning to understand our connection with the cosmos, as scientists are only beginning to understand the nature of the universe. So we should positively expect things to change and develop.

A deeper criticism is that this approach to the science is picky about what it makes so much of. It's an à la carte approach to physics. For example, adherents dislike the notion of fine-tuning, unlike with the emergent option of Paul Davies, because it seems too anthropocentric. A similar reaction is provoked when the notion of emergence is suggested to imply that human consciousness exists at the top of a hierarchy of being. Conversely, the New Age reading doesn't take much notice of another striking feature of the subatomic world: it's colossal destructiveness.

In general, it does seem as if these movements are more swayed by what they take from ancient mystical traditions than from modern science, reading the former into the latter.

Spirituality has a determining role in assessing the science, which means that the spiritual intuitions are not produced by the science, but rather, the tail wags the dog. Paul Davies put it to me like this: 'There is a lot of flaky stuff in this area, where people present quantum physics in a mystical light and then draw all sorts of dubious "spiritual" conclusions. I am reluctant to get involved because the field is so vague.'

A middle way

We arrive, then, at the fifth position. It can be thought of as seeking to establish a middle way between the New Age readings and the Platonism of Penrose, or quasi-Buddhism of Davies. It's been most clearly articulated by John Polkinghorne, an Anglican priest who first made his name in physics for his work in the discovery of quarks.

He is quite clear that he finds contemporary physics remarkably resonant with spiritual imperatives. Part of the joy of science for a believer is that its brute facts point beyond themselves: the sheer multiplicity of the stars and galaxies, say, raises the possibility of a hugely fruitful creation. As early scientists like Galileo and Newton concurred, God has written two books, the Book of the Bible and the Book of Nature. Both need to be read, and when done aright, apparent contradictions dissolve since they have the same author. During his career, Polkinghorne has also seen that many who are interested in fundamental physics and the beginning and end of things in cosmology are also interested in the big questions like God.

However, while both science and religion are looking for truth, they are different kinds of activity. The wise observer is therefore someone who does not confuse the two, who seeks a middle way. Polkinghorne calls science and religion 'intellectual cousins': the Big Bang is not the same as the doctrine of creation out of nothing, though there are analogical connections. Alternatively, religion, unlike science, is transpersonal. Thus, Polkinghorne confesses, he meets God primarily in religious practice not mathematical equations: 'Science only gives a thin notion of God.'

Further, it's quite possible to read too much into physics. An example of that would be equating the singularity of the Big Bang with the creative moment described in the book of Genesis. Or looking at quantum mechanics and deriving, say, an ethic of relationship, or a basis for telepathy from the phenomenon of particle entanglement. That is going too far because the quantum world is so manifestly different from the macro world of our reality. It'd be like recommending the planet Mercury as a lovely place for a holiday because the sun always shines there. Polkinghorne writes: 'Physics is showing the world to be both more supple and subtle, but you need to be careful.'

That said, reading too little from physics is the other extreme he rejects. Hence notions such as the multiverse to explain away observations like fine-tuning, seem to him like 'desperate' measures to do away with the theist possibility with which physics is commensurate. This critique is also made by the theologian Hans Küng, in his book, *The Beginning of All Things: Science and Religion*. He talks of a kind of political correctness against religious connotations derived from science, and an 'instinctive opposition': for these folk, there is a sense in which any scientific explanation, no matter how wild, is preferable to a theological reflection.

The key is to realise that science has its limits when it comes to these deeper human concerns, Polkinghorne believes. He argues that if you want to pursue the search for understanding – 'a quest that is most natural for [us] to embark upon' – then we have to be prepared to go beyond the domain of science. And this, surely, is right. It's the conclusion I've reached in my look at the meaning of modern physics and the possibility of cosmic religion.

The truth is that although modern physics is imaginatively inviting, it is not proof positive of any particular metaphysics. This is the cause of the diversity among our physicists: though they look at the same science, the science alone can't decide which of their interpretations is the most plausible. If you put an atheist in, you get an atheist out. And likewise for a Platonist, Buddhist, New Age follower, or Christian. The science can be made to fit with a number of bigger pictures. The positions I've outlined are all pretty respectable, given the current level of understanding. And it's possible to have a debate about where each runs into difficulties. But they all do at some point, and so you have to bring other considerations to bear on the issue when deciding which makes most sense to you.

It has always been so. Newton's discoveries – the new physics of his day – generated a not dissimilar plurality of speculations and levels of excitement. The theory of gravitation was popularly perceived as being about the influence of all bodies on one another, no matter how distant. This seemed to be not only a boon to astronomy but to astrology too. Newton's work apparently validated the notion that the distant stars and planets might act upon human bodies so as to determine their course through life, much as it does the course of heavenly bodies through the skies. And it did not stop there. Newtonianism lay behind developments such as mesmerism, spiritualism, phrenology and vegetarianism. None are completely arbitrary but exploit real ambiguities and apparent implications of the physics. But they are only apparent. Science must be in dialogue with religion. The physical needs to be related to the spiritual. But the question is always: how?

Sacred biology

It's worth noting that similar speculations are now emerging from within biology too. Some are venturing the physicist's old question: is this a new source for the sacred? It begins with the same experience, the wonder life on earth can inspire quite as fully as cosmology. The TV naturalist, David Attenborough, made a series, *Life in the Undergrowth*, in which he turned his camera on the world of invertebrates. It was both beautiful and fascinating to watch. However, it was not just the giant millipede that can kill a baby, or the exquisite film of running ants that was gripping. There was a profound sense of awe that pervaded the programmes. This led naturally – and without the sentimental anthropomorphisms that are so easy to read into more cuddly creatures – to the contemplation, first, of the insignificance of human beings in relationship to the insect world, and second to a more profound appreciation of the value of these creatures than a strictly scientific analysis allows.

Attenborough pointed out not just that invertebrates were the first creatures to colonise the land. Nor that they established the foundations of the land's ecosystems and were able to transcend the limitations of their small size by banding together in huge communities of millions. He said that if the invertebrates were to disappear today, the land's ecosystems would unavoidably, and rapidly, collapse. If human beings and all other back-boned animals similarly vanished, the world would continue without faltering. He was also amazed at the behaviour they caught on film:

> I think the thing that surprises you is that when you watch invertebrates normally, say spiders, you think, 'well, they're just spiders and mechanical little creatures'. But when you start to film them, you discover that they have individual personalities. I mean, you can watch spiders of the same species, and some are lazy, some are hard working, some don't like light. They all have personalities, there's no doubt about it.

That is a wonderful thing to say of such creatures. It also leads Attenborough to agnosticism. He doesn't think there's a divine force that designed the system of natural selection. But he has talked about looking inside a termite hill, and watching a million bugs toiling away, each at their own task.

> I know perfectly well that they can't see me because they are blind... And I sometimes think that maybe we're a bit like

that. We don't have the perceptions except very, very dimly that there maybe something beyond there and bigger there and that we can't conceive of... I think it unscientific to rule out the possibility that there may be things there that we don't know about.

Set Attenborough's thoughts alongside a few more lines from the poet Thomas Traherne. He was also fascinated by the world opened up by new optical techniques – in his case not cameras but microscopes – and the way they revealed hidden wonders. The magnified sight of the 'curious and high stomached' fly caught his imagination in particular. Their 'burnished and resplendent' bodies like 'orient gold or polished steel' evoked a virtual encomium from his pen.

> The infinite workmanship about his body, the marvellous consistence of his limbs, the most neat and exquisite distinction of his joints, the subtle and imperceptible ducture of his nerves, and endowments of his tongue, and ears, and eyes, and nostrils; the stupendous union of his soul and body, the exact and curious symmetry of all his parts, the feeling of his feet and the swiftness of his wings, the vivacity of his quick and active power...

Traherne continues at some length. And the effect of his praise, not unlike the natural history film, is a growing admiration, even fondness, for the 'sucking parts' and 'buzzing wings' of these dipterous beasts. That would be remarkable enough. But, like Attenborough contemplating the spider, Traherne's thoughts lead him further. So amazing is the fly, he writes, that it 'would make him seem like a treasure wherein all wonders were shut up together, and that God had done as much in little there, as he had done at large in the whole world.'

The point is that the 'personality of spiders' and the 'divine treasures' of the fly are not and never could be scientific descriptions. Write like that in a scientific journal, and you would be

Illus. 2.3: The 'burnished and resplendent' fly, as drawn by Robert Hooke, in 1667.

thought ridiculous. But these expressions of wonder do, none-theless, convey real insight about the insects, the experience of studying them, and their significance in the world at large. One may ask why the fly has such 'infinite workmanship about his body'? The strictly scientific answer would incorporate details like the properties of chitin, the material from which insects' exoskeletons are made, and the evolutionary adaptation of its parts. But might one not also ask why the microscopic ridges of chitin on a butterfly wing, for example, refract light to produce colours that we spontaneously and admiringly call iridescent? Or why the chitin of the cicada produces a noise that we say can sing? Is it going too far to suggest that it is because they are not only wonderful to the human imagination but, in some unimaginable sense, aesthetically attractive to an insect mate? Just what that might mean is impossible to fix. It is an example of a natural mystery within biology. A strictly evolutionary 'explanation' that the wing and the song are sexually selected implicitly dismisses the wonder. But capturing a sense of it is surely part of the reason that Attenborough and Traherne's portraits of invertebrates are so compelling.

Some biologists are going a step further. Simon Conway Morris, a leading paleontologist who is also a Christian, is one thinker to speculate on. He is known for his convergence theory of evolution. It argues that many times the evidence shows that evolution has come up with the same solution to biological problems via different paths of Darwinian processes. One of the better known examples is that sabre-toothed cats arose on at least three different occasions from different ancestors. Or there's the evolution of camera eyes, which we share with octopuses, though they evolved quite independently. Conway Morris has tracked dozens of examples across a wide variety of biological phenomena. Even divergent solutions to the same problem show such convergence, since the divergent solutions themselves repeat themselves. It's a bit like an equation that admits of more than one solution: evolution finds them all.

The implication of this is that if you rerun the 'tape of life', in Stephen Jay Gould's phrase, life would turn out quite like it does now – not very differently as Gould had insisted. Moreover, Conway Morris believes that in terms of biological engineering, evolution has arrived at pretty much the best solutions possible. Such conclusions offend neo-Darwinian orthodoxy, which resists seeing a weak kind of necessity in evolution, and believes strongly in radical contingency.

But Conway Morris's evolutionary argument is powerful. He believes that when it comes to understanding the mental characteristics of organisms – not only primates but further down the ladder of psychological complexity too – contemporary science has run up against a brick wall. It has no capacity whatsoever to explain mental phenomena that begins with the cognition of sensations, moves to consciousness, and in the case of humans, and possibly a handful of other animals, ends up with self-consciousness. He's quite open to the possibility that some higher animals have a kind of culture too. He wonders whether the singing of whales is such an 'artful' exploration. It's all highly speculative, of course: he knows that. But not unreasonable, given what is emerging about the individual nature of the music different whales produce, and the way it develops. If you accept evolutionary convergence, it might even be expected: why shouldn't the music of different species be similar, in the way that their camera eyes are too? To put it another way, and to stay with that one example, people are drawn to whale music since in some basic way it is like human music.

If you accept that, then you might be inclined to make a Platonic turn. This would suggest that evolution can be thought of not only as a bottom-up process of adaptation to physical environments, but as a top-down process that, in effect, leads to the discovery of non-material realities. Using the music example again: both whale and human music could be thought of as reflections of a kind of 'cosmic music'. Or to put it a different way, evolution is a kind of search engine, powered by Darwinian mechanisms. The human mind is the best search engine that has emerged so far, to our knowledge at least. In a further striking analogy, Conway Morris has likened the brain to a radio antenna, seeking, as it were, aesthetic and spiritual 'signals'.

Once you get going along these lines, why stop there? For as our mental life is personal, and the mental life of other animals shows signs of being personal too, then maybe that is merely a reflection of the personhood that might run through the cosmos. In short, and as with physics, it is possible to develop a full-blown evolutionary theology.

Conway Morris is not the only biologist exploring such ideas. Stuart Kauffman is another. He's developed a complex argument in his book *Reinventing the Sacred*, writing, 'So the unfolding of the universe – biotic, and perhaps abiotic too – appears to be partially beyond natural law.' The world is, instead, a place of ceaseless and genuine 'creativity'. He's not a theist, like Conway Morris, though he is happy to take the natural creativity he believes he's identified in evolution as a reinvention of notions of God. He believes biology can resacralise life and the planet.

And yet, for all the allure of such speculations for the spirituality inclined, the biological routes to an apparently scientific spirituality fall foul of the same problems we found with the physics. In particular, different biologists will look at the same evidence and come to radically different metaphysical conclusions – including those who find support for their materialistic and atheistic convictions. It will inevitably be that way because science's success is linked to the modesty of its ambition, namely to study the natural world, not the spiritual. Sacred and secular conclusions alike can be read analogously from it, and mythologically into it, but not, strictly speaking, empirically out of it. What we must do, then, is take account of what the limits of science might be.

The limits of science

This is hard to do. If you read a newspaper, or many of the popular books written about science, you could be forgiven for thinking that scientific knowledge is effectively limitless and straightforwardly cumulative. Like doing a jigsaw, that may take time and involve taking pieces out as well as putting them in place, they tend to describe science as a process of assembling a picture of the world that grows and will one day, all being well, be complete. Such a marvellous achievement is laid at the feet of the scientific method. It rests on induction: scientists collate sets of empirically verifiable premises from which a conclusion, that is more than could have been anticipated from any one of the premises, can be induced. For example: the sun rises one day, and then the next, and then the next, from which it is concluded that the sun will rise every day.

The trouble is that the history of physics over the last 100 years, and arguably now biology too, has not looked anything like this cumulative idea of scientific discovery. Physics has undergone a series of revolutions, and today arguably awaits a revolution again, to deal with unknowns like dark energy. There are biologists who venture the same prognosis for their science too. How else is it going to tackle apparent imponderables like consciousness? So philosophers of science question the all-powerful cumulative view.

Various alternatives have been formulated. Thomas Kuhn thought that the apparently cumulative periods of scientific endeavour were only one part of the story. He called this normal science, when scientists pursue their line of research on the assumption that it fits into the great puzzle of knowledge that awaits completion. However, there is another part of the story, when science undergoes a paradigm shift. As the uncertainties of one paradigm become irresistible, scientists fight it out to establish a new one. When that has happened, a new round of normal science is initiated and the illusion of cumulative truth returns. This is arguably what happened to physics at the beginning of the twentieth century. Scientists then thought that they were just putting the finishing touches to the picture of the world that originated with Newton, were it not for a handful of experiments that kept throwing a spanner in the works. These experiments confounded the wave theory of light by showing how light could behave as if it were particles of energy too. Some took this conundrum to be a result of errors; they took the 'flawed' experiments to be addressing the wrong questions. However, eventually, the weight of evidence became unavoidable. From what seemed a mere glitch, a whole new paradigm in science was born, namely, the indeterminate, probabilistic world of quantum mechanics.

Kuhn's alternative model of science is the one most widely accepted by those who reject the accumulative one. His normal science looks very much like the industrial processes under which science is carried out in commerce and universities. However, Kuhn's model also entails that social forces play a part in the determination of scientific truth too, when science is undergoing a paradigm shift. Which is to say that science is not wholly 'scientific'. In questioning the traditional model of science, an ambiguity as to the veracity of science has crept in. Science is neither seamlessly cumulative nor can it wholly account for the processes through which its results are derived.

A different model of science was proposed by Karl Popper. He rejected the method of induction, following David Hume who argued that it was no more reliable than a belief: thinking of the rising sun again, Hume pointed out that just because it rose yesterday and today is no proof that it will rise tomorrow, for all that it seems very likely. Popper thought that induction was more like a process of informed guesswork. The way science works, he argued, is that scientists come up with hypotheses based on their intuition. They then test them by observation. These tests do not verify the hypothesis, as the traditional view of science would have them do. Rather, all they can do is show that the hypothesis is not false. So, the best scientific theories are the ones that are most easily falsifiable for, if they stand up, they are more likely to be right.

However, in offering this model of science, Popper also implied that science is never quite true, though it may come asymptotically close. (In practice, because the best falsifiable theories depend on the quality of the method used to test them, which is also hard to get right, scientific theories will routinely be overthrown by other ones.)

Kuhn and Popper are both philosophical heirs of Immanuel Kant. He famously pointed out that our image of the world around us could not be a mirror image of things as they are in themselves because the human mind imposes its own structures of thought onto the world in order to see the world. We cannot do otherwise, for without our own concepts of things we would not be able to understand anything. As the philosopher Hilary Putnam puts it: 'Scientific theories are not simply dictated to us by the facts.' The wave/particle duality of light is again a case in point. When viewed using one set of theoretical spectacles, light looks like a wave. When using another, it looks like particles. But what light is in itself is another question entirely. More generally, quantum physics shows that science doesn't actually know the cosmos as it is; that lies behind what the physicist Bernard d'Espagnat has called a 'veiled reality'. Instead, there are various models that a scientist can use to describe what's observed – what philosophers call equivalent descriptions. All in all, be it by paradigm shifts or discarding falsified theories, it might be said that science evolves by rejecting ideas when shown wrong and by taking as much account as possible of the interaction between these theories and the human conventions within which they arose. This produces tremendous technologies and astonishing insights. But it can never be absolutely right.

A veiled reality

So what model of science's relationship to spirituality is right? Personally, I don't think Stephen Jay Gould's formula of non-overlapping magisteria adds up, as science so readily inspires religious wonder. Further, there is quite a debate at the moment about whether materialist models of reality or idealist philosophies work best. Biologists tend to opt for the materialist, although they run into the conundrum of consciousness. Physicists are more open to idealist possibilities, not only because of Platonic inclinations, or an awareness of the role that 'observers' and measurement might play in quantum mechanics, but because information seems as good a possibility for the fundamental stuff out of which everything is made as any material stuff. So, as Polkinghorne concludes, while there's got to be a dialogue between science and religion, you've got to be careful.

No less a figure than Einstein implied something similar. He was the individual who raised the possibility of a cosmic religion so powerfully in the twentieth century, and he also seems to have pitched his answer about right. He was quite happy to talk about God, though the exact nature of his religiosity is continually contested. Walter Isaacson, in his biography of the genius of relativity, concludes that he was religiously-minded and probably an agnostic. But he believed that science was not possible without a spiritual sensibility. He concluded: 'Science without religion is lame. Religion without science is blind', and wrote:

> Behind all the discernible laws and connections, there remains something subtle, intangible and inexplicable. Veneration for this force beyond anything that we can comprehend is my religion.

I think it would be fair to say that Einstein was pious in this way. He did not fear being caught on the boundaries between science and spirituality where the sense of wonder and a useful force of intuitive suggestion are at play. But he was also conscious of the limits of what science can tell you. 'Enough for me,' he wrote in *The World as I See It*, 'the inkling of the marvellous structure of reality, together with the single-hearted endeavour to comprehend a portion, be it never so tiny, of the reason that manifests itself in nature.' His piety is expressed in the suggestion that the greatest achievement of science is not to explain it all, but is to point more clearly to that which is beyond its scope:

> The most beautiful and deepest experience a man can have is the sense of the mysterious. It is the underlying principle of religion as well as all serious endeavour in art and science. He who never had this experience seems to me, if not dead, then at least blind... To me it suffices to wonder at these secrets and to attempt humbly to grasp with my mind a mere image of the lofty structure of all that there is.

How To Be Human: Science and Ethics

> We feel that even when all possible scientific questions have been answered, the problems of life have not been put to rest.
>
> Ludwig Wittgenstein

The allure of cosmic religion is not new. Way back in ancient Athens an optimism not dissimilar to our own was in the air. The movement now called pre-Socratic natural philosophy was becoming known for its investigations of the world. And these ancient 'scientists' had good reason to be wowed by their achievements. Its amazing power was being made manifest in the construction of the Parthenon – a technological wonder that has inspired awe for 2500 years.

One should not underestimate the remarkably prescient nature of their discoveries too. Parmenides realised that the moon reflects the light of the sun. Democritus postulated the basic units of nature as atoms existing in a void. Pythagoras, who may not have originated his celebrated theorem, may have worked out that day and night were far better explained by the earth going round the sun, not vice versa. Empedocles argued that the natural world was made up of elements, and although he considered that there were only four (earth, fire, air and water), he was right in presuming that the material world could be explained by a continual flux of elemental integration and disintegration.

These searching minds also anticipated many of the philosophical problems with which science wrestles to this day. Democritus, for example, knew that there was power in his postulate that atoms formed matter and that matter, in turn, formed the world as we experience it. But his atomic theory was also limited as an explanation: at the atomic level it can account for the material world around us, but it cannot account for itself, because that, in turn, would require an explanation involving particles smaller than atoms to account for atoms. This search for ever smaller, more elusive forces and particles is one that quantum theory is still caught up in to this day. The problem is that particle physics – ancient or modern – begs the question of what accounts for its fundamentals.

A different persistent problem was anticipated by Parmenides. What survives of his work includes two explanations of the world, called the *Way of Truth* and the *Way of Seeming* – titles that on the face of it chime remarkably with the thought of Kant. The *Way of Seeming* includes his astronomical achievements and simultaneously throws them into question: how do we know, he implies, that the way we divide the world up, as any reductionist science must do, actually reflects the world as it is? Are the divisions purely arbitrary or would a true map of reality show similar divisions? Put in the modern idiom, is the universe truly mathematical or is mathematics just very successful at describing certain aspects of it? In other words, Parmenides understood that science needs theories in order to interpret observations, but whether these theories correspond with reality is not something that science can itself answer.

Another speculation with a contemporary ring can be heard in the thoughts of Empedocles. He felt that the integrating and disintegrating cycles of the elements implied the need for a moral interpretation alongside the physical. After all, is it not as if the universe is moving from harmony to discord, and then back again, and perhaps according to some fundamental forces – he called them Strife and Friendship – he asked?

A twofold tale I shall tell: at one time it grew to be one alone out of many, at another again it grew apart to be many out of one. Double is the birth of mortal things and double their failing; for one is brought to birth and destroyed by

Illus. 3.1: The Parthenon has made the wonder of technology manifest for 2500 years.

the coming together of all things, the other is nurtured and flies apart as they grow apart again. And these things never cease their continual exchange, now through Friendship all coming together into one, now again each carried apart by the hatred of Strife.

It came quite naturally for him to slip from the realm of scientific theory into the realm of spiritual speculation. But then, in the following generation, a different question arose, and we'll turn to it now. It was, in fact, raised by Socrates at a defining moment in his life. What he wanted to know was not whether science could fill the God-shaped hole: he knew it could not because God-talk is always, ultimately beyond us. Inspiration, perhaps; certainty, no. But maybe there is something else, equally importantly for us human beings, with which science can be of assistance. Can it inform us with how to live? Plato preserved Socrates' change of direction in his dialogue the *Phaedo*. Phaedo was an intimate of Socrates, and their conversion helps take our discussion a stage further on.

Causes and conditions

The dialogue recalls the last conversation Socrates had with his friends – a poignant time to reflect on the nature of meaning. In these hours, Socrates pondered the significance of life and death, and how one might rejoice in the former and prepare for the latter. And he recalled his first forays in the world of ideas. 'When I was a young man I was wonderfully keen on that wisdom which they call natural science, for I thought it splendid to know the causes of everything, why it comes to be, why it perishes and why it exists,' he recollects. He sought answers to questions again remarkably similar to those asked by us moderns. What matter is it that allows us to think? Is it our brains that hear, see and smell? And when our brains perish, do our memories and insights – do we – perish too?

At first he thought that science was a good way of enquiring into our wellbeing because, as it claimed, it did indeed seem to explain life's causes. However, his optimism did not last. For upon further inspection, the explanations it offered seemed really quite easy to unravel. Socrates offers a simple example in Plato's dialogue, a parallel to the modern question asked by Wigner about the unreasonable effectiveness of mathematics. Does $1 + 1 = 2$? There are, in fact, good reasons to doubt it. For one thing there are examples in nature when $1 + 1 \neq 2$, as when two raindrops coalesce. Alternatively, there is, strictly speaking, no mathematic proof that $1 + 1 = 2$. Today, mathematicians would say that it is, rather, something that follows from the definition of natural numbers $(1, 2, 3, 4 \ldots)$. This is Socrates' tussle with cosmic religion: it's fascinating – he admits – compelling, but not very practical. For how should we live? The dialogue continues with Socrates reading another pre-Socratic natural philosopher, Anaxagoras.

Anaxagoras followed an atomic theory of matter, similar to that of Democritus. However, he realised that although atomic processes might more or less explain how matter can appear in so many forms in the inanimate world, its weakness becomes increasingly pronounced when it comes to living things. His point is that living things do not behave like dead matter. Plants, for example, grow. Animals show intention. And when it comes to humans, physical causes are almost neither here nor there when it comes to explaining what we do and why we do it. With people, desires and instincts – conscious and unconscious – are the causes that count. That clearly has something to do with our biology. But actually, and given certain obvious constraints, far less so than you might first think.

Put it this way: human beings want not just to exist, but to live and live well. So even when doing 'animal' things, we loathe living like animals: we prefer, say, to eat tasty food, not just muck; to sleep in a comfortable bed, not just on the floor; and to make love, not merely copulate. This is what bothered Anaxagoras too, and so he postulated an all-controlling force that he called Mind – 'the finest of all things and the purest, and it possesses all knowledge about everything, and it has the greatest strength.' Mind, he thought, is what lies behind the world, and that we see particularly in living things that demonstrate purposes and desires. It might seem a superstitious, unscientific belief to us. But it had the advantage, Socrates at first thought, of implying that the world was ordered in the best possible way – a principle of economy, simplicity and beauty that, if in a disenchanted form, is in fact still compelling to scientists today.

The problem Socrates had with it, though, was that for all its aesthetic appeal it actually explains less than it appears to and, therefore, leads to little practical advice. Take an obvious situation, Socrates asks himself, again in Plato's dialogue: why he is sitting in the prison with his friends awaiting death. Following Anaxagoras, he might say it is due to his mind and the way it controls his body. However, this seems a somewhat reductive assessment of the situation. It would imply, Socrates continued:

> I am sitting here because my body consists of bones and sinews, because the bones are hard and are separated by joints, that the sinews are such as to contract and relax, that they surround the bones along with flesh and skin which hold them together, then as the bones are hanging in their sockets, the relaxation and contraction of the sinews enable me to bend my limbs, and that is the cause of my sitting here with my limbs bent.

As might be suspected from this shaggy dog story of an explanation, Socrates thinks it foolish. You can imagine the modern equivalent from neuroscience of neurons, synapses and nerves firing. Science fails to explain his situation in another sense too. If the body's chief aim is survival, as might seem reasonable from a biological point of view, then it would suggest that Socrates should have escaped prison. According to the scientific worldview, his sinews and bones should have been miles away.

So why am I sat here, he asks again? The answer is only indirectly to do with his body or mind. It is actually to do with the fact that the Athenians have condemned him to death. Moreover, Socrates could have escaped and lived. But he has decided it is right to stay and die. In other words, Socrates is sat in prison, awaiting the hemlock for a reason that science does not begin to get a handle on. The 'cause' of his predicament is fundamentally moral. He believes this is the right way to die because it reflects what he also believes is the right way to live.

Socrates goes on, speculating that someone might retort, well that may be true, but, at a basic level, you could not be sitting in prison without your sinews and bones having moved in certain ways. That is right, Socrates admits: 'But surely to say that they are the cause of what I do, and not that I have chosen the moral course, is to speak very lazily and carelessly.' A much better way of putting it is to say that it is a condition of his sitting that

What he's saying is that because the answers that science provides are so compelling, so successful within their own sphere of competence, it is too easy to forget that and slip into thinking that what you have at your disposal is what Daniel Dennett has called a 'universal acid.' Dennett is referring to evolutionary explanations of ethics, the approach which puts our behaviour all down to adaptation and the scattering of genes. Thus, the finery of the peacock's tail is aimed at attracting a mate, and the finery of Shakespeare's prose follows more or less the same logic too, as it must have got him the girl. But to conclude thus is precisely what Atiyah means by giving up your soul, for the soul is found not in sexual success but in the poetry and fine prose.

I simplify, of course, though remarkably not that much. Consider the way biologists talk about DNA. The four nucleotides of DNA are represented by letters AGCT. They arrange themselves in what are called codons. These, in turn, are taken to be the 'words' of the genetic instructions for the cell. Now, clearly an organism like a human being, consisting of trillions of cells, is going to be a fantastically complicated product of the DNA double helix, mixed up with even more subtle intercellular and environmental factors – to say nothing of the psychosomatic. But DNA's descriptive similarity to a code, coupled to a technological age's trust in data, inevitably leads to the assumption that DNA is not only the determining factor in life – the notion captured in Richard Dawkins's metaphor 'the selfish gene' – but is nothing less than the meaning of life. The loss of soul does not stop there, for the idea that human beings are merely information-processing machines is not the only metaphor at play. Remarkably, when coupled to genetic determinism, DNA comes to look very much like the immortal soul it seeks to displace: it embodies in nucleotides an essence of life that survives the death of the body by being passed on, incorporeally, from generation to generation.

It is sometimes argued that these metaphors are passive: when deployed, they are used as analogies, serving to popularise science, as opposed to informing hard-core research. However, metaphors are powerful for a reason. Tell yourself a story that you are but the outworking of your DNA – a reproductive machine driven by selfish genes – and even if you insist it's just a metaphor, the metaphor is likely to take over and shape your understanding of life.

Policies for happiness

Not everyone engaged in science is a follower of such scientism, of course. However, in terms of public discourse, you can see that it holds great sway. There's a struggle on, with some arguing that science's contribution to moral matters should not be ancillary but axiomatic. Even for those who sense the dangers of Atiyah's Faustian pact, a weaker version of scientism, sometimes called naturalism, might well appeal. While appreciating that full-blown scientism is overblown, naturalism places great store on empirical discovery, saying that it overshadows other forms of knowledge as a way to certainty and truth. But Socrates' challenge was aimed at naturalism as much as scientism and is still pertinent today.

Consider as an example some of the hopes and expectations people have for contemporary neuroscience. Anyone who reads a newspaper will be familiar with reports of brain scans revealing the secrets of anything from consciousness to altruism, often reported as if no one before had anything much to say on the subject. Wild headlines are often misleading, of course (as headlines about genes being discovered for this or that are too). However, there is more substantial evidence that the philosophical mistake identified by Socrates is being made again: science is being treated as if it can tell us how to live.

A case in point is the science of happiness. This new discipline stems from the identification of regions in the brain that are associated with good and bad feeling. Place individuals in brain scanners, and instruct them to perform certain tasks, and you can show that there is a part of the left frontal lobe that fires when good feelings are experienced and a part of the right frontal lobe that fires when bad feelings arise. The result has been interpreted by some as of key interest not only to brain scientists but to moral philosophers too, because it apparently provides an objective indicator of what people are feeling. This, they say, is needed to overcome the scepticism that derives from certain traditions that doubt it is possible to know what is going on inside another person's head (because I can only observe you, and not see into your brain, and from that only infer what you are experiencing). The hope is that because individuals can be wired up and monitored as, say, they laugh or cry, confidence can return to interpreting the meaning of tears: if the left brain lights up, they are indeed tears of joy; if the right brain lights up, they are tears of sadness.

The science has been taken out of the laboratory and into government. Its advocates say that it provides firm foundations for social policies that aim to promote the ways in which people can live more happily. Richard Layard is one to explain how in his book, *Happiness: Lessons from a New Science*. He argues that as a result of the philosophical scepticism, policy-makers had lost confidence in the idea behind Jeremy Bentham's utilitarianism, that a good society is one in which happiness is maximised for the greatest number of people. However, says Layard, happiness can now be put back on the agenda as a goal of government because the days of uncertainty are over. Today, happiness can be measured: it is made tangible by 'solid psychology and neuroscience', he writes.

Utilitarianism was an honourable invention when it first emerged in the eighteenth century. Then, many folk did not enjoy a decent dose of quality pleasures. However, as became apparent almost as soon as Bentham published his ideas, it is very difficult to say for sure what it is for people to be truly happy. And this is where the Socratic point kicks back in.

Is not pleasure very different from contentment which is again very different from joyfulness which is similarly different from happiness – and yet all would be called good feelings? And underneath all that lies the fundamental question of what happiness is? Today it is generally taken to mean a peak or sustained experience of positive feeling – the aspect that can be measured. A quintessential example might be the sensation an athlete has having won a race. However, Aristotle convincingly argued that this notion is inadequate. He said that a happy person is one who is good – note the moral quality of that – and good in two senses. First, they are good at what they do. And second, they are good because of the person they become in doing it. In short, happiness comes to a life lived with an overall good purpose. This explains his use of the otherwise rather puzzling maxim that a person cannot tell whether they were truly happy until they die: happiness is a reflection of the shape of a life as a whole, not a measure of isolated or even extended moments in it.

Another important point was made by John Stuart Mill who realised that happiness is one of those things in life, like love, which has the property of becoming more elusive the more doggedly you seek it. Better, Mill concluded, not to think about happiness at all, for only then might you have the chance to 'inhale happiness with the air you breathe, without dwelling on it or thinking about it, without either forestalling it in imagination, or putting it to flight by fatal questioning.' It was partly for such reasons that politicians after Mill focused on things like maximising people's rights or opportunities – legal entities that are tangible in ways that the pursuit of happiness is not.

One cannot question the frustration that lies behind Layard's hope. Why, he asks, have human beings in the West become no happier over the last 50 years, a period that has seen unparalleled economic growth? Add to that, the aftermath of the global economic crisis of 2008, the pain of which will be long lasting, the damage profound. The problem here is that for too long, we ceded our ability to decide what we want to markets. Isn't it time to re-organise how we live so that instead of relentlessly pursuing efficiency and growth we pursue what actually makes us happy? He also rightly laments the limitations inherent in the kind of politics based mostly upon rights and opportunity. They are endlessly contested and make people highly individualistic. All in all, Layard wants neuroscience to 'vindicate' Bentham's approach so as to make for a new politics. But it cannot. We need to think ethically, not scientifically.

Kinder than we think

Science is being sourced as a moral fixer in other ways too. One area about which a lot is currently being written concerns empathy – the capacity to feel another's pleasure and pain. Cultivated as sympathy, the hope again is for a scientifically grounded approach to our wellbeing. The moral element becomes explicit when it's stressed that the ability to sympathise with others, to step into their shoes, is vital for the good life and a kinder society. The claim is that we can genuinely feel what others feel, rather than just guessing about their experience from our own, and that leads to the kind of sympathy for others, which, when cultivated, is the basis for our wellbeing.

I asked Chris Frith, Emeritus Professor at University College London, now working with the Interacting Minds project at the University of Aarhus, Denmark, about this. A leading player in the area, he confirmed that when we see or know that someone is in pain, the same brain areas are activated as when we are in pain ourselves; similarly, when we see someone being touched – although most of us are unaware of this and don't consciously feel that we are being touched. This capacity is a result of mirror neurons – though strictly speaking they've so far only been shown to play a role when we observe actions, like seeing others being touched, not feelings, like seeing others in pain. But there certainly seems to be a mirror system for emotions in the brain, and hence perhaps a scientific basis for an ethics of empathy.

Except that it then gets more complicated. Frith believes there are three levels of empathy. A first is called emotional contagion. It's the most basic and is involuntary. Emotional contagion is automatically detecting the emotion felt by someone else, and while that may or may not fully reach the level of awareness, it affects us. It's the cause of the inchoate feelings that arise from witnessing another's exhilaration or distress. And it can lead to action, though mostly in order to minimise the contagion: you might fetch someone a plaster not so much because you care about their pain, but because you can't stand the sight of blood.

A second level of empathy is when we consciously feel upset by seeing someone else's pain and determine to do something in response. What's interesting about this level, though, is that it might equally lead to a 'good' moral response of sympathy, or it might lead to a 'bad' one of fight or flight. In other words, empathy of itself can only take us morally so far. Because we empathise, we know we're with others. But how we react to others is another question entirely – though it's the important moral question, because following empathy alone, we might well react badly.

The limitations of empathy become even more clear at a third level. It concerns how we empathise with those whom we perceive to be not in our in-group but in another group. 'In an imaging study of Caucasian and Chinese volunteers,' Frith explained by way of example, 'the Causasians showed empathy, detected as brain responses, to Causcasians; but not to Chinese and vice versa.' The general point is that empathy-as-ethics fails in such contexts. And that's particularly significant because this failure occurs when you are confronted by people who are what we might otherwise called strangers, foreigners or enemies – occasions when the nature of our response makes all the difference between harmony and unrest, even peace and war. Once more, an ethics based on empathy alone won't work. You need the moral dimension, not just a study of feelings.

Fair is fair?

There's a final area of investigation that's worth bringing into our discussion since it highlights a wider issue too. It's to do with the study of fairness and an apparent aversion to inequality among primates.

Various experiments, involving monkeys and apes, appear to have shown that a sense of fair play is innate – a product of our evolution. One involves two capuchin monkeys who are rewarded with different foods for performing the same task: the first gets some cucumber and the other a grape. But the grape is more desirable to the monkeys, and so the one who is offered only the cucumber will refuse to eat it. It seems as if the creature is aware that its fellow is being rewarded more generously, and that it is protesting at the inequity. It seems to have a natural sense of fairness. This is seized upon as another indicator that morality has biological roots and that those roots can inform the way we live. The science, it is said, is providing an account of our good behaviour and that account goes something like this.

Many animals, perhaps most, don't live in isolation; they co-operate. Even bacteria work together for the sake of the group. There is good reason to think that this co-operation gives rise to behaviour that can be called altruistic: it's good for others but not necessarily for the individual. The story develops further when it's observed that higher animals, like chimps or dogs, don't just behave in ways that might be called altruistic. They have social emotions too. They feel shame; they empathise; they take pleasure in pleasing others.

The implication for the human animal is that our morality is based upon an evolved set of predispositions. Cognition has a role to play, as there are often quite complex trade-offs to assess when different values conflict. But when we take pride, feel guilty, act honestly, show trust, we are experiencing social emotions that steer our behaviour by playing on our feelings. We go for the pleasurable and avoid the disagreeable, which implies, in turn, that it's not moral reasoning that underpins our good behaviour, but feeling. Socrates was, in fact, wrong.

Except that, again, no such conclusion is warranted. Recall the experiments with the capuchin monkeys. Further control experiments have been done in which a single monkey is offered cucumber when a grape is lying in view but out of reach. No second monkey is being rewarded with a grape, and yet, still the single monkey will refuse the cucumber. In other words, it's not inequity that's the problem: the monkey is not demonstrating its sense of injustice. It just prefers grapes.

That capuchins could have no moral sense, just food preferences, undermines what is often presumed in the interpretation of such experiments, namely that human moral sensibilities are just more intense, or perhaps refined, versions of primate moral sensibilities. But these monkeys, at least, may well not display moral behaviour. They just know what they like. There's a moral break between us and them. In a paper for the scientific journal *Nature*, biologist Johan Bolhuis and psychologist Clive Wynne, put it like this: 'A close look at many of these studies reveals, however, that appropriate control conditions have often been lacking, and simpler explanations overlooked in a flurry of anthropomorphic overinterpretation.'

The scientists will fight on. But the wider point for us here is that the evolutionary story that underpins this kind of naturalism, and the ethical speculations that follow from it, are far from secure. The science is likely to change. And if it's overly relied on, the Faustian pact will come back to haunt us: with no offence to the monkeys, it'll be reductive of our humanity. We will sell our moral soul for the sake of a deluded scientific certainty.

To state the obvious, though it's often overlooked, the human predicament is always more complicated than first meets the eye. 'There is indeed much talk about the relevance of all this for understanding morality,' Frith continued with reference to empathy, though making the wider point too. 'I believe the new science may well help us to understand people's feelings about morality and how they choose when confronted with moral dilemmas. It may well help us to understand why people feel that some actions are more moral than others, but it does not help us to decide whether some actions are more moral than others.'

But if it's really quite straightforward to show that science can't provide us with a basis for ethics, something that people have known about at least since Socrates, then why are there still projects determined to demonstrate otherwise?

A scientific basis for ethics

The worry that lies behind the desire for a new ethics is a perceived failure of the way we've done ethics until now. The old foundations – be they philosophical or religious – are perceived as inadequate, undesirable or pernicious.

That religion might be regarded an undesirable basis for ethics is not hard to understand. It's not so much that religious beliefs and passions have historically been implicated in all kinds of human horror, from war to persecution, though they have. (Then again, they've also been historically implicated in all kinds of human good.) More subtly, for a plural democracy to function properly, you need a public moral discourse that is conducted by reasoned argument, rather than divine fiat: no single group of individuals, like the religious, can claim to have privileged access to moral truth. Everyone must be heard, and that means everyone speaking the same language. Science, today, can look like it offers such a language. Further, as Mary Warnock has argued in her book *Dishonest To God*, if you do tie morality to religion, and religion becomes a voluntary pursuit, then morality tends to lose out in public discourse, because people assume that moral discourse has suffered the same fate too.

When it comes to philosophical foundations for ethics, they look unattractively problematic as well, not least since they are so hotly disputed. Broadly speaking, two traditions have dominated the moral scene in the West since the Enlightenment. A first is the one preferred by the advocates of happiness, Bentham's utilitarianism – only, it's clear that happiness, though desirable, is not the right target for our moral aims and is not a big enough notion to inspire us to be all that we might be; to reach our potential. It does not make any weighty call on our nature.

The second philosophical tradition focuses on duties and rights, and while it is of real value, it too ultimately falls short because duties and rights can't speak to our full humanity, and thereby enlarge it: what's good for us is conflated with what's obligated for us, and while the human animal no doubt needs to be carefully managed, it's the spirit that gives life, not the law. In addition, the demand for rights increasingly sets us at odds with one another, creating a grievance culture of conflicting demands and uncaring assertions.

So if neither religion nor philosophy will do it, science's promise – though a false one – is inevitably attractive. It appears to offer a universal language, substantiated by evidence, thereby providing an unequivocal basis for an ethical view of life. We should all agree and live more happily ever after. Only it doesn't. The science of empathy, of happiness and of fairness are being asked to do more moral work than they really can. Wider considerations must ultimately decide what counts as good. Like Socrates, we need to ask the moral questions when we are faced with those moments when we grapple with the meaning of life.

Virtue ethics

Aristotle made a distinction that is useful, between merely existing and living well. It was based upon two uses of the word 'life'. (He was helped by the fact that in Greek there are two words for life – *zoē* and *bios*). Aristotle noticed that there is animal-like life (*zoē*), that is life as in being healthy, fed and housed – what could be called 'zoological' existing. And there is social-like life (*bios*), that is, life as in not merely living as animals do but living well as human beings aspire to do. *Bios* includes such aspects as being happy, as well as, say, being fulfilled, educated, inspired and having purpose. The confusion implicit in the search for a scientific ethics could, then, be put this way: the science upon which it is based operates in the realm of *zoē*, while a good life is mostly about *bios*. The distinction is useful because science is an excellent promoter of life in the zoological sense: technologies from science have clearly made countless humans healthier, better fed and housed. But science falls short when it comes to the moral matter of not merely existing but living well.

The tradition of ethics that Socrates picked up on when he became disillusioned with science has much to contribute here. It was also followed by Aristotle, and substantially developed by Plato too. It's known as virtue ethics – virtues being those skills, habits and excellences that enable us to flourish, if we can nurture them. They are those qualities that, got right, ensure you're headed more or less in the best direction, though for us agnostics our exact destination is never entirely clear. It aims at what is good, though without having to know what is good ahead of time: that can't be discovered by deliberation but only by living itself. Simone Weil put it this way. We need indicators of 'gravity' in life, the things that would drag us down, and indicators of 'grace', the things that lift us up. Like Hercules, who myth tells us came to a crossroads in life when he had to make a choice, a sense of gravity and grace can help us decide what to commit to in any particular moment.

Further, virtue ethics is not primarily interested in whether some isolated action is good or bad in itself, but in what kind of person someone is becoming as a whole – of which their actions are but a product. It does not seek definite answers, but rather a way of life, much like the musician who orientates their life around practice, learning and performance. It seeks to understand how to nurture good character, skills and habits. Happiness plays a part in this. So does empathy. However, virtue ethics takes us much further.

Illus. 3.2: Aristotle, who articulated a way of thinking about how to live known as virtue ethics.

This is because, while always conscious of our animal nature, Aristotle believed we can surpass that nature – never completely, but often substantially: we also have the capacity to transcend the constraints of our biology, at least to a degree. Understanding is the beginning of that change, coupled to training and practice. Hence, alongside the question of happiness, Aristotle discusses the moral virtues, particularly those that require self-reflection, such as prudence and restraint. These are known as the cardinal virtues, and they are those upon which any distinctively human ethics hinges because they enable us to question the limitations of our animal instincts, such as empathy, and behave not just according to our biology but to the best in our nature. Charles Darwin made a similar observation when, in *The Descent of Man*, he noted that while animals have 'well-marked social instincts', it is 'intellectual powers', such as human beings have, that lead to the acquisition of the moral sense of right and wrong. (Darwin also presumed that the primates have similar intellectual powers, but although experiments like those with the monkeys call that into question, his fundamental point about the link between cognition and morality is right in the virtue schema. It is the one Socrates made too.)

To put it another way, the ethical life for the human animal is a question of what Aristotle called practical and rational intelligence, and is learned by engaging in life. It requires the cultivation of good habits, and a greater awareness of our personal flaws and inconsistencies. Needless to say, this is a lifelong task and, unless you are a saint, never comes to an end. Moreover, it's a journey powerfully influenced not just by our reflection and effort, but by the stories we tell ourselves too, about what makes life good and full. Such stories speak to our humanity and inspire us to keep at it. They stir up moral sensibilities in us and fire our moral imagination. It's why moral heroes and morality tales are so important. They're often complex and ambivalent, mirroring our own struggles to live well. Religion will have a vital part to play in this, even for agnostics. It is just too rich a resource of parables and myths to discard.

Indeed, there are times in life, notably at momentous moments – such as birth and death – when religious stories and traditions hold the excess of feeling that comes to us then better than anything else. 'We are haunted, we need somewhere to put certain bits of our humanity and there's nowhere else except religious language and imagery,' Rowan Williams, Archbishop of Canterbury, has noted. 'The piles of flowers that you see on the site of road accidents are the most potent symbols of a society haunted by religion and not clear on what to do about it. The church is still a place where people have got the emotions that won't go anywhere else.' I can't help but agree.

Stories and the like that speak from the messiness of life are of immense value, therefore. They move beyond the reductive, Faustian accounts of what we are because they can address the complete range of ourselves as persons; they help shape us as moral beings. Moreover, the best stories represent an ethics that, in a sense, transcends us: we don't understand ourselves fully, for all the advances in knowledge we make. As Socrates put it, we are the in-between creature. Aristotle expressed it like this in the *Nicomachean Ethics*:

> We must not heed those who advise us to think as human beings since we are human and to think mortal things since we are mortal, but we must be like immortals insofar as possible and do everything toward living in accordance with the best thing in us.

If we are not to restrict what we might become, by imagining ourselves as information-processing machines or grape-preferring monkeys, we need a way of shaping how we live that remains open to that excess.

Diminishing humanity

Agnostics may, at this point, be feeling nervous. They may go along with the argument that science provides an inadequate notion of wellbeing. But they may also worry at what I am smuggling in here, with my 'celebration' of the power of religious story-telling and the like. Biblical tales may inspire us to love our neighbour, but they've also inspired the suppression of women, say. Parables may speak of the highest virtues – of faith, hope and love – but they also speak of eternal condemnation if you find yourself in the wrong group when the sheep are separated from the goats.

That's true, but that's no reason to dismiss them all. Rather, it's to note that human beings simply cannot understand the world without resorting to myths, stories or a vision of life – and that this goes for scientifically sourced myths of what it is to be human too. So a better question to ask is how conscious, and therefore critical, we are of our myths, stories and the visions that we deploy. 'If we ignore them, we travel blindly inside myths and visions which are largely provided by other people. This makes it much harder to know where we are going,' writes Mary Midgley in *Science as Salvation: a Modern Myth and Its Meaning*. Her point is made against the myths that arise from an over-interpreted science, but it applies equally to the religious stories that may serve us better – a critique we'll shortly come to.

For now, though, we'll conclude our discussion of the many scientific accounts of human nature that do the rounds these days. The fundamental problem is that they take human nature to be simple, in the sense that we can explain ourselves to ourselves in relatively simple ways. It's a particularly powerful fantasy, perhaps because modern technology puts within our power not only the ability to manipulate the world around us but, with genetics, our very selves too.

The pervading technologism leads us to think that we are on the brink of a great leap forward that will cause us to 'mutate'. It would become so easy then (and nearly 'automatic') to make objection to every reference to humanity, its weaknesses as well as its merits: 'All of that is overcome! We are in a new era! An entirely different race is born!

105

So wrote the philosopher Dominique Janicaud in his book, *On the Human Condition*. His aim was not to knock the science but to point out the dangers of being led by utopian talk of a post-human future, nourished by a myth of ethical conundrums solved. The fear is that the ethical naivety that can exist in the scientific worldview leads us into a future that, far from improving our wellbeing, will actually diminish us.

In fact, life's complex: we are essentially many-sided. And we know that really. Think of a game of football. Physics can tell you a lot about the dynamics of the ball, but it can tell you nothing about the dynamics of the team; you need psychology for that. How much more do you need when it comes to life.

The issue at stake is that while science is good at what *is* the case, it can tell us little about what *ought* to be the case. To assume otherwise is known as the naturalistic fallacy, which is the tendency is to support your pre-existing moral values with your scientific evidence of choice. Hence good liberals quote research on empathy, more or less reinventing the golden rule about doing well by others. But the golden rule doesn't actually follow from empathy alone: it is a moral imperative precisely because it is often quite unnatural, irrational and unpleasant to defer to strangers and enemies.

What would work better, because it would reflect our nature, would be to take ourselves as objects of 'complex and difficult elaboration', as the philosopher Michel Foucault put it. We must invent ourselves, not in the sense of just making it up, but by a treating ourselves like 'obscure texts' to be worked upon, whose secrets may be discovered. The implication is that we today need more of the mystery about what it is to be human, and it's only when taking account of that, that we may build an ethic that is both intellectually satisfying and humanly enriching. It's what the Christian revolution brought to our culture, though its resources feel rather depleted now, at least to agnostics. So if you're serious about the good life, how are you going to go seriously about it? Virtue ethics is a vital start. But there's this troublesome spiritual dimension too. We're coming back to the question of religion.

Socrates or Buddha? On Being Spiritual But Not Religious

I've found that Buddhism is best. But that does not mean Buddhism is best for everyone. That's clear. It's definite.

The Dalai Lama

Anger is the mood I usually sense. Or if not anger, then frustration. Sometimes sadness. I'm referring to the occasions when I talk about having quit being a priest, having left the church. It might be after an event at a book festival, or during one of the classes I teach, on matters such as how to fill the God-shaped hole. Individuals approach, a little angry, frustrated or sad to ask more about my experience and share theirs. Typically they have a link to institutional Christianity in their past, perhaps through parents, perhaps via school. And they've rejected it. It may be that church values did not chime with their values of inclusion or quest. It could be that the religion of their youth strikes them now as overly negative, obsessed with guilt or purity. Sometimes, they'll have had a vexed personal experience. There's the man who married a divorcée, which led to his parish priest excommunicating him. There's another who studied for a PhD in quantum physics, and realised that her wonder at the subatomic world sat uneasily alongside the wonder she was supposed to show at the biblical miracles of Jesus.

It's a traumatic experience because once such doubts set in, it's not just a change of preference that's at stake, as if one had gone off cornflakes in favour of a cereal with a little more bran. To be religious is to take a holistic attitude towards life. It is to be involved in a comprehensive story about the world and the way things are. Once a trickle of concern is unleashed, it tends to become a flood, and to ask one question feels like questioning it all. You're not just risking your opinion but your community, the place where you once belonged. The issue or experience that caused a fine fissure quickly becomes a visible crack and then an existential rupture because everything is connected. There are totemic issues – often associated with sexual morality because sex is about intimate matters which, by virtue of being so intimate, are explosive and powerful. To transgress them is almost unforgivable. Every religious community has such lines in the sand. Cross them and you put yourself on the outside.

The psychological theory of attachment between parents and children helps illuminate the experience. A good-enough parent is one who provides the child not only with a secure base, but also with the encouragement to explore beyond that base. The child, thereby, learns who they are as an individual, while at the same time remaining confident that parental concern for them will survive their moves away, towards independence. The quality of the attachment needs, therefore, to be accommodating not rigid, characterised by trust not just rules. Trust is particularly important since it tells the child that they will not only continue to receive love but that they will continue to be worthy of being loved too.

But things can go wrong. The psychologist John Bowlby lists the kind of behaviour in parents that causes children to question their worth and which leads to a breakdown in loving trust. It's remarkably like what goes wrong between religious institutions and believers. The parent may be unresponsive to the child's sense of what it needs. Does not so much ecclesiastical moral teaching feel like that too? The parent threatens the child with a withdrawal of love, in order to control it – which seems not unlike crude tales of divine judgement. The parent scares the child with physical violence, actual or intimated – a bit like the god who would punish you forever. The parent induces guilt in the child. Do not churches do all these things to those of whom it disapproves? Is there a religious institution that is not more than capable of doing the same? The analogy suggests that priests and rabbis, ministers and gurus frequently become like bad parents. They don't trust enough to let be. It also posits a theory as to why that happens: the parent/church is unable to be a good-enough parent/church because it is too anxious about itself. It's unsure of its own secure base, probably as a result of feeling threatened by the secular world. And so it plays out that insecurity on those who look to it for security, the game becoming more destructive with those who are most vulnerable – children, gays, divorcées, women.

The result in the child – and by extension the individual who has fallen out with their community of faith – is anxiety. At first, this may well be repressed, in a doomed attempt to maintain an attachment with the institution. But eventually the resentment that builds up becomes uncontainable, whence the anger. This is often shown in essentially adolescent behaviour. For myself, I can remember this phase quite vividly. When I was still a priest, the church newspaper I read arrived on a Friday and I would rush to the doormat to open it, searching for stories that fed my discontent – news of a bishop who'd uttered illiberal views, or a vote that had rejected progressive reforms. It was a kind of self-harming, and a symptom of an inability to take responsibility for myself, also called growing up. For a while, it was compulsive.

Bowlby describes such activities as 'aberrant forms of care-eliciting behaviour'. I turned to the paper ostensibly seeking comfort, but simultaneously seeking to have my fears confirmed. What this also means is that it is the person who has turned their back on the church who is most likely to become the most vociferous campaigner against the church: it is as if they want to destroy the parent that has rejected them, a rage that is consciously expressed as disgust at Christian values. The individual who is merely indifferent to the church, who has never had a parent-like relationship with it, is hardly likely to find the energy required to write the books, issue the press releases, march on the streets, maintain the websites. It's a vicious circle, as well as frequently being vicious in tone. But alongside the hurt, there's a more subtle feeling too: a sense of loss.

Lost souls

Former church-goers, ex-believers, the sometimes religious often become conscious of this loss. They miss the good things a community of faith can give them. One such good thing might be belonging to a tradition, a body of insight, practice and thought upon which they can draw. It's found in texts, rituals and great buildings, and its gift is that your own life might gain from the many lives of others, the echoes of which can be heard in the music or architecture. You yourself only have one life, and there's simply not enough time to ask and answer all the questions, to forge new patterns of life, to reinvent the stories. So you had submitted to, and engaged with, the wisdom of the tradition. Plus, there are some individuals – the moral heroes of traditions, the theological virtuosi – who are inevitably going to have much more profound perceptions than you or I could ever have. To turn your back on that, as you feel you must because you've lost confidence in the church, can therefore not only be felt as a liberation but also as a kind of waste. After the thrill of rejecting has died, there may well be a sense of emptiness, and exhaustion at the thought of having to go it alone.

Another way in which loss can be felt arises from the loss of the community to whom you belonged and within which you could address life's problems, find direction, and take yourself seriously. Where else in the public square today are there spaces to ask what is good, outside of religious buildings? Art galleries and book shops offer a partial substitute, though the nature of the relationship we have with them is shaped by the commercial imperatives that keep them open: they are inevitably more interested in attracting us as consumers of a product than participants in life.

These losses are expressed in a common formula. Individuals will describe themselves as 'spiritual but not religious'. They've given up on church membership – or going to the synagogue, temple or mosque – which is what is meant by the 'not religious' bit. But they've not given up on wanting to pursue the spiritual dimension. It's that nebulous impulse, though no less crucial for that. It comes from this sense that the other models of what it is to be human – as consumers, as gene-machines, as workers, as citizens – may be partly right, but they're not big enough. There's an excessiveness to being human that needs to look beyond what the biologist, the psychologist and the economist together describe. Life comes to us as a mystery, one deepened by all that we know. So we seek an eternal, infinite or perfected horizon that lies under or through the everyday: it might find expression in anything from an interest in astrology and crystals, through alternative practices like meditation and yoga, to converting to other traditions, particularly when perceived as non-doctrinaire.

Being spiritual but not religious responds to a crisis that is both personal and cultural. It's as if the old ways of nurturing the spiritual dimension are failing many today, notably in certain parts of the Western world, and so people are searching for new ways of feeding it. It's what Jung called 'the spiritual problem of modern man'. He argued that we live in a time of shock, because while the benefits of technology and consumerism are obvious, their failures are obvious too, be that manifest in the wars of the twentieth century or the ecological fears of the twenty-first. That troubles at a cultural level, and at the personal: the birth of psychology and psychoanalysis are a product of a corresponding desire to embark on a meaning-yielding inner search. It's a search that has become necessary because we've become disconnected from the historic ways by which we fed our souls – in the West, from the Christian story. Are tales of Mary as the virgin mother of Jesus only slightly less strange to us now than tales of Isis the incestuous mother of Horus? Is the blood of the cross, as a symbol, going the way of the blood of the bull of Mithras? These elements of the Christian myth no longer feel immediately part of us. They tell us something of where we've come from, for sure, but do they speak of where we're going? 'The modern man has lost all the metaphysical certainties of his mediæval brother, and set up in their place the

ideals of material security, general welfare and humaneness,'
Jung concluded. Only while security, welfare and humaneness
are great goods, they are not enough.

This is a crucial part of the agnostic predicament. I recognise
it in myself. And I've also become increasingly aware of what's
lost. When it comes to asking how to be an agnostic, there's
more to attend to here.

The secular predicament

For most of human history, a claim to be spiritual but not religious would not have made any sense. 'Spirituality' was just
the more existential side of religion, and 'religion' the practical side of spirituality – the confessional element demonstrated
in a way of life that was owned by the community to which

Illus. 4.1: Carl Gustav Jung wrote of the spiritual crisis of modern people.

you belonged. Credal beliefs were incomprehensible aside from that way of life, and theology was the attempt to distil and discern the spiritual experience: a theologian who didn't pray would be as debilitated as a writer who doesn't read. Similarly, the meaning of saying you believe in such and such was much more like saying you trust it, or are committed to it: 'I believe in you', is closer than the propositional, 'I believe that'.

Now, though, to be religious means, most commonly I think, an individual affirmation of metaphysical beliefs, rather than a way of life that is practised. So when individuals today refer to what historically is a religious practice, they tend to use the description 'spiritual'. Beliefs will, of course, emerge within and from that experience. But out of a desire to own beliefs – to affirm that they spring from one's own experience, and are not sprung upon one by a tradition or church – being called religious holds little appeal. I've noticed that even individuals who go to church prefer to talk about being 'people of faith', not religious. To be religious may, in fact, be seen as antithetical to being spiritual, an inauthentic because inherited confession, which an individual of integrity would resist and, quite possibly, reject. We don't want to submit, to recall the origins of the word 'religion' from the Latin *religare*, to bind fast.

Sociologists call this process secularisation. It is a complex phenomenon and one that is hotly contested. But it adds to an understanding of the agnostic age.

Karl Marx is in one corner. Religion, he famously observed, arises as the 'opium of the people', a palliative against the horrors of alienation in society. It is the 'sigh of the oppressed creature, the heart in a heartless world, the soul of soulless conditions,' as he also said of theistic belief. What's interesting about Marx is that though avowedly atheistic, he did not believe that simply arguing against religious belief would be enough to throw it off, should that be thought desirable. Only when the material realities of humankind's alienation had been addressed would religion disappear, for it would then be no longer necessary. It would become redundant, like ink in an age of LEDs.

Marx believed that that time would come with communism. That clearly hasn't worked out. Also, while the notion that there's a link between material improvement and spiritual decline is an idea that still has currency, you increasingly struggle to find sociologists who believe it. In fact, if Jung is right, the opposite is the case. As the material benefits of modernity become more widespread, they delude us into thinking they can satisfy the spiritual side of us too. But they can't. Which leaves us increasingly in search of heart in a heartless world, and soul in a soulless condition, not less.

A different account of secularisation is found in the processes described by the sociologist Max Weber. He talked of disenchantment. The key idea here is that as scientific and rational explanations for things become more available to human beings, so spiritual, mythical and supernatural explanations become redundant: theology and religion go the way of the supernatural and irrational. Weber argued that this process of disenchantment had come about in the Western world.

Think of our ancestors on the savannah, watching a thunderstorm approaching across the plain. As the dark sky splits with light, and the turbulent atmosphere howls with thunder, they feel fear. And in an enchanted world it makes sense to connect such natural events with matters human and divine. Hence in Shakespeare's *King Lear* the 'deep, dread-bolted thunder' signals Lear's own demise. In the scientific age, though, such meaningfulness is lost. We no longer interpret the thunder; we understand it – as massive discharges of electricity.

And yet, it is still spectacular and, in a different sense, enchanting too. It's what we've questioned as cosmic religion. A physicist does not look at the lightning and see a portentous sign, but he or she may well wonder at the extraordinary nature of electrical discharge. For modern individuals nature is still a mirror for meaning. It is the meaning articulated by the Romantic poets who wrote of the sublime – the awesome mountains and terrible waves that reflect the mix of fright and beauty we feel when facing our mortality, say. Hence, science has a capacity to instil a new kind of wonder in us.

What is probably more accurate to conclude, therefore, is that the scientific revolution and the birth of modernity have not led to the end of spiritual sentiments. What they have done is force religious tradition to engage with new understandings and, often, that leads to theological changes which distance us from the old myths. Hence, there are religious liberals who worry about issues like the virgin birth – or the historicity of Moses, or the origins of the Koran. And there are conservatives who reheat cold myths by emphasising a purely emotional and deliberately anti-intellectual connection with them. One sees this, in Christianity, as the extraordinary growth of individuals who feel they have a one-on-one relationship with Jesus, quite as immediate as their best friend. Perhaps more so. It's a conceit that would have shocked most Christians in history, for whom Jesus was lord and judge.

These are not entirely unprecedented problems. Theologians have long realised that negotiations between religious wisdom and scientific insights are inevitable. As far back as the thirteenth century, Thomas Aquinas addressed contradictions between our understanding of the natural world and the literal meaning of the Bible. A case he considers is when the psalmist wrote that there are 'waters above the heavens'. That cannot be the case, Aquinas reasoned, as water is heavier than air. He concluded that the literal meaning of the Bible must give way. But whereas in Aquinas's day, this was no reason to doubt the basic truths of the Bible, today it is, especially when linked to another feature of modernity, its pluralism.

What's happened in the modern world, according to pluralistic accounts of secularisation, is not the disappearance of religion but a massive diversification of belief and non-belief. A plural world is one in which every day you can meet people who think radically differently from yourself. It's a context with real options. We must choose what we make of assorted beliefs and how we might pursue spiritual matters, or not. There's a freedom in that. It's an individual quest. Again, one way of signalling that you are on this journey yourself is to affirm that you are spiritual but not religious. But it also raises difficulties, not least when you are unsure about which option to choose. Pluralism feeds the sense of loss, as every choice not made is a possibility that's lost – and what if you've made the wrong choice? What to do?

A religion of humanity

The most radical way of responding to this predicament is to invent a tailored set beliefs, and associated routines, rid of the elements that you find objectionable. It's inevitable to a degree, but it's been tried more formally on a number of occasions too. Thomas Jefferson was an early advocate. In 1803 he wrote to a friend: 'To the corruptions of Christianity, I am indeed opposed; but not to the genuine precepts of Jesus himself. I am a Christian in the only sense in which he wishes anyone to be; sincerely attached to his doctrines, in preference to all others; ascribing to himself every human excellence, and believing he never claimed any other.' What Jefferson does to Christianity is extract what he regards as the best bits, dropping the rest.

Auguste Comte went a stage further. This French philosopher, who invented the term 'sociology' and was as famous as Marx and Darwin for a while, developed an account of historical progress known as positivism. He argued that human beings exist, first, in a theological stage, characterised by superstition and doctrines. Second, we move into a metaphysical stage, during which reason and deism gain dominance. However, that gives way to a third moment – the one he believed had dawned in his own time. It's the positivistic, and it emphasises individuality and freedom. This stage reaches maturity when even the affirmation of God's non-existence has ceased. 'Atheism even from the intellectual point of view, is a very imperfect form of emancipation,' he wrote, 'For its tendency is to prolong the metaphysical stage indefinitely.'

Ironically, Comte was a great admirer of Roman Catholicism, not for its theology, but for its power. It had global reach and was astonishingly able when it came to giving shape to social life. So, as his own contribution to the positive stage, he set about creating a 'Religion of Humanity'. It came complete with secular clergy, and Comte himself as the Grand-prêtre de l'Humanité; liturgies and rites of passage, marking the important moments across the course of life; and saints who exemplified moral and educative excellence, and commitment. Followers met in buildings that were part chapel, part temple. Inside were images of the Great Mother, carrying inscriptions like 'The worship of Woman is a preparation for the worship of Humanity.' There were also triptychs, showing human figures representing Supreme Being, Supreme Earth, Supreme Destiny.

Some of these temples still stand. The organisation was particularly influential in the creation of modern Brazil: the words 'Order and Progress' inscribed on the Brazilian flag come from Comte's motto, 'Love as a principle and order as a basis: progress the goal'. It sounds rather sinister now. And there are historical reasons for that. Comte's ideas were influential in the formation of the various totalitarian experiments of the twentieth century too, which turned to him for insights in how to maintain social order once the revolutionaries had stripped religious institutions of their influence. The iconography of Stalin and Mao are visible manifestations of the links. Comte's religious invention is worth pondering as a political warning. And also because its failures highlight certain issues still faced by the spiritual but not religious.

Revealing truth

Thinking of Comte's iconography, there's an observation made by the philosopher Martin Heidegger that's illuminating. He drew a distinction between bad and good art. Bad art merely represents things, or tries too obviously to express truths. It's bad because it has a linear relationship to what it seeks to express: it presumes that the truth of things is relatively straightforward and can be conveyed without the complexity and confusion that actually characterises our attempts to grapple with what's true. Hence, this kind of art looks shallow, or it has a message that one gets at a glance, and it doesn't take you any further. It can't see beyond the smallness of its own self-confident horizons. Comte's art was like that.

Good art, though, does something different. It reveals truths. It shows, not tells. It makes 'raids on the unspeakable', as Thomas Merton put it. It's art that knows it's not the truth itself, but is attempting to point to that which is beyond it. It does not sit in judgement allowing only what it counts as convincing, like Thomas Jefferson did with Christianity, but allows itself to be judged in the creative process too. It acts like a window, or an icon. In so doing, it becomes genuinely creative, not just reproductive. The insight is implicit in the Greek for truth, Heidegger observed: *aletheia*, which means disclosed or unveiled.

Other philosophers have picked up on the theme. Wittgenstein, for example, made a parallel distinction. Facts, he noted, can be said. They can be captured in the propositions we utter. But everything else must be shown, or glimpsed, or pointed towards. It's obvious when you think about it. If I tell you that the sun set last night in Greenwich at 7.36 p.m. I express everything that needs to be said about that fact. But if I want to convey the glorious sunset that occurred at 7.36 p.m., as I gazed westward across an orange Thames towards London, I must resort to less direct methods – metaphors and descriptions that always narrow the experience, so that eventually I find myself resorting to exclamations like 'You know!' or 'I wish you'd been there.'

Think of the large canvases of colour painted by Mark Rothko. He was self-consciously working in the period described by Nietzsche as following the death of God, and diagnosed the fundamental problem as the draining of religious symbolism's former power to liberate our spiritual energies. He was addressing what Jung had discerned too. His abstract blocks of purple, red and black don't represent anything, instead functioning as aesthetic midwives to spiritual sensibilities. They are large, since that allows the viewer to be in the picture. 'It isn't something you command,' he once commented on his art, adding: 'The people who weep before my pictures are having the same religious experience I had when I painted them. And if you ... are moved only by their color relationship, then you miss the point.'

Similar observations are made by writers of religious music. The composer Howard Goodall once found himself unable to write a mass setting, though the deadline was looming. Then, in the depth of the crisis, the music emerged, not unlike a dream, from an imaginative part of himself over which he had little control. It was like a revelation. In his book, *The Big Bangs*, he writes:

> Music, because it is by and large mysterious and inexplicable itself, seems to edge back to the heart of it, to step cautiously towards the feeling of a spiritual dimension ... It is not really under our control, it has a chemistry all its own that composers tinker and dabble with. Composers are merely carriers, drawing water from a gigantic well to some parched and needy tribe, stranded far away from their natural homeland.

Goodall references the mysterious. What's absent from Comte's religion, and must be part of any spirituality that is to be liberating not oppressive, is Schleiermacher's 'sense and taste for the infinite' or Tillich's commitment that warrants 'ultimate concern'. The human creature is one for whom his or her own existence is too small. We need to be able to expand into regions beyond our own concerns. If Man is made into God, as Comte seeks to do, then Man will disappoint at best, and at worst become a tyrant. As the poet Wallace Stevens wrote, we need to hear 'a tune beyond us, and yet ourselves'. We need something more than ourselves to be ourselves.

Jung wrote of the two parts of the individual – the ego, which makes our particular place in the world; and the Self, which is our connection to what is traditionally called the divine. The story of our lives is, first, the establishment of the ego, an ability to function, perhaps succeed, in the ways of the world. It's a secular tale and necessary, so that we can find security and gain a sense of who we are. Then, second, comes the integration of the ego with the Self – that wider participation in life, variously referred to as embracing the flow of life, a fuller consciousness, the Way, God. It's the spiritual aspect. One needs the other: the Self needs an established ego fully to be in the world; the ego needs the Self to find not just biological, psychological and economic purpose, but spiritual meaning. The goal of the human life might be defined as connecting the two, to create a synthesis.

Transcendent causes

Comte, then, made a fatal mistake. He believed that we make meaning when, in fact, we discover it. Though he was right about one thing: human beings need rituals and stories in order to live well. Reason and science alone are not enough. They aid discernment and shift our frames of reference but, always seeking facts, miss deeper truths. So where is the individual who regards themselves as spiritual but not religious to look for that which can only be glimpsed on occasion, that which must be shown or revealed?

People try various options that we've already explored – not least science – and there are others. For a few years myself, I turned to the countryside, to find a rural retreat. I repeatedly returned to the same place in order to get to know something of its rhythms, that which you don't see directly but appreciate only over the course of seasons. The great thing about nature is that it cares nothing for you, and that forces you out of yourself. I've watched the point on the horizon where the sun rises as it shifts south during the winter, and then back north again as summer comes – things like that. I've no unchecked notions about gorgeous blue peaks and cool green glades. Across the valley there's a plant that raises cows. That's quite enough to disabuse a city-dweller of the romance of farming. But the rural landscape is relaxing for the city-dweller because, at least in part, it takes you out of your immediate con-cerns, away from what Jung called the ego.

Maybe it's just that your eye is drawn to the horizon in a way it can't go in the city, and that draws you to patterns and processes that are nothing to do with you. They are ones that chart a slower, circular passage through time. In contrast, in the city, my mind's eye is repeatedly drawn to my own projects: the urban social imaginary is ego-aggrandising not ego-transcending. Time is fast and linear – good for activities like earning a living, less good for contemplation.

Another possibility has been identified by the philosopher Peter Singer, as 'transcendent causes'. These are concerns that reach beyond your struggle to establish your place in the world by attending to matters that are not in your own interests. They will be ethical: Singer himself is known for his involvement in animal rights and ecological activism. The point about both is that they do not benefit him directly, and may well curtail his pleasures in life – those of eating meat, say, or flying regularly. But that sacrifice carries his concerns elsewhere, towards what Jung called the Self.

Singer puts his money where his mouth is: he gives one-third of his income away to his transcendent causes. Speaking about it, he's said: 'The first donation was the hardest to make. The first time I wrote a check that had at least a couple of zeroes at the end – that was the hardest thing.' This is impressive. But there is a problem with transcendent causes: how to avoid pursuing them not because of the good they do to others, but because of the spiritual meaning you hope they'll deliver to you?

It's a question of how not to put the cart before the horse, of not being too calculating about it. In order to sustain you in your devotion to them, you'll need to want to pursue them genuinely for their own sakes, or else you'll readily become discontented with monitoring what you're receiving in return. This is why, generally speaking, giving everything up and travelling to Africa, say, to offer up your services, is not a recipe for happiness, but for disaster. Your motivation has to be right. (And if you've got to ask, it's probably already too late.)

Meditation

A different option is to turn to the practices of Eastern religions, particularly Buddhism. Insight meditation, or mindfulness, is the obvious case in point. It is an option that I have pursued myself. I came to it not for directly spiritual reasons, though; more philosophical. As I read about the life of Socrates, it seemed to me pretty likely that meditation of some kind was at the heart of the ancient philosopher's way of life. Parmenides' appreciation that all is one strikes me as primarily a mystical reflection not a metaphysical theory, gained by meditation. Plato's account of Socrates often standing still to think, and his discussion of philosophy as a preparation for death, seem to be references to a practice of brave reflection. Aristotle took contemplation to be the highest activity of the good life. Or there's Marcus Aurelius' Meditations, which can be read as a record of his attempt to detach from the past, not to attach to the future, and to live in the present.

If that's so for ancient philosophy, then I found it hard to resist the thought that exploring meditation may be as necessary as reading books, if I was to take these seminal figures seriously; contemplation as the philosopher's equivalent of the theologian's prayer. Mindfulness meditation was the way I went, as it is relatively easy to find introductory instruction in its techniques. And I quickly found that it's conducive to the agnostic mindset too.

There's always a debate about terms when it comes to talking about meditation, which is a reflection of how it too is best known not described, best experienced not told. There are techniques to be learned, though the basics can be conveyed in a few minutes. My best teacher was actually the one who said the least: we'd meet once a week, and rarely did he do more than invite us to sit still for an hour. I take this to mean that meditation is not for anything more than to meet a desire for awareness; its instrumentality does not reach beyond patience and perception. Only, it then achieves more.

As I understand it, mindfulness can be construed as a way of keeping questions of life open. By paying close attention to something simple, though symbolic – like the in- and out-flow of breath – you nurture a curiosity that does not try to explain, but rather to comprehend. It's not esoteric experience that counts, but the astonishing quality of the everyday. Stephen Batchelor, in his book *The Faith To Doubt*, puts it characteristically well: 'It was not an illumination in which some final, mystical truth became momentarily very clear. For it gave me no answers. It only revealed the massiveness of the question.' It's a path or means through which to experience what Heidegger called the 'throwness' of being alive: we find ourselves in the midst of existence. It does not seek to figure things out, as if life were a problem to be solved. Rather, the source of its release is found in better questioning, which in turn stems from a growing love for the extraordinariness of the immediate – why there's something, not nothing.

I was drawn to the centrality of doubt in this process. That's not meant in a passive sense, as if the goal were the cultivation of an indifferent, detached state of mind. Rather, it's doubt as an active engagement and, so, source of energy. The Chinese adage captures that, when it notes that when there's no doubt, there's no enlightenment; when there's little doubt, there's little enlightenment; and if there's great doubt, there's great enlightenment. It's the kind of doubt that arises with discovering more. The ancient Greeks sometimes used the analogy of an expanding circle. The circle represents knowledge, which as it gets larger also has more extensive contact with the unknown, represented by what lies beyond the growing circumference of the circle.

This is a process of knowing that is simultaneously one of unknowing, revealing how fundamentally ineffable things are. The goal is interest, not explanations. It proceeds by saying not this, not that. Negation is, in fact, essential to being open to this newness. We can only fully say 'yes' to what we already know and grasp: if you don't entirely know what you're saying 'yes'

Illus. 4.2: Buddha as depicted at Kamakura, Japan

to, you are in part not saying 'no' to it. So a negative dialectic, paradoxically, has the capacity to lead us to new worlds, towards that which is beyond our comprehension, to the transcendent. It's like the sculptor who works by removing material from the block of wood or stone, saying 'no' to this chip; and who leaves some material, not saying 'no' to that. The result is a revealing of the form.

Or remember Socrates and his daemon, the inner voice that only ever said 'no' to him, telling him not to do this or that, and thereby leaving him open to new experience and the wisdom to be found with an awareness of the limits of your knowledge. Or you could relate it to the falsification thesis of Popper, that nothing can be proven to be true, only proven to be untrue. That which remains, that which we cannot say 'no' to, is the best approximation.

Existentially, this feels like a process of letting go. Active doubting is like shedding layers or peeling off skins. Often meditation teachers will talk about that discarding in relation to emotional perceptions: something upsets you in life, say, and rather than obsessing about the pain of the experience, as is easy to do, you should treat it like a wave that dissolves back into the sea and passes. There's value in that. But I think this might be equally true of our cognitive perceptions. Meditation seeks to draw attention to what you think you know, and then asks whether that's right. It can be a tough process, as witnessed to by the life of Socrates, the man who said, 'One thing I know, that I know I know nothing.' The key to wisdom is not how much you know, but is understanding the limits of what you know – an understanding that he failed to find in the politicians and poets of his day. If Plato is right, Socrates devised a method of questioning, now called the elenchus, that brought people to a position where they realised the profundity of their not knowing: it's what his relentless questioning called individuals to do, leading them to an existential precipice. It was a kind of meditation that would ask what something is – say courage, or friendship, or charm – and then would show that everything that might be said about the matter, or any experience that might be brought to bear upon it, failed at some point. There's always more.

For some this was too much, and they turned away stung. They called him the gadfly. For others, though, it revealed a deeper sense of what it is to be human, what it is to be uncertain and conscious of that ignorance. You might say that he developed a verbalised version of mindfulness, and took it out of the meditation hall and into the marketplace. There, in the public square, he found some fellow spirits, though among the powerful, he found himself in trouble too.

Selfless or selfish?

Mindfulness is not envisaged in such a form today, at least in the West. It's not a Socratic encounter of careful unsettling. It's presented as a private, inner journey, one primarily conducted in silence not in debate. You may well meet to meditate alongside others for support, but the core activity is internal. It's about you yourself. And I came to feel that this raises problems. In fact, as I continued with mindfulness, I came to feel that this solipsistic quality might be a major issue in its technique when it bumps up against powerful notions of autonomous individuality.

The thought became unavoidable for me when I went on a longer retreat. It was, in many ways, a positive experience. I'd recommend it. The meditation centre I attended is serious about addressing the spiritual problem of modern man. Silence is the watchword of the house. Visitors are pretty sternly requested to respect it. Even reading was banned, as it would disturb the inner stillness that the outer observance is designed to engender. It would spoil the quality of the silence that together we were pursuing.

You go to meditate, and not a lot else. Apart from mealtimes and an hour doing household chores, the day is devoted to it: three quarters of an hour sitting in the meditation hall, followed by three quarters of an hour doing walking meditation in the garden – the same activity of concentration conducted while walking very slowly and focusing on the sensations in your feet. Then back to sitting meditation. Then more walking. It adds up. The mind repeatedly and routinely wanders, of course. But you're not asked to attempt to control it. Rather, you are to become aware of the fact, and then draw your attention back to the breathing or the walking. Most of the meditation periods pass easily enough. A handful are a struggle. One or two are a real joy. The retreat was led by two teachers. They topped and tailed the sitting sessions with a few helpful words, and were also on hand lest any participants become unsettled, an important safeguard when embarking on prolonged silence. My time in the place was good. However, I came away with these nagging questions more clearly formed.

The *raison d'être* of the meditation we were nurturing was not Socratic but was focused on the wellbeing of those who practise it. That seems like a pretty good *raison d'être*, and it is to a degree, though it comes with this solipsistic risk. Meditation-as-self-help flirts with narcissism when it is devoted to observing yourself. The dynamic it sets up makes for self-absorption and self-obsession. I suspect this is a key paradox with which Western Buddhism is currently grappling: the practice that tells you your strong sense of individuality is damaging could, in our cultural context, entrench the very attitude it seeks to dislodge.

I've put this point to Buddhist friends and they have broadly two responses, one metaphysical, the other practical. The metaphysical response is to refer to the Buddhist doctrine of 'no-self', or *anatta*. It's a complex concept, not least because of variations from school to school. There's the literal interpretation that our perceptions of who we are as selves are delusions, for there is nothing substantial about us as persons at all. The goal of meditation is therefore the emptying of the self, snuffing it out. That strikes other Buddhists as too nihilistic, and they prefer to talk of how everything is conditioned – everything being caused by something else, and so everything is connected. This means that to make a presumption of your self-sufficiency is deluded, and this, they aver, is the true insight gained by meditation. A third idea is that *anatta* is better translated as 'transfigured self', the transfigured individual being one who sees things clearly, who is enlightened. Whichever version you prefer – if any – does not, though, address the issue of narcissism because, of course, the problem with narcissism is not that you love yourself, but that you don't know in which way to love yourself. Mindfulness might perpetuate that battle by meditative means.

The second, practical response is to point out that there is a supplementary meditation that's taught alongside mindfulness, called *metta bhavana*, or loving-kindness meditation. It is designed to nurture a loving attitude towards yourself and others, a kind of sweeping compassion for the world. Only no action is required: the primary activity still goes on inside your head. It's a kind of I-love-myself-while-loving-you-while-loving-all. This is very different from Plato's account of love, which is not first an inner attitude but is first a desire that reaches out beyond the individual. It's self-aware but seeks to talk with others by asking awkward, life-deepening questions.

I thought some more, and reminded myself that self-obsession is a danger inherent in any community devoted to a particular task. I'd seen it in Christian religious communities too. Though, perhaps there's a greater risk in communities that lack a reference point beyond the individuals involved, as is the case at the meditation centre. Religious houses in a theistic tradition would be different, in theory at least. They have their problems and idiosyncrasies. But, ultimately, they don't exist for the wellbeing of the occupants, but for the service of God. That nurtures a way of life that approaches your own wellbeing indirectly, by focusing on something greater, something other than just the problems of your own existence. The 'more' here is referred to as God, of course, which for the spiritual but not religious, may feel like more of a hindrance than a help. It's why non-theistic Buddhism appeals. But even as an agnostic, I was surprised by my longer meditative retreat: it lead me to wonder whether a God-centred spiritual practice might offer a better way.

Mindful of problems

There are other worries to think through too. One issue revolves around the pic'n'mix that comes with focusing on mindfulness and mindfulness alone. I'm instinctively wary of the pic'n'mix approach to belief and spirituality, mostly because I'm quite a pic'n'mixer myself. At one level, it's unavoidable in a plural age, but the fear is of never engaging the wider aspects of the tradition that your personal selections exclude. This problem is implicit in the Buddha's original teaching, for it turns out that mindfulness is just one of eight components of the path he reportedly discovered. Buddhism is often represented as a wheel, and there's no wheel that has only one spoke.

The complete path also involves 'right way', seeking to understand life, nature and the world as they really are, as a whole; 'right intention', about the aspirations you have, not least concerning self-renunciation; 'right speech', refraining from grumpiness and gossip (the Christian monk Benedict thought this a crucial issue too); 'right action', about living morally across all spheres life; 'right livelihood', about what job you do and the social context of your life; 'right effort', on how hard this path is, though conversely right effort is about not taking yourself too seriously too; 'right mindfulness' (number seven: we reach it at last), about awareness and consciousness of body and mind; and 'right concentration', being focused, in the moment. Several of the other elements are to do with your engagement with others and how you are in the world, not the meditation room, and yet Western Buddhism tends to prioritise what goes on in there alone. I've heard the defence that doing one component is better than doing none. Though I'm not sure that this is what the Buddha would have said, partly because practising mindfulness alone is of questionable effectiveness and efficacy: what tensions exist between the attitude you're attempting to cultivate in meditation and the opposed ones you unavoidably cultivate at work, say? Mindfulness alone fails to address our wider cultural context, which profoundly forges and shapes us, by taking us out of that embedded context. The net result may be a contemplative withdrawal. It's not a risk Socrates ran, as the everyday, and your presence in it, was the raw material for his philosophy.

This separation is heightened when you find yourself negotiating the cultural hurdles that arise because of Buddhism's non-western origins, most strikingly in the religiosity that surrounds it. Advocates of mindfulness are often careful to minimise such trappings, aware that, while it is far from a fringe interest anymore, Buddhism in all its diversity can seem pretty alien in the West, especially if you were brought up in the restrained Church of England. (We all have our crosses to bear.) But if you seek more than a beginner's class, activities such as prostrations to the *bodhisattvas* start to creep in, and can become a serious hurdle. Similarly, you may gradually notice that beliefs in doctrines such as reincarnation and karma come to be more or less assumed. Discussions about this or that sutra, and what the

Buddha did or didn't say, become common – even as Buddhists insist that theirs is a non-doctrinaire approach, with nothing taken on trust, for all must be experienced. Or there's the question of whether you attend a Tibetan class, Zen or something offered by the Western Buddhist Order, or one of the subdivisions therein. It's quite as confusing as choosing a therapist.

You can ignore these elements, more or less, and just stick with the mindfulness, glad for the silent company of others – a substantial aid it must be said. There will be some of your fellow meditators who will believe the whole thing, drawn by the very exoticism of Buddhism. Only then, I wonder whether there is not an element of donning a Buddhist persona in a desire to belong to the group, to become attached to a new community – a 'good church'. While entirely understandable, given the alienation from Christianity that is so prevalent in the West, it feels inauthentic. Not infrequently do you see the glazed look of the convert in such settings, a face adorned with a *Siddhartha* smile or *Gautama* grin. Such are the ungenerous directions in which my mind wanders while sitting, though I suspect that a similar critique lies behind the frequent exhortations, given by Buddhists like the Dalai Lama, to find a way that originates in your indigenous cultural context. Then, you will be dealing with who you are as a whole person.

A related concern arose for me when I noticed how converts to mindfulness are often evangelical about its benefits. There's nothing wrong with that per se but the desire to sell it, and make it acceptable for a Western audience, can distort. Hence, it's increasingly common for mindfulness to be advanced as a remedy for stress and anxiety, or for the worried well, as a path to a richer happiness. (I've seen it offered as a workshop at one conference under the euphemism 'wellbeing services', which made it sound like a manicure for the mind.)

Buddhism is interpreted in this way via the doctrine of suffering. Suffering here is meant in a broad sense, everything from the faintest emotional perception that something is wrong, to the manifest psychological injuries that human beings inflict on themselves and each other. It's a worldview that is humanistic and tragic. The first of the Buddha's noble truths is that life is suffering – a 'noble' truth since that realisation is also the first step towards an ennobled life, namely one in which the suffering can cease.

This is where meditation comes in, on this understanding of it at least. It's to develop an awareness and acceptance not so much of our limits, à la Socrates, as of suffering existence. Meditation itself needn't always be painful. It might be pleasant, even elating. But the aim is neither to cling to experience, nor to reject it, but rather to know it as it is. Hence, the 'insight' of insight meditation. Something profound is shown to the meditator. 'To understand all is to forgive all,' the proverb says, and the Buddhist version would be, 'To understand all is to let go of all'. It just takes practice.

This is a spiritual practice – a religion, if you accept the metaphysics of suffering – presented as a kind of therapy. It's no doubt one of the reasons that Buddhism is finding such a ready audience in the West. Modernity has damaged many egos, perhaps as a result of the Enlightenment teaching that we are autonomous selves, capable of self-creation, control and consolation. Only, it turns out that we are not so self-sufficient. Hence, if that's right, another way of understanding the spread of loneliness and alienation, stress and depression. Western Buddhism is developing a radical remedy for this condition. Look closely, it says, and you'll see that's an inadequate account of what it is to be human. Let go of that, and liberation follows.

In this area, mindfulness increasingly rides on the coat tails of CBT, or cognitive behaviour therapy, the practice that encourages individuals to be aware of destructive patterns of thought. CBT aims to disrupt these habits of the mind in order that the individual might return to their normal life. There's clearly value in that. Mindfulness in this context does something slightly different, aiming to develop a conscious of these patterns of thought and feeling, not so much to arrest them as to let them come and go without gaining a grip on the individual suffering from them. Claims for its benefits are backed up by a growing body of evidence derived from scientific trials, and there's no doubt value in it too.

But there are ironies inherent in this turn to science. Trials are appealed to partly in order to validate the insights, while at the same time, the science is patronised, *soto voce*, for only just beginning to grapple with the deep things that the Buddhist tradition has otherwise known for centuries. Again, maybe it's just a question of strategy: advocates of mindfulness are bound to turn to the forms of language and investigation that have currency in the West. Science controls the imprimatur. But there's a further concern.

As mindfulness submits to the assessment of neuroscience, and deploys the language of psychology to understand and promote itself, it also risks being formed by the instrumental worldview of these sciences. It will have to prove itself successful at alleviating suffering, at delivering measurable results, at being cost-effective – all of which may well be at odds with what the broader Buddhist tradition has held, not least that life is not fixed by a six-week course but – if you hold to reincarnation – perhaps over countless rebirths. It'd be hard to secure government funding for that.

If this tendency to turn to science is a product of the possibility that Buddhism can only really make sense in the West as a mind cure technique, then it seems destined to become diminished and to dissatisfy like any other form of self-help. If Jung is right, as well as the Buddha for that matter, then the psychological approach to life alone is not enough. We seek that which addresses us as whole persons. We need the spiritual dimension.

Socratic mindfulness

Stephen Batchelor is fond of noting that it took 500 years for a distinctly Chinese Buddhism to emerge, when the religion left the Indian subcontinent and made it's way east. It found an audience because Confucian communitarianism had created a crisis of selfhood by undermining people's sense of their individuality. Buddhism could address this – interestingly, in a way that looks like a mirror opposite of the remedy it is developing in the West today, where a conversely over-powerful notion of separate individuality is doing the damage. But it took five centuries. The difficulty is that we're only some way into the second century of Western Buddhism, if you mark the engagement of philosophers such as Schopenhauer and Nietzsche as the start of the process. There's a long way to go. And this, perhaps, is the core reason for current incongruities. On the other hand, if you care about the spiritual life, and the place of meditation in it, then they are difficulties that should not be sidelined – though I suspect that they often are, because individuals who turn to Buddhism, and invest themselves in it, resist the anxiety that questioning their new spiritual home might entail.

My sense, for what it's worth, is that the letting go of mindfulness is best not aimed at the lessening of suffering in the individual, though that may happen by and by. Rather, it is about this process of constructive doubt – questioning what you take to be the case, so that what you didn't know can emerge, no longer held at bay by the too small worries of the ego. It might be called a Socratic form of spirituality. The meditative attitude is like the elenchus: they are midwives to what can be discovered by the individual which, like a child in the womb, is both of you and not you. It's a tune beyond us and yet ourselves.

This means that mindfulness needs to go along with other forms of agnostic questioning, and together they'll take on the character of waiting. What's admitted is that you yourself are not up to the task of fixing your own life. That's let go of. And instead of just giving yourself to yourself, you aim to give yourself to the transcendent. You have no power to determine how it will arise within you. As an agnostic, you have no certainty anything will arise within you. But you are prepared to wait, driven by an intuited conviction that there is more to life. It's a kind of letting go that is not nihilistic because it is also an attempt at letting in – by a glimpse, by what might be revealed.

It's a pattern that is found in the Christian tradition. Take Augustine, and his diagnosis that the human condition is a restlessness of the heart that seeks God. His spiritual journey, which he writes about in his Confessions, is characterised by doubt: everything that presented itself to him in life as a satisfaction for this restlessness, as a solution to this suffering – the love of another, the Manicheism of his youth – fails him. They frustrated and disappointed, intellectually and emotionally. Augustine's journey only ends when his heart finds its rest in God, and what's striking about this moment is that it comes about with the realisation that his search for himself requires an outward dynamic. It is not just an inward turn but is also, simultaneously, a discovery of God. He finds what it is to be human when he finds God. It's a discovery that, far from alienating him, makes him. In Jungian terms, the ego of his youth exhausts itself – we'd call it a mid-life crisis. And in letting go of itself, finds the Self. 'But you were more inward than my own inwardness,' Augustine writes. 'You were within me, and I was outside myself.'

So here's the nub of the issue for the spirituality-inclined agnostic as I see it. We have a desire for more than biology and psychology can describe. But we also find it difficult to put our trust in the religious discourses that might address our restlessness. We know that being spiritual but not religious is limiting, because it makes spirituality too much like shopping – signing up for this meditation class because it's good for our happiness, or pic'n'mixing over this truth and that. And yet we are also rightly unsure about believing – meaning trusting – in a religious tradition if only it were true, that might carry us to wider horizons and satisfy the restless heart. However, I think that Plato's Socrates offers us help again with this apparent impasse.

There's this link between his awareness of his ignorance and his way of love – philosophy, the desire for what he lacked: he said both that he knew nothing for sure and that he knew about love, and that's no contradiction. Plato's Socrates embraced ordinary human searching and doubt and fashioned it into a flourishing way of life. It was a disciplined desire to reach out for more, in a refinement of love's energy. It was a developed sense that what lies beyond us powers our humanity – the longing to understand, to discover, to become enlightened. Iris Murdoch wrote a dialogue called *Above the Gods*, and at one point, Plato – who's a key character – becomes increasing excited until he rises to his feet and exclaims: 'You see, love is energy. The soul is a huge vast place, and lots of it is dark, and it's full of energy and power, and this can be bad, but it can be good, and that's the work, to change bad energy into good, when we desire good things and are attracted magnetically by them.'

I like the way that the philosopher Anthony Price has described it too: 'Love may be the best helper not because it provides reasons, but because, in a promising soul well prompted, it is receptive of, and responsive to, the opening of new vistas.' Similarly again, there's the way Plato defines love as the child of two parents, 'poverty' and 'cunning resourcefulness'. Love, then, is never more keenly felt than when it lacks what it loves, which is as good a description of the agnostic predicament as any. To my mind, it also makes better sense of the Buddhist intuition that suffering must cease. It's not actually suffering that's the problem. Suffering is rather the symptom of something else, namely that underneath our existential discontent lies love. It's not first and foremost the love of compassion, but rather the love that seeks more, that draws us out of ourselves. In fact, if we weren't the creature who loves, we wouldn't be the creature who suffers, at least in the existential sense. Or to put it another way, if you want to stop suffering, you're also committing yourself to giving up on loving, to becoming detached from life.

Love, then, doesn't promise an end to suffering but it also always has tremendous strengths to draw on: whether bravely, impetuously, mistakenly or intelligently it never ceases to seek what it is compelled by. Loving is to be awakened to the more of existence. Love is, if you like, promiscuous. Wake up to love, and it can lead you elsewhere. It is the fundamental issue, as Socrates seems to have realised.

It's at this point that Plato's philosophical way of life comes close to the spiritual impulse that lies behind religion. To know Socrates was tantamount to a religious experience, to realise something in the deepest part of your being that an encounter with him, the midwife, would reveal as true. It's illuminating to note that Socrates is portrayed by Plato as a messenger from God.

But there's that 'G' word again: God. It is the crux issue to which we must now turn. It's forced its way back into the quest, if you buy the recognition that to be serious about the spiritual is ultimately to let go and wait on the transcendent. We concluded as much in our discussion of cosmic religion: science of itself isn't spiritual, since it seeks to understand that which is within its comprehension, though it may inspire a spiritual response with the realisation that it can't understand everything, particularly in relation to the big questions. I've argued now that non-theistic spiritualities seem problematic since, in the West at least, they trip up over our robust notions of individuality which, when stoked by an inward self-concerned turn, doesn't save us from ourselves but traps us in ourselves. As Nietzsche put it, after the death of God, Man can't avoid trying to make himself into God – the locus of meaning, value, wellbeing. Only that's too small for us. It turns spirituality into self-help or a contemplative withdrawal from the cultural nexus that makes us, thereby leaving us with a depleted not a fuller humanity.

So if you're still with me, we're now at this point. A spirituality-inclined agnostic is like being a believer to this extent: we are individuals who think that God is not a silly question, as the conviction atheist must have concluded, but rather one that our experience demands we keep asking. To put it more concisely: for us, God is not the answer, but the pressing spiritual question. But can God still be thought of as the question, in a mystery-dissolving age of science and certainty? It depends on what you mean by God.

Bad Faith: Religion as Certainty

Ah, what a dusty answer gets the soul
When hot for certainties in this our life!'

George Meredith

That Sunday in September ostensibly began for me like many others since I had been a curate at St Cuthbert's Church, Billingham. I arose early. Few people were about. To my back was the huge chemical works that employed the parishioners and poisoned the air. In front of me was a scene from the country. I could see the row of cottages, uneven with age, including the one I lived in. At the end was the handsome vicarage with its own drive. And then there was the Saxon church itself, so old that some of its stones had been moved to the British Museum on account of their Celtic inscriptions.

I walked in through the vestry door. The vicar had already arrived. I made my way down the north aisle to the bell rope in the tower. Its thick walls were a little damp, the source of a moist smell that somehow linked the present with the past. I rang the Angelus, the call to prayer that had once stopped labourers in their fields, and was now, at least, keeping the rumour of God alive.

After morning prayer, we prepared the vestments, the altar, the sacred vessels and our stalls. St Cuthbert's was what is called Anglo-Catholic: it was inspired by the famous sermon of Bishop Frank Weston of Zanzibar who closed the Anglo-Catholic Congress of 1923 with the following stirring words: 'You have got your Mass, you have got your Altar, you have begun to get your Tabernacle. Now go out into the highways and hedges where not even the Bishops will try to hinder you. Go out and look for Jesus in the ragged, in the naked, in the oppressed and sweated, in those who have lost hope, in those who are struggling to make good.'

That Sunday, I reflected upon the first time I celebrated the Mass myself, two and a half years earlier. Then was a time of optimism, when my hope was as strong as the incense that hung in the air; when my faith mirrored that of the people. I had entertained intellectual doubts about Christianity at theological college. However, once ordained, at least at first, worrying over the literal veracity of this or that doctrine seemed a distraction from the certainty of the mystery they tried to express: God is love. We could sing because our future, and the world's, was destined to be caught up in that divine and constant care.

But it turned out that that Sunday was my last. For the next one was very different. I did not ring the Angelus or lay out the vestments. I was 200 miles away, in Bath, staying with friends, having left the church. I felt free. I felt that, perhaps for the first time, I had made a decision that could be called grown-up. I had converted – to atheism. Now, my notice had been served, pastoral niceties had been performed, and my new Sunday ritual was bedding down fast: newspapers, coffee and conversation. Did I miss St Cuthbert's? A little but at first only in the way a teenager misses the presence of parents during their early days away from home. No more did I need to breathe an atmosphere thick with theism, I thought. I would rely on the heady drafts that were human and only human. For the next while a new certainty framed my life: life is all there is. The challenge is to live it.

So what had happened in between Billingham and Bath? How could it be that an individual with a sense of God clear enough to be ordained moves, within months, to the other side? What brings about such a change of heart?

The answer, of course, is complex and can be told in many ways. It was, in part, loneliness on the job. It was, in part, anger at the conservative attitudes of the church. It was, in part, the shock of wearing a dog collar and having to be an ambassador for the institution. And it was also, in part, the apparent triumph of the rational over the theological.

However, at another level, the leap was not so large or particularly complex. Before, my faith had depended upon the maintenance of a certain certainty. After, my newfound conviction re-established certainty, just in a different guise. Like a politician crossing the floor of the House, I may have switched parties but I was engaged in the same debate. 'How can you believe that?', the atheist berates the believer. 'How can you not believe that?', the theist despairs of the atheist. In terms of their convictions, theism and atheism are not worlds apart: epistemologically they may well share the same assumptions – that the world can be understood, that truth corresponds with reality, and that one can decide for or against God. 'Science offers the best answers to the meaning of life,' says Richard Dawkins. 'Is there more to life than this?', asks the evangelical Alpha Course – and you know they are not going to say no.

The atheist's God

To be fair, there are some atheists who are not so sure. Julian Baggini is one. In his book, *Atheism: A Very Short Introduction*, he makes a rational case for not believing in God, or gods, not because he believes it is irrefutable or because of some militant need to do so. Rather, atheism is the opinion he finds himself holding and, alongside the non-rational forces that inform his convictions, he believes he should have reasonable grounds for doing so. In fact, he opposes militant atheism because it undermines his more subtle position:

> I think that my opposition to militant atheism is based on a commitment to the very values that I think inspire atheism: an open-minded commitment to the truth and rational enquiry ... Hostile opposition to the beliefs of others combined with a dogged conviction of the certainty of one's own beliefs is, I think, antithetical to such values.

However, Baggini is striking because he admits uncertainty. Many atheists who put their thoughts on paper are quite sure about the God they do not believe in. It is for this reason that the effect religion has on them is nothing short of emetic.

The journalist Martin Krasnik, who secured a rare interview with the novelist Philip Roth, made the mistake of asking him whether he was religious? 'I'm exactly the opposite of religious,' Roth erupted. 'I'm anti-religious. I find religious people hideous. I hate the religious lies. It's all a big lie.'

Polly Toynbee, a leading British newspaper columnist, routinely rounds on religion as a cause of evil. After the bombs in London on 7 July 2005 she wrote: 'All religions are prone to it, given the right circumstances. How could those who preach the absolute revealed truth of every word of a primitive book not be prone to insanity? There have been sects of killer Christians and indeed the whole of Christendom has been at times bent on wiping out heathens.'

The polymath Jonathan Miller felt so strongly about it that he made a television series on the history of disbelief. He represents those for whom religion's supposed supernaturalism and belief in life after death is offensive. 'The notion is infantile. I'm amazed that people who can find their way to the toilet without advice can entertain such logically incoherent ideas,' he said in an interview with the London *Times*.

These champions of the Enlightenment are often far from rational in the way they bludgeon belief. Could someone who has sifted even a little of the evidence available still say with ease that religion is simply a lie, or that Christianity will inevitably spawn suicide bombers, or that the theology which has engaged various intellectual giants is logically incoherent? Maybe the assertions are made only for the sake of their rhetoric force. But, if so, that only pushes the irrationality back a step for it raises the question why faith requires such overblown refutation. One is tempted to call into question the atheist's faith in reason.

There is also, I suspect, a deeper reason for their frustration and for God's irritating refusal to die. It is paradoxical. Like many religious people, many atheists want certainty in a sphere of existence in which certainty is not to be found. This means, in turn, that they focus their attacks on a series of man-made deities about which they can be certain because they have made them. Of course, these 'gods' – of lies, killers or infantile fools – are sometimes the same gods to which some religious people are prone. However, a moment's reflection shows that they are clearly false gods. The real challenge for the atheist, then, is to establish a knock-out blow for a decent conception of God. Even Julian Baggini, who resists the demonising way of attacking religion, still insists that religion is at fault for refusing to be judged by 'the standards of proof and evidence that intelligent discourse relies upon'. He would require a god he could believe in to be less than God, namely, subject to human reason. Little wonder that he remains an atheist.

The challenge for atheists has been articulated with great wit by Denys Turner, now at Yale, but before Professor of Divinity in the University of Cambridge. His inaugural lecture to the Norris-Hulse chair was entitled 'How to be an atheist'. He has never met, he declared, an atheist who does not believe in a god that would be worth believing in to start with.

As an example of what he means, consider the idea of God implicit in Nicholas Fearn's book, *Philosophy: the Latest Answers to the Oldest Questions*. It is a good book in many ways, seeking to take a general audience on a journey through what the greatest living philosophers have to say about being human. Fearn, who I presume to be an atheist, does not consider God a question to address head-on. Like belief in flying saucers or the power of crystals, I imagine he would say that to pay it serious attention would only be to pay it respect. However, given that God is one of the oldest questions humans have asked themselves, and that it is certainly a question plenty of philosophers are still asking, theological matters inevitably make several appearances in his book. This forces Fearn to get theological on occasion, which in turn exposes the divinity that he objects to as woefully reactionary and narrow-minded. His deity is an absolute principle that would underwrite human beliefs, guarantee meaning in life, and determine what everyone would do in the future. Conversely, it is divinity as inviolate moral will, punishing those who do wrong, and patting on the back those who do right. In other words, Fearn's theology says more about his atheism than it does about the question of God. It is a mirror opposite of the beliefs of a fundamentalist. Such believers certainly exist. But they can hardly be taken as the best of the community of faith, or even typical. Their theology might be sure but it is trite. It is a reactionary conception of God.

God unknown

So what is it that atheists are missing? What would it be to have a reasonable conception of the divine? What idea of God might they have that any decent theology would not deny too?

Thomas Aquinas, the giant of medieval philosophy, provides the key. For any normal subject of human investigation, he says, there are two steps to take. First is to identify what the matter in hand is about, and second is to define its nature and scope. Hence, biology is about living things and its domain is the material world of the animal and plant kingdoms. Or, physics is about the natural world and its domain is the fundamental constituents of the universe. However, theology is different. It can say what it is about – God. But God is not like other things in nature and scope. If God could be investigated like living things or the natural world then God would not be God. Aquinas wrote, 'since we cannot know of God what he is, but [only] what he is not, we cannot inquire into the how of God, but only into how he is not'. Aquinas is, in this sense, radically and insistently agnostic about God. 'It is extremely difficult for readers of Aquinas to take his agnosticism about the nature of God seriously,' wrote Herbert McCabe:

If he says 'Whatever God may be, he cannot be changing' readers leap to the conclusion that he means that what God is is static. If he says that, whatever God may be, he could not suffer together with (sympathise with) his creatures, he is taken to mean that God must be by nature unsympathetic, apathetic, indifferent, even callous. It is almost as though if Aquinas had said that God could not be a supporter of Glasgow Celtic, we supposed that he was claiming God as a Rangers' fan.

All that, though, would be wrong. Aquinas is merely but profoundly insisting what God is not. A thought experiment develops the idea further. Consider someone who decides to count up all the things that exist in the world. Calculator in hand, they start on everything they can see around them – trees, insects, people, buildings, books and so on. Eventually they reach a number, let us call it N. But just as they are sitting down, they realise they have missed something out. It happens that they believe in God. So they conclude, there must actually be N+1 things in the world.

This is wrong, says Aquinas. The answer is, in fact, N because God is not a thing at all. If that was the case, then the divine being could not also be the creator of all other things – something that is a minimal requirement for God to be considered a worthwhile deity. As Turner sums the thought experiment up: 'although the word "God" is not the proper name of an individual, but a word we use in the way in which we use descriptions, still we have no proper concept which answers to it. Having no proper concept of God, we have no way of identifying God as an instance of any kind.'

Proofs of God

This is also the meaning of Aquinas's five so-called 'proofs' for the existence of God, which are better referred to as 'ways' as that is the word he uses: they represent the ways the thinkers of his time tended to talk about God, and he is going to explore them, to establish what they mean. They can be put into two groups: the first four are called cosmological; the fifth is teleological.

The cosmological ways arise from looking at the cosmos and asking what lies behind it. Aquinas saw that the cosmos exists, that it is full of movement, and that it is full of causes of movement. So he concluded that this way of talking about God is to infer that there must be a necessary being, an unmoved mover and an uncaused cause behind it all, and that this being must have the attributes of a deity, whatever else that God might be. In a modern idiom, Aquinas's questions are a bit like asking what caused the Big Bang, and concluding that we don't know because there was nothing before it to cause it. So, whatever was before the Big Bang, if that's even a reasonable question, must have been something divine-like because before the first event there could not have been normal being. That said, we don't know what it means to be divine-like, only that it is not thing-like.

The teleological argument also arises from looking at the cosmos but, rather than looking at its origins, it looks at its purpose. It argues that the universe appears to be designed with an end in mind – whether that end be taken as the 'pinnacle of creation', namely human beings, or simply the intricacy of the universe itself (the version put most famously by William Paley in the analogy of finding a fine watch and concluding that there must, therefore, be a watchmaker.)

As positive proofs, the cosmological arguments are highly vulnerable to critique. For example, one might ask what this God looks like, for clearly the unmoved mover and uncaused cause does not look at all like the personal God people claim to believe in. Someone else might think that if God can exist without a cause, then perhaps the universe can come into being without a cause too – though whatever the universe might be, it is a thing existing as time and space; and whatever God might be, God is not that.

The teleological argument can be made to look flimsy too. Most obviously, Darwinian theory articulates a mechanism by which plants and animals can come to look designed, but are not, since the 'design' is actually adaptive. By extension, the Darwinian supposes that the universe itself evolved according to natural, indifferent processes.

Aquinas is exploring ways, though, not proofs. To try to refute the so-called arguments for the existence of God as if they were exercises in logic is itself to mistake their purpose. His five ways are certainly supposed to show that it is reasonable enough to look at the cosmos and intuit a God behind and before it. But at the same time – and this is the crucial point the atheists miss – the five ways are simultaneously supposed to prove the impossibility of knowing anything positive about God. What Aquinas intends is to instruct believers in why it is simply not possible to say much about what it means to confess that God exists.

Say that the universe did spring from nothing in a random fluctuation of the quantum vacuum. For the believer – following a modern version of Aquinas's 'proof' – the implication is not that quantum theory disproves God, but that God's 'uncausedness' must be more mysterious still. Or consider the teleological argument from design. As Hume pointed out, thinking that a watch is made by a watchmaker presupposes that we already know who or what makes watches – namely, the fore-mentioned watchmaker. So while design in the universe might apparently be seen all over the place – from the fine-tuned organs of the senses to the fine-tuned constants of cosmology – the argument should also highlight the fact that any designer of the universe would be way beyond anything of which we might have experience. As Turner summaries again: whatever might show God to exist equally shows God's unknowability. The 'proofs' are meditations on the mystery, not scientific hypotheses.

Missing this fundamental point is to make the same mistake as taking Socrates' question in the *Euthyphro* as an argument for atheism. This asked whether things are good because the gods say so, or whether they are good because they are good in themselves. If the former, then the suggestion is that this makes morality arbitrary. If the latter, as seems right, then it supposedly negates the gods' role in morality – which would seem to be a major blow. What is routinely missed is Socrates' point that the conundrum is not an issue for the gods, but for human beings. The importance of the question is to show up the limitations of human conceptions of morality. It says nothing about the gods' involvement with it.

The loss of contemplation

No doubt the unknowability of God is very annoying to conviction atheists. Rather than see the conundrums it poses as an invitation to grapple with the limits of human knowledge, they reject them as incoherent. Another so-called argument for the existence of God, the ontological argument, makes the point directly. Formulated by St Anselm, it was meant by him as another kind of meditation on God. It is found in his work, the *Proslogion*. It is the sort that has the aim of trying to invoke as profound a sense as is possible of the enormous mystery of God in the human mind. The formula that Anselm derives to do this is that God is 'something than which nothing greater can be thought'. He suggests a meditation: contemplate anything at all, and God is greater.

Anselm's ontological argument is often today summarised thus: if God must be greater than existence, God cannot, therefore, be thought not to exist. QED – God exists! Little wonder it comes across as nothing more than a trick of logic, which most philosophers agree as a proof it probably is. The atheists then set on it. They point out that it is only about the concept of God and God's existence, and this says nothing about what exists in the real world. Under the same logic, someone could develop a concept about the perfect example of anything – say a perfect car or a perfect flower – and then ask why its perfection should not entail its existence too. Clearly, it would be a fool who then set out to find this perfect car in the showroom or perfect flower in the meadow. Therefore, they say, it is the fool who thinks the ontological argument proves God exists too.

The problem for the medieval 'proofs' of God is that, in the present day, it is easy to lose sight of the religious milieu in which their authors expected them to be pondered. The cloister has been replaced by the classroom; flickering candles by fluorescent lights; the prie-dieu by the projector. With these changes, the meditation comes to be taken as a strict argument – for the existence of God. If you are a believer, as Anselm was, then this is the start of a reflection on the nature of God's existence – since existence is the greatest attribute God can have. Certainly this is a reflection that would take the believer beyond reason, which is to say that it will throw up all kinds of rational conundrums. But then that is the whole point: if someone's thoughts on God seem logical, reasonable and clear, then only one thing can be said for sure; the meditation is not on God but on some reduced concept of divinity, an idol.

After atheism

I can remember being similarly irritated by the insistence of theologians that to read the proofs about God in a literal way was to misread them. Logic is logic, I thought; bad logic is bad logic. By implication I also believed that reason was supreme, and human reason had replaced God. For a while, I concluded that if God's unknowability meant that anything that may be said about God is also a reason for not saying it at all, then that itself was good reason to be an atheist.

However, in time, atheism ceased to be, for me, such a desirable thing to assert, though not because of any proofs. After all, proofs tend to confirm minds not change them. Rather, the complex of irrational and psychological ire that had fired my revulsion of God abated, and then died – for equally elusive and poorly understood reasons as it first arose. Having said that, at least one thought did stand out in my mind during this time that is perhaps worth remarking upon. Part of the reason that atheism lost its appeal was because I became increasingly conscious that to be an atheist seemed to entail denying more than

Illus. 5.1: St Dominic, depicted by Fra Angelico, from the period in which the practice of prayer and the exercise of reason were indistinguishable.

I really wanted to or, in truth, felt. This question kept occurring to me: like the atheist who refuses to see Anselm's argument as a meditation, and so misses the point of it, was my atheism refusing all sorts of imaginative possibilities in life?

I recall being on holiday in Egypt and being truly amazed not just at the remains of the temple at Karnak, but also at how they inspired a sense of religious awe in me – and no doubt thousands of other tourists – for all that we live 4000 years later in time. In the guide book, I read about the social and economic significance of temple architecture and the religious system. But this description, though interesting from the perspective of the historian, seemed to miss the most significant element that strikes the visitor: the awesome spirit of the place. Did I want to limit my appreciation of these other, ancient people to essentially atheistic discourses? It is not that an agnostic or theist could have an experience of ruins that is not open to the atheist. But there did seem to me to be something in atheism that would prefer to turn its back on such an experience, because to embrace it would be to be embarrassed by the confession of being so moved by an ancient people's expression of the transcendent.

I had a similar sense in relation to religious music – the music that has an ability to speak, without words, directly to the soul, suggesting at the same time that, through the senses, the soul is being opened to that which transcends it. Clearly such an understanding of music can be debated. But it does express how I felt that religious music seemed different from other forms of art, even secular music. A Mozart aria of passionate intensity might make you weep in the way it captures the longings of your heart; a Hopper painting of solipsistic isolation might do as much by reminding you of your own loneliness; a movie might make you cry through empathic sentimentality. But sacred music need not say anything that can be connected to your past or present, but still it can move you to tears in apparently nameless ways.

I felt this as a result of playing the piano and organ myself. I've never been very good, but I've been good enough to have the sense that, when you know a piece really well, you don't play it, so much as it plays you. I suppose professionals have that experience all the time. It comes after all the practice, when the piece is not just learnt but internalised; it wholly and utterly makes sense. This is why you no longer need the notes written down in front of you: it's not that they are memorised so much as that they could go in no other place. The music can speak through you, which is to say that it's as if the music has come from elsewhere. Quite where that 'elsewhere' is – the right-side of the brain, some link between composer and player, a Platonic realm, heaven – is one for debate. But I wanted to have that debate and not foreclose it.

Again, an answer determined by the human sciences alone seems too parochial. It would ask the question what music is for, as if its effect can be summed up by saying it binds people together, like a nationalistic hymn. Or it might adopt a psychological explanation, saying it evokes some altered state of consciousness, as if the altered state were all. However, such understandings alone, while illuminating to a degree, seem to necessitate certain 'no-go' areas of thought – those that invoke the spiritual. Again, this is not necessarily to say that only believers can fully appreciate the perfection of Bach's B minor mass or Mozart's Requiem, for clearly believers do not gain some extra musical faculty upon turning to God. There is no divine hearing aid – though as an aid to hearing the divine it might mean more. And that's the point: the atheist mindset appears forced to put a cap on the appreciation of such things. At the very least, a degree of agnosticism in relation to the value of spiritual yearning would seem to be necessary to be open to the music that speaks of divinity.

The gift of creation

Turner's advice to atheists on how best not to believe in God adds to this sense of the imaginative poverty that conviction atheism seems to entail. Turner has shown that, contrary to what many atheists might think, their denial of certain kinds of divinity is, in fact, exactly the same denial any reasonable theist would make too. The difference comes because the atheist stops there, whereas the theist will go on to see whether anything affirmative can be said about this unknowable God. In other words, if theists would deny most of the things about a deity that atheists deny too, then when does the point come at which theists affirm something that atheists would still deny? The positive thing that theists would assert, and that atheists presumably would not, Turner believes, is that the world is created. The world is not 'just there', as the atheistically inclined Bertrand Russell put it.

Of course, the belief that the world is created does not mean that the theist can offer anything about how the world is created. Neither does it make any difference to the way that, say, the sensible theist will want to do science; this is not an argument for Intelligent Design. However, there is more entailed by the atheist's denial than merely the assertion that the world is brute fact.

The difference comes because if the atheist denies that the world is created, they also resist the idea of existence as gift. Turner explains it this way:

> In saying that the world is created out of nothing, you are beginning to say that the world comes to us, our existence comes to us, from an unknowable 'other'; that is to say, you are claiming that existence comes to us as pure gift, that for the world to exist just is for it to be created.

One might think about the difference this makes in a thought experiment. Imagine a customer who logs onto their bank account one morning and sees an unexpected balance of $1 million. Being an upright individual, they alert the bank. However, after an investigation, the balance stays the same: no mistake has been made, they are told. The customer can reach one of three conclusions. The first is that the money is a gift from some unknown benefactor. The second is to conclude that the new balance is the result of a glitch but that, luckily, the money is now theirs. The third is to be unsure about what has happened: it could be luck or it could be a gift.

The first conclusion is like the theist's response to existence: they are full of gratitude for the gift. The second conclusion is like the atheist's response: having no one to thank, they merely count themselves very lucky. The third conclusion is like the agnostic's response: thrown into wealth, like existence, they would perhaps spend some of the money trying to find a benefactor to give thanks to, though they never completely puzzle it out.

The difference between a response of gratitude and a response of luck to existence also carries implications for how an individual thinks about the world around them. For the response of luck tends to contain the exploration, particularly when that involves entertaining thoughts that bring up theological problems. They will tend to think that there is little point in asking questions for which answers 'in principle' cannot be given. So, and recalling the money analogy again, the question of life becomes mostly how to spend or use it. The response of gratitude, in contrast, is in practice more expansive since it longs to know more about this gift of existence and what lies behind, above and through it – for all that such questions can never be wholly satisfied.

Back to church?

Now, it would be fair, after my rejection of the certainties of atheism, to ask why I did not return to some kind of Christianity. I'd moved from the certain world of the young priest, to the certain world of the turncoat atheist, and had now seen through both. Mightn't the discovery that any decent talk about God should include a sense of God's unknowability – indeed must make that its main objective for fear of worshipping lesser gods and idols – signal a return to a more mature theistic commitment?

The answer, in brief, is that moving on from atheism gave me permission, as it were, to re-engage a religious imagination – Schleiermacher's sense and taste for the Infinite, Tillich's quest for the ground of being. However, it did not easily re-engage a belief in the Christian God. The position I had come to was an appreciation of the unknowability of the divine. This left me passionately agnostic. As it happens, I do fairly regularly go to church – trying to pick the times and places that attend to the mystery of things in great architecture, music and silence. However, what you still have to reckon with are the repeated expressions of doctrinal certainties that pepper the vast major-ity of liturgies. They are not the same as the assertions of the fundamentalist. But to an agnostic, they are still felt.

The very first words you are likely to hear upon attending a mass, communion, worship or family service are either, 'In the name of the Father, the Son and the Holy Spirit', or, 'The Lord be with you' – phrases that immediately encompass all sorts of assertions about God. Then there will be the prayers of interces-sion, the part of the service where the concerns of the world and the people are rehearsed. It is a natural thing to want to do. What doesn't often seem to be asked is what kind of answer God might be thought to give. Personally, I also find the words of many hymns problematic – when they read more like pop lyrics than poetry. And then there is the main stumbling-block in the service when people are invited to recite the creed – 'I believe in God …' and so on. Even uttering the credo – the 'I believe' – leaves me wanting to add qualifiers. By the end – 'the holy cath-olic church, the communion of saints, the forgiveness of sins, the resurrection of the body, and the life everlasting' – I have run out of fingers to cross. (For which reason my strategy has become just to go with the flow, to allow the whole experience to affect me: it's church, not a law court.)

There are a number of rejoinders that the minister or priest would suggest in response to these complaints. First, it might be said that a church is a Christian place of worship – for believers – and so one should only expect Christian language to be used there. That is fair comment. But my difficulty is not so much with the Christian nature of the language. After all, there is no such thing as generic religious language: it always originates in specific traditions that inevitably have a certain hue. This is why agnosticism and atheism are recognisably related to the religious systems that they are struggling with or objecting to. I don't seek a perennial philosophy, so generic as to have lost any particularity and colour. My difficulty is more with the tone of the language; its seemingly unguarded affirmations.

There are services that are exceptions to this. At the midnight mass of Christmas the story of the birth and the time of day both work to put a narrative in the foreground, not statements of belief. Alternatively, cathedral worship, with its glorious aesthetic, gains the advantage that the action of the liturgy transcends its literal content. Might it be that the persistent popularity of these kinds of service, amid otherwise declining congregations, has something to do with the way they allow the spiritual search of the agnostic? (In similar mood, I sometimes wonder whether a return of older forms of language might do wonders for numbers. It would be an advantage to hear the wonder of God conveyed in the poetry of the words themselves.)

A different rejoinder would emphasise the point that religious language is always part of a tradition. Take the creed. It is a historic formulary that originated at a particular moment in the church's history. Today it should be read as an expression of the church's connection with the past and its continuity over time. That is true. But as a historic formulary, it was specifically designed to define who was orthodox and unorthodox. It not only achieved its purpose then but achieves the same effect today – forcing the agnostic out of their closet. I have also heard it said that the creed should be read – or even better, sung – as a hymn of praise. There's something in that: I remember reciting it to the melancholy chant of Merbecke in my grandmother's church, and that just about conceals its bureaucratic origins.

A final rejoinder would want to correct the perception of religious language as straightforwardly affirmative. The fundamental point here would be that all religious language is metaphorical, in keeping with the insight that God is radically unknowable, and there are various strategies that religious language deploys to underline its metaphorical nature. Sometimes negative language is used. For example, God may be said to be 'immortal' or 'invisible' – that is, not mortal and not visible, with the emphasis on the not. Alternatively, when positive statements about God are used, they should never occur in isolation, but should be set alongside other statements that unsettle any direct inferences. For example, when God is called 'Lord', it is quite clear that he is not a lord in any usual sense – dressed in ermine or lording it over an estate – but that the word is metaphorically trying to express something of God's authority or power. Similarly, when God is called Father, Son and Holy Spirit, the idea is to convey insights in the way that God is manifest to human beings, at least as the Christian tradition sees it. The emphasis, again, is on the way God is manifest to human beings – that is, though divinely inspired, this is human language about God. What God is in Godself is as mysterious as ever. As the Archbishop of Canterbury, Rowan Williams, put it in a lecture entitled 'What Is Christianity?', at the international Islamic University in Islamabad: 'When we speak of "the Father, the Son and the Holy Spirit", we do not at all mean to say that there are three gods – as if there were three divine people in heaven, like three human people in a room.'

The Archbishop's thought must be right. However, it is one thing to say that technically speaking the doctrine of the Trinity does not include the idea that there are three gods. But it is another thing entirely for the language to take the individual beyond the idea that God is literally Father or Lord. I can only speak from experience, but I doubt whether many Christians think that, or would even think it right to think that. Most think of God as a Father, as Lord.

The modern use of religious language has sidelined God the question – in favour of more accessible notions of the divine. Further, this, I suspect, is part of a general historical shift in which a full sense of theological agnosticism has largely been forgotten – not only in the sense of having been marginalised but even in the sense of having been lost. To see this, we must take a step back and look at the history of ideas that lies behind modern Christianity, the path that has led to contemporary Church language and practice.

Myth and *logos*

It was a few hundred years ago that it first started to look as if a gap might be opening up between a scientific understanding of the world and the Christian one, after Copernicus displaced the earth from the centre of the universe. What we now call the scientific revolution had begun. It's clear that it would be a mistake to think that from that moment on it was only a question of time until atheism ruled the day, as if the earth's demotion obviously entailed God's destruction too. Many scientists continued and continue to see God in their observations and experiments. Like Newton, they thought that the new science revealed God to them more clearly.

However, something profound has shifted in this time. A scientific way of talking about things has gained the upper hand. This began with the tremendous success of scientific descriptions of the natural world – a success that some would like to see extended to every sphere of life, usurping the spiritual once and for all. However, while science can now, I believe, be seen to have lost this war over explanation – because it overreaches itself when it claims that everything is explicable by a rational materialism – the arrival of modern science has not left things unchanged.

It's this difference between the discourse of the social sciences and that of the spiritual. It's a move described very well by the historian of religions, Karen Armstrong. In a nutshell she sums it up by saying that the scientific revolution led to the triumph of *logos* over myth. *Logos* – Greek for word, argument, speech and reason – favours the worldview that latches onto facts and,

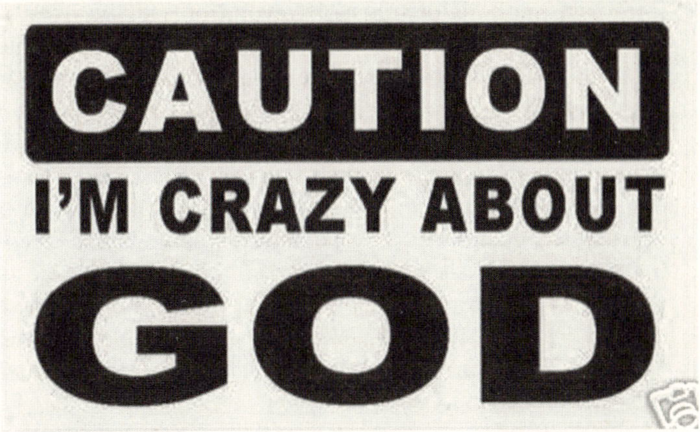

Illus. 5.2: Apophatic religion was a life-long search. Fundamentalist religion is stick-on statement.

in particular, those facts that have practical application. It is the natural language of the sciences. Myth – from the Greek *muthos*, meaning a story that is symbolic, traditional or paradoxical – favours the worldview that grapples imaginatively and intuitively with the significance of patterns, vision and values. It is the natural language of religion. Myth does not sit easily alongside a strident *logos* if it repeatedly asks myth to declare whether its stories are realistic and logical, true or false. This is the impact of science. It forces a focus on pragmatic outcomes – results, measurements and evidence. It squeezes out and displaces insights that are indissoluble, irreducible and uncertain.

The distinction offers another reason why science, the mode of thought that quintessentially exemplifies *logos*, fails as meaning. In *A Short History of Myth*, Armstrong writes:

Thanks to their scientific discoveries, [people] could manipulate nature and improve their lot. The discoveries of modern medicine, hygiene, labour-saving technologies and improved methods of transport revolutionised the lives of Western people for the better. But *logos* had never been able to provide human beings with the sense of significance that they seemed to require. It had been myth that had given structure and meaning to life, but as modernisation progressed and *logos* achieved such spectacular results, mythology was increasingly discredited. As early as the sixteenth century, we see more evidence of a numbing despair, a creeping mental paralysis, and a sense of impotence and rage as the old mythical way of thought crumbled and nothing new appeared to take its place. We are seeing a similar anomie today in developing countries that are still in the earlier stages of modernisation.

So the relationship between *logos* and myth is not a matter of choice – as if for certain parts of life one can resort to the scientific, and for other parts one can turn back to myth. Because scientific *logos* compromises the potency of myth, modern people in search of meaning appear to be presented with a zero-sum game with a lust for certainty winning out.

Myth, though, holds many things that remain unputdownable for us – an aesthetic, an openness to that which is beyond us, a response to the vicissitudes of life, a communal or ethnic identity, an expanded remembrance of historical events, as well as a set of stories. Individual myths of a virgin birth, or of blood and a cross, may lose force, but the human need for myth does not. They're too good at speaking to us of the more, and science itself is no mean generator of cosmic religious myths, as we've seen.

This means that there is good news and bad news for the believer. The good news is that, when *logos* gains the upper hand, it does not bring Christianity to an end: challenging the power of myth is not the knock-out blow that the atheist may hope because Christianity has plenty of other *raisons d'être*, not least its unique abilities as a response to life and as a provider of identity. It is for this reason that it continues to be a major force in the

the responsibility of saying whether or not the Trinity is true: *logos* demands a decision. Thus, when Christians confess belief in a Triune God now, they do not take it as a reminder that God should not be thought of in personal terms, because the personal dimension to the human-divine relationship comes from human beings, not God. Quite the opposite: God, it is said, must be personal to be relevant to me. So the Trinity is taken as describing God in Godself: in practice, and reflected in the writings of some theologians, God is literally a Father, literally Son, literally Holy Spirit. To do anything else would mean that the doctrine fails according to the rules of *logos*, which in the modern age is to say it fails, period. (This is also why theological apologists, like the Archbishop of Canterbury, are forced to tell other monotheists that, in spite of appearances, Christians are not polytheists.)

The pressure to drop myth and take up *logos* explains many other features of modern Christianity too. It explains the extraordinary success of evangelicalism. This is nothing if not religion as fact and with direct personal applicability. In evangelicalism, the individual must decide what they think about Jesus – who he was – not as part of some lifelong engagement with a tradition, as Christian writers of the past thought of it, but as a one-off assessment of the evidence. As the TV evangelist demands, look at the witness of the Bible: the rational person can only come to one of three conclusions – either Jesus was mad, bad or who he said he was! The thought that the Gospels of the New Testament might have been written not to provide factual evidence but as the struggles of four uncertain individuals, or groups of individuals, continually working out who this figure called Jesus might be for them, does not occur to this school of thought (or, if it does, it is branded liberal nonsense). Indeed, that there are four Gospels that in part do not agree should be a source of inspiration for Christians, not a cause of obfuscatory embarrassment. The disagreements remind the reader that the Bible points beyond the words it contains. You are supposed to read between the lines.

Having delivered on the factual requirement for modern belief, evangelicalism also delivers on the requirement of relevancy. 'Do you accept Jesus Christ as your personal Lord and Saviour?', 'Are you born again?', 'What would Jesus do?' – these are the questions of a personal religion that must be seen to be applicable to the modern, autonomous individual. Similarly, courses on being a Christian at work, being a Christian at home, marriage as a Christian, singleness as a Christian – these are the self-help programmes that a church must run to be relevant. Or again: this kind of Christianity conveys the idea that you can talk to God as easily as you can call your mother. It is an idea of prayer that is more or less absent in the spiritual traditions of the past. Then prayer was perceived as entering a cloud of unknowing or a dark night of the soul. Now, though, prayer is the activity so entertainingly parodied in Wendy Cope's poem, from her collection *Serious Concerns*:

> When I went out shopping,
> I said a little prayer:
> 'Jesus, help me park the car
> For you are everywhere.'

Even within more liberal churches, the *logos* is profoundly shaping the nature of the church. Paul Fletcher's book, *Disciplining the Divine*, explains why from a historical perspective. He points out that one of the key tenets of the Reformation was that the Bible should take precedent in matters of doctrine and salvation, over the tradition and the church. *Sola scriptura* was the slogan. Unless something can be proven in the Bible, it cannot be taken as 'gospel truth'. The element that the Bible could provide, and that the diverse tradition and a corrupt Church could not, was the new, post-Copernican need for fact, decision and proof.

However, treating the Bible in this way is a risky strategy because the Bible itself could be put under the microscope and subjected to the rigours of scientific investigation – as, indeed, it was – and as, indeed, it was found to be wanting. What then? How might the integrity of the Bible as a source of authority be preserved? It came to be thought of as embodying a different sort of reason by the Reformers – a divine reason that contains certainties of which secular science knows nothing. No longer was Jesus the Word (as, paradoxically, the Bible itself testifies); the Bible was. 'This is the Word of the Lord,' Christians now say after the Bible is read out in services – in mainstream practice, not just fundamentalist churches. In other words, the scientific revolution forced Christians to turn to the Bible, and it forced them to say that the Bible was above the critique of the scientific worldview.

This, in turn, sheds light on crises churches face today. Consider the issue that appears to be tearing the Anglican Church apart – that of homosexuality. It is often a puzzle to people why gay relationships should be so divisive. Jesus himself said nothing about same-sex activity. It should not be a 'first-order' issue, like say the Trinity or the Incarnation. Surely, it would be thought, an essentially liberal Church ought to be able to find an accommodation within which homosexuality is treated as a matter of private conscience. However, homosexuality has become a schismatic issue today because it has become a test case of this need for biblical reliability. Liberal voices contest this, arguing that the Bible condemns the consumption of shellfish and the practice of usury, or that the word homosexuality is a modern one and has little to do with the same-sex activity objected to in the New Testament. But, to the conservative, that misses the point. Homosexuality, they say, is against the order of creation described in the Bible, expressed no more succinctly than in the book of Genesis. The argument that the Pope, Archbishops, Chief Pastors and Moderators make in mainstream churches is that God created humans as man and woman in a complementary relationship, and that this narrow ordering of human relationships represents a line beyond which a Christian cannot go. To condone homosexual relationships, as if they were a similarly ordained part of creation, is therefore read as a rejection of the Bible in toto. This is what religion as a transcendental science puts the liberal Christian up against.

A similar rationale also explains why creationism carries such force in the US. A literal seven days of creation is taken as a key test of faith; if you believe in it, you believe in the Bible; if not, you do not.

Sexuality is not the only issue over which churches are forced to draw the line. One of Pope Benedict XVI's favourites is relativism. The growth of relativism is another paradoxical product of the scientific revolution. In the search for facts and certitude, philosophical certainty is itself called into question, and flounders. Only one thing is sure, relativism says: nothing is sure. That this is itself a contradiction does nothing to lesson the fear of the nihilism relativism implies. The Pope objects to this. But what is particularly surprising, for a man who confesses faith in God, is the ferocity with which he rails against it. 'We are moving towards a dictatorship of relativism which does not recognise anything as definitive and has as its highest value one's own ego and one's own desires,' he said in a sermon on the eve of his election. 'From Marxism to free-market liberalism to even libertarianism, from collectivism to radical individualism, from atheism to a vague religion, from agnosticism to syncretism and so forth.'

Rampant relativism is a good candidate for demonisation. Everyone fears it a little. And the Pope is issuing a powerful challenge with his concern for the erosion of the moral foundations of the modern state. Consensus is not enough, he argues, because consensus is weak. There must be principles upon which life is based that are 'pre-political', not subject to the ups and downs of democratic agreement.

But the reason this is surprising from the Pope is that talk of God – theology – is itself bound to embody a kind of relativism because anything that can be said about God is provisional – relative to human beings' incapacity to know God. He might do better to make us more comfortable with 'right relativism' and thereby more equipped to resist its destructive forms. But in a world dominated by science, lines must be drawn in the sand. If the price is the rejection of religious uncertainty, and forgetfulness about the ultimate unknowability of God, then that is a price worth paying. So, strange as it may seem, papal infallibility is as much a product of the scientific revolution as neo-Darwinism. It is surely no coincidence that the doctrine was formulated in 1870, just 11 years after the publication of *On The Origin of Species*.

Other fundamentalisms

My discussion has focused on Christianity, and Western Christianity at that, reflecting my own experience. Western Christianity is, arguably, particularly prone to the influence of science because, although it has a fantastically rich, if increasingly forgotten, mythological heritage, it has always been the case that what makes someone a Christian is assenting to creedal statements. In this way, it is unlike the other religions of the book – Islam and Judaism – within which what one does, as well as what one believes, counts. For them, orthopraxis – the correct performance of rituals – has always counted alongside any orthodoxy in determining faithfulness.

However, the culture of certainty is radically shaping contemporary Judaism and Islam too. In Islam, it is Wahhabism that is the parallel to fundamentalism and that sets the tone. As the Muslim scholar Reza Aslan says in his book, *No God but God: The Origins, Evolution and Future of Islam*, Wahhabism should have been 'a spiritually and intellectually insignificant movement in a religion principally founded upon spiritualism and intellectualism'; 'it is not even considered true orthodoxy by the majority of Sunni Muslims'. Yet its ideological certainty has an appeal that is seriously compromising what Aslan takes to be Islam's historic pluralism.

> Islam is and has always been a religion of diversity. The notion that there was once an original, unadulterated Islam that was shattered into heretical sects and schisms is a historical fiction. Both Shi'ism and Sufism in all their wonderful

manifestations represent trends of thought that have existed from the very beginning of Islam, and both find their inspiration in the words and deeds of the Prophet. God may be One, but Islam most definitely is not.

Indeed, the central doctrine of *tawhid* in Islamic theology – the profession that 'There is no god but God' – is itself in part a formula for preventing ideas of God becoming fixed. Notice how the first phrase, 'There is no god', sits uneasily alongside the second, 'but God'. On the one hand, it is a statement of the truths the Muslim believes were revealed by the Prophet. But, on the other hand, it is also a statement that God is greater still – *Allahu Akbar!* (literally, God is greater). 'Tawhid suggests that God is beyond any description, beyond any human knowledge', explains Aslan. He laments the fact that bigotry and fanaticism are the new false idols in Islam.

The same can be said of Judaism. Although there is no equivalent movement that stands out to the extent of Wahhabism or Christian fundamentalism, there is an issue around which religious conservatives can rally and exert influence, that of the politics of the state of Israel. Thankfully, there is a lighter side to this too. I was once told the joke, by a rabbi, about an orthodox Jew and a gentile caught in a lift on the Sabbath. Being in Jerusalem, the lift had two sets of controls. One control had normal switches to operate the lift. The other had a set of buzzers, that did not start the lift, but prompted a non-orthodox operator to do so. Why the buzzers? They meant that, on the Sabbath, the orthodox Jew could still use the lift and not work (for operating a lift counts as work). 'But that is ridiculous!,' the gentile exclaimed in rational indignation. 'Ah,' replied the Jew. 'It is God's ridiculous ways that remind me that He is unknown.'

Although many Victorians struggled with the implications of the new sciences for their beliefs, it was not until the twentieth century that fundamentalism as a religious movement emerged and, more widely, that words like conservative, orthodox, ultra-orthodox,

Bible-believing, traditionalist and infallibilist became virtually synonymous with Christian, Islamic and Jewish commitment. It was in a similar time-frame that modern militant atheism took hold as a cultural force.

It is sometimes said that science gives rise to a world of 'two cultures' – one is the culture of science and the other is the culture of art (or perhaps religion). However, I believe that the polarisation is somewhat different today. If my experience is anything to go by, and the analysis of this chapter is right, then positions that might be thought of as on opposite sides of the two cultures divide are actually just different aspects of the same culture – the culture with a lust for certainty. This is the reason why it is surprisingly easy to make the leap from belief to disbelief. It also lies behind the various forms of intellectual closure that lurk in both atheistic and theistic discourse – a rejection of possibilities both human and divine in favour of apparently sure grounds to stand on. The question, then, is where the opposite of this culture of certainty can be found, a worldview that embraces uncertainty, wise ignorance and unknowing – God the question.

Christian Agnosticism: Learned Ignorance

The word 'God' is a label for something we do not know.

Herbert McCabe

Thomas Aquinas was known as the 'Dumb Ox' at school, probably on account of his substantial frame. He is second only to Augustine among heavyweight theologians, and was the lynchpin in the thirteenth-century embrace of Aristotle. His great achievement was the harmonisation of the writings of the ancient Greek – whose authority was such that he was referred to simply as 'The Philosopher' – with Christian thought. Aquinas has been called a 'genius' in leading philosophy journals; 'one of the dozen greatest philosophers of the western world', by Anthony Kenny, one of his keenest contemporary readers; he was canonised by the Roman Catholic Church in 1323.

However, just three months before his death, something remarkable happened to this man of words. On 6 December 1273, he was celebrating the mass of the day, for St Nicholas, in the priory of San Domenico, Naples – where he was responsible for studies. The mass ended. But instead of continuing with his usual habit of calling for his secretary to continue writing, he stopped. From that moment on, he neither wrote nor dictated a single word again. The man whose intellect had grappled with the philosophy of nature, logic, metaphysics, morality, mind and theology was now silent.

It was not as if 6 December 1273 was a particularly good date upon which to put down his pen. His magnum opus, the *Summa Theologiae*, was far from complete in its Third Part. Modern biographers have put the abrupt halt down to a stroke or a breakdown caused by exhaustion. Others have said he had a mystical experience at the altar. But perhaps the truth of the matter is found in the response he gave to the colleague who begged him to continue: 'Reginald, I cannot, because all I have written seems like straw to me,' Aquinas said.

The comment has been taken as a rejection of his oeuvre, from the master's own mouth, as if for 'straw' one should read 'rubbish'. But that would be to misunderstand what was said. Straw was, in fact, a conventional metaphor for a literal reading of the Bible. It expressed the conviction that a straightforward treatment of scripture might provide the believer with comfort, or some basic material upon which to build their faith, but that such a use of the Bible was only a first step. The implication of Aquinas calling his work straw is therefore positive, not negative. His goal had been to understand God. He had made many attempts at the summit. But while they had produced wonderful insights – such as the reflections around the so-called proofs – he had reached the point at which he was able to appreciate the most profound truth of all. The peak lies beyond the clouds. God is unknown. Not in spite of, but because of, all his efforts – with its theological sophistication, subtlety and seriousness – the best interpretation of what happened to Aquinas on St Nicholas's Day, 1273, was that he had reached as profound an appreciation of this mystery as was possible. Even his enquiries into how God is not would now stop. His new silence was not a rejection but the culmination of his life's work.

Bonaventure, Aquinas's contemporary, had argued something similar. If God can be said to sustain the universe, then God would also have to be invisible in the universe. As God said to Moses, no one can see God and live. It's that notion of God as the ground of existence. If God is such a ground then God cannot be said to exist. Neither can God be said not to exist. God is somehow beyond existence, being the reason for existence.

Move forward just over 800 years, to a seminar room in an Oxford college. Richard Swinburne, Emeritus Nolloth Professor of the Philosophy of the Christian Religion, is about to continue with the explication of his account of the existence of God. The session had begun well. One student, tape machine in hand, had asked whether he might record the seminar. 'There is no copyright on truth,' came the permission so to do. The hour proceeded in an orderly, if intellectually challenging, manner.

Until, that is, another student sat up in his chair. He had been reading a new book about the religious writings of the French philosopher Jacques Derrida. His inquisitive mind had been particularly gripped by the idea summed up in the phrase 'religion without religion'. Derrida seemed to imply that any experience worth talking about – that is, a moment or an insight that was not merely humdrum – has a religious character. This is because, for it to be such an experience, it must happen at the limits of what is possible. After all, is it not the case that the most amazing experiences of life are when what was thought impossible actually occurs? The book argued that this structure of experience, this 'becoming possible of the impossible', might even be a good definition of God. It was religious but without the usual trappings of religion. Perhaps, the student wondered, this might have a bearing upon Swinburne's argument about the existence of God.

He was wrong, or at least he soon got the message that he was wrong. For having explained the point, he received the abrupt response: 'I believe they offer a course on Derrida in the French department.' The seminar continued as before. That line of thought about God, on the becoming possible of the impossible, was curtailed – though not because of any inherent failures in its logic. Rather, it had simply been declared off-limits. The silence that the reprimand left in its wake was a negative one, not full of possibility, but conspicuous by its emptiness.

These two anecdotes, the first famous in the history of medieval theology, the second mostly trivial though standing out as not atypical of half of my experience of studying theology at Oxford, illustrate two approaches to the subject. The former is an embrace of uncertainty. The latter aims to meet the demands of fact, application, veracity and coherence – the demands of *logos*. Thomas Aquinas, of course, was nothing if not rational: much of his work reads like logical puzzles and another of his titles could easily have been the Father of Scholasticism. However, he had the good fortune, theologically speaking, to live before the scientific worldview took hold. He understood that words, reason and argument must at some point give way before God, lest the divinity it discussed ceased to be God. His theology was a means to an end that it could not itself express. He could enter into a positive silence having exhausted all possibilities and sit with the impossible without shame or retribution. For many modern-day theologians, though, such a move is unspeakable – in the negative sense. Along with the atheists, the attempt to use words to throw the individual onto the unknowability of God is dismissed: different conservative religious parties would variously declare it 'continental', 'relativist', 'liberal' or 'heretical'. The atheist's preferred putdowns are 'incommensurate' or 'incoherent'.

Varieties of silence

The story of Aquinas opens up a whole new dimension to what Christianity has lost since the scientific revolution. In a word, silence. It is why someone can graduate with a degree in theology never having once written the word apophatic, and perhaps not even knowing that it is God-talk by negation. It is why silence is such a rarity in churches. Modern services tend to kill it with two blows; first, by filling every minute with words – be they from the missal or the overhead projector; second, by making those words 'vernacular' – commonplace in language and meaning. It is why the ping-pong between conservative religionists and militant atheists will continue ad infinitum with nothing much new being said: neither can bear the thought that, if God exists, divinity ultimately lies beyond anything that can be said of it. Or to put it another way, God to be God must be heretical and inconsistent – beyond good and evil, and for that matter existence itself.

However, and this is Aquinas's point, it is not simply true that nothing can be said about God. Everything possible, or at least a fair summary of everything that is possible, must be pursued before the move into silence.

This silence is of a certain sort: it is not empty but full; it is not a silence in which anything goes but in which nothing goes; it is not a place of resolved or dissolved argument but of irresolvable, indissoluble argument. Aquinas was not silenced but he was drawn into silence, having spoken much. This kind of silence, then, requires much to be said because it must be the right kind of silence. It is a point at which someone arrives; their mind then 'moves upon silence' in W.B. Yeats's lovely phrase.

It is worth adding at this point that this spiritual silence is subtlety different from the philosophical silence remarked upon by Wittgenstein in the *Tractatus*, where the comment we referred to before appears. His point there is a specific one about philosophy, to say nothing except what can be said with clarity. If you can't do that, then 'one must pass over in silence'. What this kind of silence does is try to show the limits of a certain kind of philosophy, to narrow it down. If the same principle were applied to religious discourse then it would imply that the 'big' questions were quite possibly empty. It'd be silence as a refusal, which spiritual silence is not.

This Wittgenstein recognises elsewhere when he remarks on what it is to talk about the unutterable, to move towards a spiritual silence. Take something simple, like describing the aroma of coffee to a friend. It is very hard to describe, or at least all descriptions will carry their own inadequacies – bitter, strong, sweet, nutty? Philosophically, you might say, the aroma of coffee is imprecise, and so, to a certain kind of analytical philosophy, it's not a good philosophical subject. But in life, the inadequacies inherent in our describing coffee – the silences – don't mean we don't talk about it. We rather look at our friend as we talk, who affirms, or questions, or denies. The aroma of coffee can't quite be told, but it can be shared. This is the showing not telling point, which the search for the divine is like. As

Wittgenstein remarks in another place, 'The unutterable will be – unutterably – contained in what has been uttered.'

Needless to say, moving upon silence is not easy, perhaps suggesting again why it is a road less travelled. We've talked about the letting go to let in of meditation. Another is the silence practised by the Society of Friends or Quakers, to whom many who regard themselves as spiritual not religious also turn. It's valuable in that. However, Quaker silence is of a different sort to that of the Catholic Aquinas and of the Socratic mindfulness of before. The central doctrine of the Quakers, as I understand it, is the 'Inner Light'. This is a sense of the divine, held collectively, that is superior to scriptures or traditions. Meetings are conducted in silence in order to facilitate discernment. Someone speaks when they feel stirred. All outward forms of worship are rejected as a hindrance to this discernment, this silence. But silence in the Catholic tradition works in the opposite way. Aesthetically rich liturgies draw the Christian into silence because God is beyond even the very best in words, images and music that the church can offer. It is a silence of superfluity, not simplicity. It is rooted in the specific things people have discerned of God, and the practices – writing, performance, symbols – that have stood the test of time, while also acknowledging that all fall short; which is very different from short-circuiting an engagement with those traditions in an attempt to surface perennial truths, as if they can be readily stated.

The tried and tested way in the Christian tradition is to approach such silence by the way of negation. This *via negativa* is applied to your God-talk – to say what God is not. It offers a method for understanding something more about the nature of the silence itself too.

It is not, for example, the silence of the oppressed. The oppressed are silenced in order to crush their humanity. Their silence is neither voluntary, but is imposed by some power, nor does it represent the inexpressible, but rather it marginalises that which, politically speaking, should be expressed.

Neither is this religious silence like the inarticulacy of brute ignorance. The brute ignorant are silent about what they do not care about, not just about what they do not understand. Their silence is not humbled and considered, but is arrogant and thoughtless.

Another sort of silence that this religious silence can be distinguished from is the vacuum that emerges when mature religions depart. This is the space highlighted in the comment, widely attributed to G.K. Chesterton: 'When men stop believing in God they don't believe in nothing; they believe in anything.' In other words, there is, perhaps, a brief moment of metaphysical silence when people stop believing in God. But like nature, people abhor vacuums, and so struggle to fill the emptiness with something else – superstitions and the like.

It is possible to speak more positively about religious silence too – using another theological method, this time of analogy. One example of a silence that has an awesome, religious quality is the silence associated with wonder. Again, science can elicit this. I remember the news coverage of a capsule called Stardust returning to earth. The probe had travelled to a comet and back, a round trip of nearly three billion miles. At its rendezvous, in deep space 240 million miles from Earth, Stardust took photographs and grabbed some of the material from the comet nucleus. These particles, roughly one-hundredth the size of a printed full stop, have remained unchanged since the solar system formed 4.6 billion years ago. The whole trip took seven years.

Needless to say the scientists were tearful at the press conference, when announcing the mission's success. It was a truly remarkable feat of technology, vision and nerve. And one can talk about it as a purely human achievement, which it is. But there is, somehow, more going on too. This probe had ridden a small but impressive stretch of the vast empty seas of space, and returned to tell the tale. One could look at the potholed, charcoal grey casing of the capsule and glimpse indirectly what that otherwise inconceivable journey might be like. I watched it on the TV – in silence.

Religious silence might be said to be like the silence following the performance of a great piece of music too. After the final notes of a Mahler symphony, Bach's B minor mass, a Mozart opera or other great music, there is, sometimes, a brief pause. It is as if the audience and musicians hang together, indeterminate, like quantum particles, between the universe portrayed in the music and the world they normally inhabit. It is a moment that cannot last; a moment that collapses with the first 'Bravo!'. But it is one that can only be arrived at having been sated, even exhausted, by the music that preceded it.

It is perhaps also like the silence that is the mark of certain close friendships. It has been said that the measure of a good friendship is not how much or how often the friends speak, but how little the friendship demands they speak even though they are together for much of the time. They say they are comfortable in the silence. If friendship can be summed up as the desire to know someone and be known by them – as opposed, say, to erotic love which is the desire to have and be had by someone – then friendship will move towards a togetherness in silence as the friends come to a kind of knowing that is beyond words.

Another positive evocation of such silence comes from religious life, not the churchgoing variety, but the community variety of monks and nuns. At the end of every day, they say or sing the office of Compline, from the Latin *completorium* or complete. Literally, that refers to the completion of the offices for that day. However, each liturgical day also symbolically represents everything that can be said about God – in scripture, in psalmody, in symbols in sacraments, in praise. So Compline also marks the point at which the monk or nun must turn to silence. This is literally the case too, since after Compline the so-called Greater Silence begins – the silence through the dark hours of the night. After the final part of Compline – the *Salve Regina*, the traditional Latin hymn before sleep – cowls are turned up, lights are turned off, and the community leaves the church in silence. From my experience of staying in religious houses for retreats, it is the most powerful moment of the day. The silence is thick with possibility. On the one hand, the office recognises that the night's silence may be full of 'fears and terrors', in the words of the office hymn – for sustained silence is a frightening thing. On the other hand, the silence portends the moment of death, the moment when words will cease forever. Compline powerfully conjures up another replete silence.

Beyond experience

The apophatic tradition, also known as mystical theology, stresses a similar process of speaking in order to clear an intellectual path through what God is not to silence. In Christianity, one of the first great articulators of the unknowability of God was Gregory of Nyssa. He argued that God was both infinite – lest God was limited by something – and unknowable, even in theory: after all, he says, echoing debates that continue to this day, we do not even know what the essence of an ant is, much less God.

Gregory taught that the inability to comprehend God forms the basis of a progress from the initial darkness of brute ignorance, through spiritual illumination, to a second darkness when the mind appreciates the mystery of God. He used the story of the encounters between God and Moses to illustrate the point. Before the Burning Bush, Moses was simply ignorant. The Burning Bush represents the phrase in which he tried to speak of God: for Moses, the high point of enunciation was in the revelation of the name of God – 'I am that I am' – though clearly, and quite deliberately, that phrase is no name. Next, Moses meets God in the pillar of cloud. This emphasises that, for all the light of his earlier theophany, God cannot actually be seen with the senses. Finally, on Mount Sinai, Moses learns that God cannot be known with the mind too. Divine darkness is the end of the journey that started with ignorant darkness.

Nicholas of Cusa, a fifteenth-century cardinal and humanist of the Renaissance, fills out the parameters of this negative way. His best-known work is entitled *De docta ignorantia*, 'Of

Learned Ignorance'. In it he pointed out that wise people from Solomon to Socrates realised that the most interesting things are difficult and unexplainable in words and that they know nothing except that they do not know. How, then, are we to interpret human beings' desire to know? The answer is that we desire to know that we do not know. This is the great challenge of the intellect:

> If we can fully attain unto this [knowledge of our ignorance], we will attain unto learned ignorance. For a man – even one very well versed in learning – will attain unto nothing more perfect than to be found to be most learned in the ignorance which is distinctively his. The more he knows that he is unknowing, the more learned he will be.

In this learning, one learns something about what one does not know, as it were. Nicholas thought that truth was unitary, simple and absolute – and this was why it was unknowable: human beings know in ways that are multiple, complex and relative. The nature of human knowledge, therefore, is that it always results in contradictions. But it is in the *coincidentia oppositorum* – the realm in which all contradictions meet – that God dwells. Nicholas's book is full of mathematical examples, which he uses by way of analogies, to make the point – triangles that are circles at infinity, and so on. His words carry challenging implications for atheists and theists alike. For atheists, he stresses that whatever they envisage God not to be, they must allow that image to be the most perfect thing possible. For theists, he emphasises that it is idolatrous to name God after created things, and that affirmative theology needs the sacred ignorance of negative theology to remember that God is ineffable. He concludes that strictly speaking God is neither known in this life nor in the life to come, since being infinity only infinity can comprehend itself. 'The precise truth shines incomprehensibly within the darkness of our ignorance' is a typically paradoxical formulation of his message.

Illus. 6.1: The greatest challenge to the intellect, according to the Socratic Nicholas of Cusa, was what he called 'learned ignorance'.

Another apophatic theologian, Meister Eckhart, makes a point that is particularly prescient: the importance of drawing a clear line between silence and an experience of ecstasy. It is prescient because there is an emphasis on experiencing ecstasy in much contemporary religiosity. This is Christianity that is authenticated by some kind of peak experience, from speaking in tongues, to being healed, to seeing a statue move. Typically, the experience is noisy, demonstrative and, qua the high, often barely distinguishable from a bungee jump or druggy trip. But this is Christianity as psychological buzz; its passion is no more than emotion. Its aims may be valid – happiness, satisfaction, belonging – but they eclipse the goal of spirituality, at least according to Eckhart, which is that of sacred ignorance.

For the pursuers of pure experience, the unknown is regarded suspiciously. They substitute the language of personal fulfilment for the language of vertiginous doubt. It is not going too far to say that Christianity as peak experience is the diametric opposite of what the great spiritual writers of the past meant when discussing the mystical life of the Christian (or indeed of other faiths). If anything they are notable for being against it: the whole point is to search for the God that is beyond experience, even esoteric experience. This is why they talk of 'divine darkness', 'emptiness' and 'mistrust of the senses'. In one sermon Meister Eckhart preached:

> If thou lovest God as God, as spirit, as Person or as image, that must all go. 'Then how shall I love him?' Love him as he is: a not-God, a non-spirit, a not-Person, a not-image; as sheer, pure, limpid unity, alien from all duality. And in this one let us sink down eternally from nothingness to nothingness.

He heaps up the impossibilities – a not-God, a non-spirit, a not-Person, a not-image – in order that God, spirit, Person, image might be left behind.

Here, then, is a tradition in which a strong, cultivated sense of mystery is the goal of its theology. It is characteristic of those who pursue it to premise everything they say on knowing that they do not know God. The aim is to hone the inability to speak of God so that things which are clearly wrong are discarded – which is to say, eventually, everything. The spirituality minded agnostic might warm to all this for it is a way of doing God-talk that is simultaneously keen on the question of God but, contra much theism and atheism, insists that God is kept as a radical question. Little wonder that mystics like Eckhart frequently found themselves on the wrong side of the religious authorities.

If contemporary Christian practice has lost this core theological strand, then it seems to me that a serious, engaged agnosticism might be thought of as a check on the apparently unchecked use of positive statements about God – God's unqualified 'personhood' or 'fatherhood', and even lovingness and goodness. In other words, the reason for spending the last chapter critiquing theism and atheism is that it has brought us to the point at which an account of Christian-shaped agnosticism could begin. However, before continuing with that, there are two questions to answer that arise from the apophatic tradition. Although for apophatic theists God is unknown and unknowable, they can still say they are theists because they profess a Christian faith in God. The agnostic cannot readily say this. So the first question is: what is it that distinguishes the agnostic from the atheist, since, without the profession of a faith, it is not always clear how agnostic belief is distinguishable from atheistic non-belief? Second, and relatedly, if mystics state that God is unknown and unknowable, they do so having made a prior commitment in faith to divine reality. The agnostic is unsure of this reality, believing it is in the nature of God-talk not to be able to settle it. So does that not undermine the integrity of the agnostic position?

Agnostic integrity

The first question was put into the mouth of Cleanthes by David Hume in his *Dialogues Concerning Natural Religion*. Cleanthes is the character who believes in natural theology. This is the attempt to gather insights about God from the world of nature and reason, on the good grounds that they are presumably both God's creation too. Cleanthes' charge is put to Demea, the character who is suspicious of what reason can achieve in theology because, for the divine to be divine, it must be beyond comprehension. He is not an agnostic though. He tends towards fideism, the belief in God by faith and faith alone. Cleanthes' complaint is that this is practically atheism since it allows nothing to be said about God's relationship with the world: 'How do you mystics,' he says, 'who maintain the absolute incomprehensibility of the Deity, differ from sceptics or atheists, who assert that the first cause of all is unknown and unintelligible?' Perhaps, they are fideists without knowing it.

I think our discussion so far provides answers to Cleanthes. For one thing, the atheist makes an assertion which the agnostic leaves as a question: the atheist says that God is not only not known or unintelligible, but is, further, non-existent. A second reason comes from something that all positions – theist, atheist and agnostic – can initially agree on, namely, that the world exists. As mentioned in the previous chapter, there are three responses to this existence. The atheist says that existence is a problem that may or may not be explained, but ultimately it is just a fact. The theist may or may not say that existence can be explained, but they will say that ultimately it is a gift. The agnostic says that existence is not just a problem, but a mystery, for it can never be explained away. They may also regard it as a gift. So, in this way, once again, the agnostic differs from the atheist.

Third, one can point to the different attitude that atheists and agnostics have to the mystics. For atheists, the apophatic is mostly gobbledegook. They may concede that some interesting insights about existential matters have been elicited by those operating on the margins of thought, but those gains to rationality are made at the unnecessary cost of an otherwise wilful obscurantism. For the agnostic, though, the apophatic not only has an integrity of its own but also is part of the valid search for ultimate things and, moreover, is an excellent embodiment of the Socratic wisdom of learned ignorance.

The second charge against the agnostic is more challenging. It is that they lack the prior commitment to faith in God, and so their apophaticism is, strictly speaking, pointless. The case can be fleshed out using another mystical theologian, Dionysius, also called the Pseudo-Areopagite. He makes the familiar moves implied by the inevitably slippery nature of theological language, moving through calling the reality beyond knowledge 'it', and even moving into the negation of negation, saying 'it is also beyond every denial'. His aim is to move his reader to a very profound silence indeed.

However, and this is where the challenge to the agnostic comes in, his multiple negations are made on the basis of a single affirmation: the negations negate the 'it'. Without that fixed point, Dionysius says, the force that drives the mystic into ever deeper contradictions becomes unstable, and the specificity of the apophatic silence disintegrates into unfocused intellectual turbulence. He uses the analogy of the sculptor, searching for the 'pure view of the hidden image' inside the stone or wood. The accusation is that the agnostic will obliterate the hidden form like a bad sculptor who chips too much away and so destroys the image.

This difference is, I think, substantial. It turns on the fact that the agnostic does not adhere to a faith; the believer does. Even if the believer's exploration of God reduces all that can be said to an 'it', and then negates that since an 'it' implies an object which God is not, faith allows the believer to affirm the 'it' knowing it is provisional, which the agnostic, unequivocally, cannot. The question then is whether there is a difference between the agnostic and the believer that disqualifies the agnostic's mysticism on the outside of faith?

Anthony Kenny has written about how both can still share the silence in relation to the poet Arthur Hugh Clough. Clough was a contemporary, colleague and correspondent of Matthew Arnold, the poet famous for 'Dover Beach', with its metaphor of the 'withdrawing roar' of the 'Sea of Faith'. Kenny shows how, of the two agnostics, Clough captures the ineffability of God more precisely, and in so doing provides an example of a genuine agnostic apophaticism.

Kenny considers Clough's poem *humnos haumnos* (a hymn, yet not a hymn) in a collection of his essays entitled *The Unknown God*. The poem begins by addressing the divine who dwells in human shrines, though immediately notes that this image of God 'Doth vanish, part, and leave behind / mere blank and void of empty mind'. The second stanza articulates the mystic's conundrum, of speaking about the unknown, and confesses that, 'The imperfect utterance fell unmade'. In the third stanza the more radical turn is taken, of negating even the negations. 'I will not frame one thought of what / Thou mayest either be or not.' The poet cannot only not say 'thus and so', but neither 'no' too.

Then, in the fourth stanza, Clough distances himself from the believer who, although similarly mystic, might have faith to receive a revelation beyond human words: 'I will not ask some upper air,' this agnostic asserts. So what is left? If the agnostic must admit that they cannot turn to faith, what shape can their agnosticism take? Oddly, a prayer:

> Do only thou in that dim shrine,
> Unknown or known, remain, divine;
> There, or if not, at least in eyes
> That scan the fact that round them lies.
> The hand to sway, the judgement guide,
> In sight and sense, thyself divide:
> Be though but there – in soul and heart,
> I will not ask to feel thou art.

The poet has reached a point of being reconciled with the fact that they cannot make the minimal, Dionysian affirmation of the 'it'. The question of God is held suspended, 'unknown or known'. Perhaps this God is only in the minds of those who 'scan' the world around them. However, even so, the final stanza concludes on this surprisingly prayerful note. The poet ends by seeking divine guidance and discernment 'in sight and sense' nonetheless. How can this be? Does this not require some positive sense that God is? Does not someone who makes such a prayer need to ask 'to feel thou art'? Kenny writes:

> No, the prayer need not assume the truth of that; only its possibility is needed. An agnostic's praying to a God whose existence he doubts is no more unreasonable than the act of a man adrift in the ocean, or stranded on a mountainside, who cries for help though he may never be heard, or fires a signal which may never be seen. Of course the need for help need not be the only motive which may drive an agnostic to prayer: the desire to give thanks for the beauty and wonder of the world may be another.

It is Kenny's last comment that saves the *via negativa* for the agnostic, that preserves a sense of radically unknowing silence with integrity. Like thoroughgoing uncertainty which regards existence as a mystery and therefore maintains the possibility that it is gift, the possibility that God 'is' – and that the whole experience and quest of the agnostic seems to require that possibility – is the minimal requirement which keeps the search via learned ignorance from spinning out of control. God is a question and a living question. That possibility means that the agnostic can return to the things that are said about God, and their negations. It is only if God ceases to be regarded as a possibility to be treated seriously that the apophatic quest loses its *raison d'être*. But then, that is to become an atheist.

This implies something else too: the agnostic is tied in a relation with the believer. Their search is parasitic on faith – though by engaging with faith from the outside, the agnostic contributes to it too, not least by emphasising the apophatic and the risks of ready assertion. It's like the relationship between the prophets and the priests in the Hebrew Bible. The agnostic historian of Christianity, Diarmaid MacCulloch, catches the mood well when he talks of his 'candid friendship' with Christianity. It's in the agnostic's interests that religious traditions thrive, for they live within them too, if from the outside of faith. Conversely, the atheist may be glad of religious traditions, as the repositories of much that is great in human art and thought, but they will not be living traditions for them, but rather points of departure towards an atheistic future.

Hence Clough's poem can end in prayer, if of a purged sort. What it emphasises is that the *via negativa* is an ongoing process. The poem begins with an invocation of God – 'O Thou'. The prayer at the end requires a return to the beginning; in calling out again to that now dimmer 'shrine', the poet repeats the process of unknowing. This is not because the agnostic is condemned to some pitiful attempt to call out to a deity who is really not there. Rather, the prayer for divine guidance and discernment requires it. Like repeatedly reading a wonderful novel, or hearing great music time and time again, each repetition changes and deepens one's relationship with the process of negation. This is, in Eckhart's phrase, a sinking 'down eternally from nothingness to nothingness'.

How may one try to think about this, for clearly it is a process ultimately as indescribable as the non-image of God it seeks? Well, there is a parallel in the process of Socratic philosophy. Socrates' insight was that wisdom is found in a knowledge of ignorance. Such wisdom is not arrived at simply by admitting that one is ignorant; that is not enough. One must explore the nature of one's ignorance as deeply as possible. Like mystical prayer, it is to this extent a process of unknowing, of letting go. This is why Socrates did not stand in the agora simply preaching a message of condemnation to his fellow Athenians for their unacknowledged ignorance, but he engaged them, to discover more about what they thought they knew. In this way he nurtured a way of life that came to be called philosophy. Similarly, mysticism is not simply an assertion that, whatever else the divine might be, divinity is unknown. Rather, it has as its goal an ever more profound appreciation of this truth. The cycle of invocation, negation, invocation, negation, that Clough's poem sets up is, therefore, the fundamental pattern of the mystical life. Replace 'invocation' with 'assertion', and one has the pattern of the Socratic life too – assertion, negation, assertion, negation.

The paradox is that this is often a highly rational process. This is partly why to read Eckhart or Dionysius or Nicholas of Cusa or Anselm is to find a remarkably similar tone to some passages in Plato's dialogues. Plato does not give thanks to Christ, of course, and the Christian theologians do not flirt with Athenian youths. Also one should remember that the Christian mystics read Plato and neo-Platonists so the observation is slightly circular. However, it is for good reason that both genres of writing play with the ambiguities of verbs like 'to be' or 'to love'. It is for good reason that in both there is a sense of identifying errors in order to establish a clearer way forward; that both use mathematical analogies and logical conundrums; that both allude to theophanies beyond words; that both admit of no final resolution. Such as they are, these similarities are an encouragement and a challenge. The encouragement is what one might call the demystification of mystery: the aim is not to nurture some esoteric experience, like a wannabe Buddha struggling to emulate higher levels of meditation; the mystical path is no more, or less, opaque than philosophy. The challenge is that learning ignorance is at least as hard as Socratic philosophy.

The problem of evil

It is sometimes said that God moves in mysterious ways. And this flags up another, disquieting, aspect of divine unknowability. It's called the problem of evil and is another common reason that agnostics, and others, are troubled by God. It's the problem of how a good, loving, all-knowing, all-powerful God could allow suffering in a world of that same God's creation. It is for many the greatest barrier to belief. Should not divine goodness require, divine love desire, divine omniscience understand, and divine omnipotence enable a world in which suffering was not necessary? Or might it be another path into a kind of silence?

The problem finds one of its most forceful modern articulations in Dostoevsky. One of the Karamazov brothers, Ivan, complains to his brother Alyosha, that he cannot understand how the world will ever find the harmony, promised in religion, of a divinely ordained reconciliation of evil with good. He takes the extreme case of a tortured child. He knows that God's ways are way beyond the power of human understanding, but he simply cannot conceive of a moment when he could forgive the torturer of such a child. He runs through various arguments that are put to dissolve the problem. A philosopher might intellectually side-step the issue by saying that the problem of suffering is really a subset of the problem of how someone can know of another's experience. A humanitarian might say that the problem of evil must be resolved in forgiveness of even the most heinous crimes, for only then can suffering stop. But Ivan resists such 'solutions'. Even if the child forgave the torturer – even if the child's mother forgave him – the tears of the child would remain spilt, screaming out for atonement. He cannot help but feel that creation is not worth it, if it costs the suffering of that child.

Various other answers are offered to the problem of evil. A philosopher might say that evil is necessary if human beings are to be moral and free. The argument here is that the corollary of a world without evil is a world in which everything people did would automatically be good. This, though, would mean we could not make moral choices – something that would lessen our humanity and make us little more than virtuous robots. Similarly, if someone else argued that any divinity worth its salt should intervene to save people from suffering, the implication would be that there were no consequences of human beings doing evil, since God would prevent it. This would morally infantilise us.

But for all these apparently unassailable arguments, the suffering, the evil and the revulsion of what happened to that child remain. The problem persists, as does the hurdle it represents for belief in God. This is arguably one message of the book of Job in the Bible, the story of the man who suffered foul calamities and foul disease, apparently at the behest of God. Although

God gains some credit at the end of the book for chastising Job's tormentors – his 'friends' who tell him his suffering must have some 'meaning' as punishment – God can appear to come out of the story as a monster who followed Satan's agenda, the angel whose challenge to God initiates Job's tragedy. The book of Job seems, in part, to say that it is better to think God a monster than to think the problem of evil can be solved and that suffering need no longer be a concern.

To put it another way, the most valid response to suffering, whatever the content of that response, is not via abstract argument but is in real experience. After all, the irreducibility of evil stems from its ever tangible presence. Cautiously, then, for to write about the problem of evil is always to risk complacency, I would offer two reflections, one from my own experience, one from experiencing a tragedy faced by others.

My own experience is that of the early death of my mother. The bare facts will be familiar to others. She had cancer and, after various treatments and the roller-coaster ride of hope and dismay, the disease became terminal. Medical science gained us two years while she was ill, and they were invaluable: as has been observed before, mortality, when one is conscious of its irresistibility, comes with the strange gift of knowing life in all its agonising fullness. I understood the wisdom of the ancient liturgy which asks to be saved from sudden death.

At the funeral, which was a requiem mass, I did not receive communion. This was partly because I was at the time still an atheist. I could appreciate the value of the ceremony as a rite of passage, and that kneeling to receive the bread and wine might be a very good way of admitting my vulnerability at her death – especially since it would be to do so with others who also mourned her loss. However, in my mind, this benefit was outweighed by also needing to express my conviction that the world was godless. At that moment in time, that seemed to be the best response to her too early death. It was not that I felt angry, just the need to be quietly resolute in the implications of my atheistic belief.

Illus. 6.2: It is better to think that God is a monster than that the problem of evil can be solved – the message of Job?

In the period after her death, though, my mind changed. What I had not expected was the way my 'dead' mother was present to me for months, and then years. For a long time, I was very conscious of what she might have said or felt in a particular moment. Some people who lose someone close, like a lover, find themselves talking to the person who has died, and eventually find a kind of happiness in doing so. This was not so for me. Instead, I had dreams in which my mother lived on, though in a kind of parallel universe. I would recognise her but also recognise she was becoming different. What this made me realise is that I would not get over her death; it would always be with me in some shape or form, and that was, in fact, good. I did not want to forget her, and not doing so entailed pain. But I would learn to live with it and even, possibly, live a little better because of it – a little more conscious of my own mortality, a little more attentive to the present moment.

The question became how to do this new way of living as well as possible? I did not want to 'get closure', as the ugly phrase from pop-psychology has it. Even if closure were gettable, it would be to move on, not live with. Neither did I want the comforts of the language of immortality for it did not feel right to simply say that my mother was in heaven or just on the other side of the veil. If pushed, even now I tend to think that I won't see her again because identity without a body is so difficult to conceive, and her body has most certainly gone. However, I also had this spiritual sense in which she has not straightforwardly 'gone' either.

An uncertain though nonetheless Christian-shaped response has proven to be the answer. As I lost my atheism, and my religious imagination returned, it was the silence conveyed through certain liturgies that came to shape the ambivalence of, on the one hand, the clarity of my remembrance and, on the other, the lack of clarity as to what death may or may not be. One such service is the ashing of Ash Wednesday. Here, the priest marks the penitent on the forehead with the sign of the cross, saying, 'Remember you are dust and to dust you shall return.' The stark reality of that act is chastening, of course, and to some might be objectionable. But it is an intimate moment: the ashing becomes an oddly life affirming assertion of one's mortality.

Another service that I found capturing my ambivalence was All Souls Day, when churches of a Catholic persuasion have a requiem mass at which the dead are remembered by name. I now look out for a service that includes a liturgical performance of one of the great Requiem Masses. Though the All Souls Mass is full of words and sound, its purpose makes it different from other services. It becomes a container for an underlying silence which I now take to be the best response to my mother's death. Christianity has become for me, in this context at least and to use Denis Potter's phrase, 'the wound, not a bandage'

Several composers have written some of their most profound music in response to this rite, capturing the mixed uncertainties of death, loss, aspiration and hope. One of the most beautiful is that composed by Gabriel Fauré, and it fascinates me that he was an agnostic. The setting was quite revolutionary at the time because of its humanity, and I wonder if it is only an agnostic, though one thoroughly engaged by their religious tradition, who could have captured the feeling of love and loss with such poignant balance.

What this has to do with the more general problem of evil is to suggest that, having been exposed to some manifestation of it and all that it implies, a final response of silence represents not its resolution but its fullest expression. Like a *via negativa*, the problem of evil provokes multiple objections, such as the sense of injustice, anger and horror. To these, part-solutions can be suggested. But, always, the problem of evil remains, its resolution unknown. I am not saying that suffering is redeemed if something is learnt from it, as if the suffering itself might be thought good. It is irreducible. Rather, it is that suffering may be an occasion for unlearning certain things that are otherwise taken for granted, notably the illusion of immortality; and more importantly, an occasion for appreciating what matters most in life, not least love of others. This may, in turn, be best expressed in a religiously shaped silence that emerges as the questions are wrestled with. In other words, theodicy – the confrontation with the problem of evil – can become another path into depth.

Someone might object that this is all very well at a personal level. It is, after all, my responsibility and right to respond to my mother's death as I choose. But what of the objective sense of injustice within the problem of evil – Ivan Karamazov's point that the sufferings of a child for the sake of creation will call out for all eternity? Again, this is a genuine sticking point that ultimately admits of no dissolution. Given that, the question becomes how to live with the impasse?

The tsunami disaster of Boxing Day 2004 is a salient event here. Witnessing this, and asking the fundamental question, 'Where was God?', offers another reflection on theodicy. Several things strike me. In the West, the disaster provoked prominent atheists to rehearse the argument for the non-existence of God. They echoed Voltaire who wrote similarly following the Lisbon earthquake of 1755. 'This is indeed a cruel piece of natural philosophy!' he cried. 'What a game of chance human life is!' It should crush the sanctimonious, he continued, for it is the mountains of human achievement that will save people from earthquakes, if anything.

However, two things stuck out in the aftermath of the tsunami which make that humanist outrage inadequate, if understandable. One was the way in which the people involved turned to religion as a response to their often terrible loss. To deploy the metaphor of the wound and bandages again, the material superiority of the Western world could and did provide the means to fly absolutely necessary aid into the disaster zones – that is, to provide the bandages. However, when it came to seeking means of expressing just what it was that the tsunami had inflicted – the nature of the wound – it was religion that people turned to. Although some people were wholly understandably angry with God, there appeared to be no objections to Buddhist monks chanting on beaches in Thailand, mosques becoming places of refuge in Indonesia, and Hindi prayers being offered in Sri Lanka. Indeed, they were wanted. Bernard Williams, the philosopher, was once confronted with the objection that religious faith might be thought of as colluding with a God who allows bad things to happen. He replied that such a position overlooks what religion does for people. 'That religion can be a nasty business', he wrote, 'is a fact built into any religion worth worrying about, and that is one reason why it has seemed to so many people the only adequate response to the nasty business that everything is.'

I observed something similar in the aftermath of the Chilean miners' disaster of 2010, when 33 miners were trapped underground for two months. For the first two weeks after the collapse that contained them half a mile down, they thought they would die. They kept themselves alive out of thin hope on meagre rations. Then, they were discovered and eventually marvellously rescued. As they emerged, their personal stories were told, and it was striking how much of a role God played in the telling. There are no atheists in a foxhole, it's said; none in a collapsed mine apparently beyond hope, either.

For those at an emotional distance from the story, and with a preference for reason not faith, this raises the familiar issues about the problem of evil. Why did God save the 33 but not the hundreds who died in an earthquake a few months previously? Why allow the mine to collapse at all? Only, such questions are for the seminar room, not the disaster zone.

Psychologically, the quick answer is to say that turning to God is about comfort: hope beyond hope. It's easy to be patronising: who could deny an individual in such a predicament the consolations of faith, even though you yourself believe it empty? But I wonder whether there's something more profound in the turn to God when your fate seems set in granite, as it must have done for the miners.

Sometimes that which is way greater than you, indifferent to you, silent, is actually a blessing. This might be called the 'no atheists up a mountain' phenomenon, when you're hit by the sublime, that which is fearful and mirrors your fear, and yet by also being indifferent to your fear helps create a distance from your fear. It's the impersonal that apparently doesn't care which may be a help in dire predicaments. This may be another meaning in the book of Job, when God 'answers', were you there when the world was created?

Put it this way. The miner who falls to his knees no doubt prays for a literal rescue. He also prays for comfort. But perhaps when you're clear you're to die, touching cold eternity is a relief for mere morals. It provides reconciliation and allows you to give up the ghost. Which, should you be rescued, paradoxically may mean you survive the ordeal better than if you'd struggled to the end.

This turn to God is unnerving to the secular mind. In fact, in all honesty, it is unnerving to the Western religious mind too since it seems to lack the resentment that is the natural response in those who have come to believe that it is almost a right not to have to suffer. Science can patch things up, so reading of people being able to get on with life in the face of terrible events is quite as shocking as the mother in Dostoevsky who can forgive the torturer of her child. As it happened, I was in Thailand during the spring of 2005, a few months after the tsunami, albeit in a coastal area that was not as badly damaged by the wave as some. I did indeed find that silence was the only final response after asking and hearing about what had happened.

I have been advocating silence. It is silence of a particular sort, since it only comes after everything has been said about the problem in hand – be that the question of God, or the problem of evil. Being thrown into silence in this way is a profoundly agnostic process. It stems from God being taken as a question, and the requirement to learn and relearn ignorance of the divine – the great insight of the mystics. Of course, believers are the chief guardians of this tradition, since they preserve the writings, liturgies and ways of life that embody it. Which is again to say that the Christian agnostic needs the Christian believer: it is, after all, hard to imagine a world of only Christian agnostics in which prayer would last, let alone flourish. However, there is also a sense in which the believer needs the agnostic. The religiously minded but deliberately undecided agnostic can ensure that the central affirmation of the faith is not reified. If, as I have argued, much Christian practice today cannot stomach this mystery, because it is antithetical to the desire for an orthodoxy that can supply spiritual certainties and peak experience, the religiously-minded agnostic has a particular role to play. Paradoxically, it is their committed uncertainty that might revivify the first and last commitments of the religious quest: God is unknown. God comes as a question.

Wagering on God

The truth of this lies behind another argument that is frequently rehearsed in debates between theists and atheists – namely, Pascal's so-called wager. Like the 'proofs' of God, it is routinely misunderstood.

The wager is usually taken to be something like as follows. If God does not exist then, upon death, the individual will know nothing of it. If God does exist then, upon death, the individual will know it for a fact. Moreover, if they believed in God, the benefits that come with faith will then be visited upon them. So, it is better to act as if God does exist, and believe, than to act as if God does not. The problem for the wager when presented like this is that it makes faith out to be not only a calculation, but calculated – an objectionable quality that undermines the value of faith.

That, though, is a gross misrepresentation of Pascal. The first point to note is that he was a believer, of a particularly conservative sort. Like Anselm, his reflections only make sense when that is borne in mind. In the *Pensées*, in which the wager text is found, he is grappling with the unavoidable antinomies of his faith – unavoidable because of the nature of God. In particular it is the undecidability of God's existence – because God is beyond human comprehension, and certainly beyond the powers of human reason to prove – that interests him. What then can reason say of believing, or not, in God?

He thinks that faith, if not founded on reason, should, nonetheless, be as rationally justified as possible. This is where the wager comes in. What he argues is that the position of believing in God makes more sense than the position of not believing in God, since although both positions are adopted in the face of an uncertainty that reason cannot overcome, the believer in God wins an infinite prize. His argument, then, is aimed not at converting the atheist but rather at the lesser task of calling their rational certainties into question which includes the assumption that theism is less rational than atheism. Using mathematical probability theory, which he takes to be something both he and his opponent would agree is sufficient for good reasoning – though clearly not for good belief – he hopes to unsettle the atheist.

The argument has other benefits for it allows Pascal to make some interesting observations. For example, if the sceptic is worried that confessing a belief in God would be to compromise his rational powers, he is worrying about the wrong thing: reason alone cannot decide one way or the other. In fact, I suspect that admitting this was as much a blow for Pascal as it may be for the atheist. Probably the most famous quote from this section, and the whole of the *Pensées*, is: 'The heart has its reasons which reason itself does not know'. As it happens, Pascal wrote this upside-down and in a margin. This is, I think, significant. It seems to be a sign of despair stemming from a keen insight: it is as if he were saying, 'for all that I can reason about my faith, ultimately my reason cannot get to the crux of it. That comes from my heart, the organ of an altogether different kind of knowledge.' (He continues the famous sentence with the far less poetic clause 'we know that through countless things', suggesting again that he did not think he was crafting a memorable aphorism, merely making a blunt observation.)

In other words, in spite of the force of Pascal's argument, he is also forced to remind himself that reason is barely a start. Like the rudder of a ship, it may point the boat in the right direction, but it is the wind of faith that fills the sails and propels the believer forward. To wager on God is therefore to do something necessary but minimal: it is to do no more or less than take the stance that talking about God is worth it. At the very least it is not unreasonable to do so; at most there is, possibly, everything to gain. Implicitly, then, the argument also gives support to the reasonableness of the agnostic position.

The charge of deism

Having said that, Pascal would have had no truck with agnosticism. His wager might cohere with the agnostic stance but, he would argue, it is no more a reason for remaining uncertain than it is a reason for believing or not believing – it is not a sufficient reason for anything. What the agnostic is accused of is what he accuses the atheist of too. It is not reason that stops you believing, Pascal says, since there is no good reason not too.

Rather it is your lack of passion – that complex of personal temperament, history and obstinacy. The charge is that the agnostic, and the atheist, do not allow their hearts to speak to them; Pascal might agree that it would be nice if reason could decide, but, given that it cannot, that is no reason to block out one's feelings.

We have a clear indicator of what Pascal's feelings told him. On the night of 23 November 1654, the feast of St Clement, he had a vision. 'From about half past ten in the evening until about half past midnight. Fire,' he wrote on a piece of paper, now known as 'The Memorial'. He subsequently sewed it into his clothes. In what followed these first phrases he articulated a distinction that mirrors the role of reason and feeling in matters of religion. The distinction is between the God of the 'philosophers and scholars' and the 'God of Abraham, God of Isaac, God of Jacob'. The implication is that the former divinity does not live, whereas the latter God does. One can easily imagine that for Pascal, far from being the beginning and end of religion, apophaticism is only a prolegomenon to faith. After all, no one could worship the deity of the philosophers. It is the God loved by the community of faith that is worth seeking.

Pascal's implicit accusation is that of deism – the belief that God can only be known through reason not revelation. Pascal can be taken as saying that the agnostic may be open to God-talk but is not open to the ways in which God may actually talk to us.

The charge is serious. Is it not reasonable to assume that if there is a God, that God would make himself known to us, one way or another? Doubly so if God is a God of love. For what is the point of a God who may have written the rules of nature, and even given the universe its first nudge as those rules kicked in, to be subsequently effectively absent. As T.H. Huxley powerfully observed:

Whether astronomy and geology can or cannot be made to agree with the statements as to matters of faith laid down in

Genesis – whether the Gospels are historically true or not – are matters of comparatively small moment in the face of the impassable gulf between the anthropomorphisms (however refined) of theology and the passionless impersonality of the unknown and unknowable which science shows everywhere underlying the thin veil of phenomenon.

There are several things to say about this. First, the agnostic spirit I am exploring is not denying that people might feel that God speaks to them, or that God is revealed through processes of scripture, incarnation and prayer. Indeed, inasmuch as it is serious about engaging with religious traditions, it pays attention to such manifestations. However, the agnostic does so without the certainties of faith. Probably the most powerful argument for adhering to this position, which is another version of Huxley's 'impassable gulf', is that even if God did want to make himself known, that would have to happen within the limits of human understanding. So whatever it may be that would signify that this 'making known' was divine, its divinity would be lost in its reception. Like Hamlet, who cannot decide whether the ghost is the spirit of his father speaking truth or the phantom of a demon telling lies, how could one know this communication was of God and not of the human imagination? Such is the human predicament.

Where I think Huxley goes too far is in suggesting that this casts the agnostic adrift. There is another distinction to draw here. Although the divine is unknown in itself – even to the extent of its existence – that is not to say that we can know nothing about divinity, as concept and perhaps as reality. Whatever God may be, we can say what God is not. Trivially, we can say that God is not, say, the golden calf that my neighbour may erect in their back garden to fall down and worship. More interestingly, we can say that God is not the idea of the divinity presented by many atheists, or indeed theists. This is the whole point of the apophatic tradition, the negations and then nega-tion of negations, that not only can be said of God but must be said in any decent theology. God-talk is not empty; the silence is full.

For the same reason, the agnostic stance need not be deist. There is nothing in agnosticism that relegates God to the margins of creation – its beginning and, if it has one, its end. In fact, I suspect that idea is itself mistaken. If the fundamental mystery in life is existence itself, why there is something rather than nothing – and one does not share the non-belief of the atheist, that existence itself is just brute fact – then the quest for God is potentially provoked every waking moment of the day. (One could also say an agnostic could not be a deist, for deism is a positive belief about God.)

Rather agnosticism manifests itself best as an attitude. It is a way of life driven by the desire for ultimate things. It is a determination, in the way that philosophy was a love of wisdom for Socrates. It is a 'passionate commitment' to a certain form of life. What marks it out is a confession of ignorance – a confession both in the sense of an admittance and in the sense of a conviction.

than that. For what happens after Peter makes his confession to Paul is not what Peter had feared. Paul is not crushed by the revelation. He does not take it to mean that his life's work has been in vain. He knows that his encounter with this man Jesus changed him. It spoke to him of far more than facts. Now, years on, even an apparently devastating exposé of what actually happened cannot remove the glimpse of truth he gained. This is the reality that is most immediate to him. Christianity had become for him a way of life, one that was powerfully transforming. In the closing scene of the play, the two apostles hold each other and prepare for the moment that they had long known their commitment would bring them to – the time to die.

Religion is not just a set of beliefs or a moral code. It is a way of seeing the world and a way of approaching what's unknown. As Theo Hobson has described it, 'Faith is a form of hope that sticks its neck out'. This is why it is so resistant to being questioned and mocked, why attacks with reason and ridicule are as likely to sustain it as undermine it. The scientific revolution may have undermined mythical ways of understanding. But while making religion forgetful of the unknowability of God, and aggressive towards its despisers, it still thrives because it is a thing of the heart first, and then the head; it is not done in abstract but in lives.

This also adds to why, although I lost my faith, I found atheism unsatisfying. Atheism is not a practice but a principle. You can no more believe in atheism than you can in science: the whole point is that you don't believe; you know. Life may be explored by the arts, offered to others in transcendental causes, mirrored in nature. A lack of spiritual belief may be supplemented by faith in the power of empirical discovery, and a conviction that materialist explanations for things will be able to accommodate everything in the natural world in the end. But what of the soul – the facet that needs to reach out to concerns aside from the material business of life, in order to connect with what is called the spiritual, the transcendent, God? There's this sense that human beings are the creature for whom our own lives are too small for us. We need something bigger than ourselves to be ourselves. My religious imagination demanded this something else. And one way of pursuing it – I suspect the richest at this point of history for those formed by Christianity – is via an agnosticism that is linked into the Christian tradition. It turns on whether God can be imagined, encountered, as the question, in all the different contexts we've explored – in meditation, theodicy, mystical theology, cosmic religion. However, there's this further element that can be brought to the table. Agnosticism as a way of reaching towards the unknown, reaches back before Christianity. It rests on the shoulders of Socrates. And he can provide a complementary resource to the Christian one.

It is not uncommon for thinkers, some Christian, to turn to Socrates for inspiration in this way. Philosophers as diverse as Hegel and Nietzsche, Kierkegaard and Montaigne have done so; as Cicero put it: 'Socrates was the first to call philosophy down from the heavens and compel it to ask questions about life and morality.' He is often associated with scepticism on account of his modus operandi – namely, inquiry. But the agnosticism that I find in him is scepticism of a particular sort. It is not like some forms of modern scepticism that, since Descartes, have practised the habit of doubting everything. This hyper-speculative doubt is somewhat akin to hyper-speculative banking: it's speculation for speculation's sake, not for human sake, and so it loses touch with reality, until reality comes crashing down on it. Socrates, though, was not solipsistic, as if he thought we are only 'brains in a vat', or the empty vessels that will be snuffed out with nirvana. As I see it, he was not sceptical about existence, nor the value of questioning reason, nor crucially that life can be about, or for, something. Quite the reverse. It's not even clear that you can literally doubt everything: with what capacity, what assumptions are you doubting? Doubt needs some minimal scaffolding to lower you into its darkness.

He was sceptical about what human beings can know for sure, on account of their in-between status between the animals and the gods. This is both a burden, inasmuch as the individual can become conscious of their ignorance. But it is also a blessing. Socrates' agnosticism meant that while using reason to understand the nature of his ignorance more fully, he also knew that reason alone was not enough; it too has its limits – most notably when it comes to matters spiritual. So Socratic philosophy did not stop at the point at which reason could go no further. It engaged the heart as well as the head. It was a more profound exposé and encounter.

But if Socrates is a key, a problem is raised. The man himself is almost lost to us. He's much written about. But he left no words that are indisputably his own. Plato's dialogues, our best source, already mythologise him. They were written far more closely in time to the life of the historical Socrates than, say, the gospels were to the historical Jesus. But like the gospel writers, Plato was not interested in providing an accurate record of the life of Socrates – though some details, perhaps many, reflect actual characteristics and events. Rather, he wanted to capture what it was like to encounter Socrates.

The historian, then, will be frustrated. But we're not primarily seeking history and facts. We are, rather, seeking precisely what Plato has left us: a vivid record of one man's engagement with the sage. We don't seek video clips of Socrates walking the streets of Athens, as if we were making a documentary; we seek the experience of what it was like to bump into him on the streets of Athens. It's Plato's genius to leave us with something very close to that. As Paul realised in Howard Brenton's play, how someone changes you is the most valuable echo of that person's life, and that can shape the lives of others.

Not that Plato's conjuring of the charism is straightforward. It should not be, for then his story could not inform your own story, which will inevitably be different. Plato does not seek to tell us what to believe and feel. Instead, he seeks to enable us to catch a glimpse of the spirit that the historical Socrates embodied, of all that he constellated so powerfully, so that something of that spirit might be kindled in his reader's lives. He presents Socrates to us in such a way as to nurture a response. As Jesus almost said to the disciples: it's good that I go, as then, if you want to follow me, you will have to do so in my spirit, not in my shadow.

Encountering Socrates

Not much is known about Plato's life before his encounter with Socrates. He was from an aristocratic, politically active family, and it is likely that his turn to full-time philosophy came after disillusionment with politics – perhaps as a result of having seen Socrates condemned at the hand of a democratic state. He may have been a wrestler in his youth, if you believe the speculation that his name was actually a pun on the Greek for 'broad' – platus – as in 'broad-shouldered'. He may have travelled in Egypt in his early life, seeking wisdom in what was an ancient culture even to the ancient Greeks. He did not marry. Any indications as to his character are tentative since, apart possibly from the so-called *Seventh Letter*, he wrote nothing in his own voice.

But after they met, everything changed. The influence of Socrates on him was massive and profound. It has been called fateful, because afterwards life never looked the same again. There is a story – and stories are what we seek for the spirit they convey – that on the day Plato met Socrates he was due to have a tragedy performed in the theatre of Dionysos, the Theatre Royal of Athens. Plato cancelled the performance and burnt the manuscript there and then. Socrates made Plato re-examine everything: this is why Socrates is always depicted in the dialogues as on the move, questioning, seeking more. And this is what made Plato wiser, not that Socrates revealed timeless doctrines to him, but that Socrates' passionate desire for what was good and true, his love of wisdom, captivated Plato too. After all, what is it that makes a person truly wise? Not that they utter sagacious words, even less that they know it all. Neither is it that they are warm or welcoming, for to meet them might be unsettling. Rather, their wisdom is manifest in their attitude, in the sense that they are digging deep. Their wisdom is appealing because, being with them, you are enabled to dig deeper too.

What was a momentous meeting for Plato could have become just a paragraph in the history of philosophy, and no more important than a detail like knowing that Kant read Hume or that

Wittgenstein argued with Popper. That it is far more important than either of those facts is not just because Socrates features in nearly every Platonic dialogue. It is because Plato constructs them in such a way as to conjure up something of the same sense of encounter with Socrates in us, his readers.

He does this partly by his inclusion of descriptions of Socrates' impact on those around him. 'I made progress when I was with you, if only in the same house, not even in the same room; and still more, so it seemed to me, when I was in the same room and looked at you (rather than elsewhere) while you were talking; but most of all when I sat beside you, quite close, and touched you,' says one of Plato's characters, Aristeides.

It is also implicit in the way the dialogues are constructed. For example, many have rather tortuous introductions: the *Symposium* begins with one Apollodorus addressing anonymous individuals who are asking about what happened at the famous drinking party. The anonymous individuals are us – reading to find out the same thing. Moreover, 'we', as it were, are not the first to ask Apollodorus this question. Another, Glaucon, has recently asked him the same thing too. And, as if to underline the point again, Apollodorus himself says that he only knows about the occasion second-hand. Luckily for him, and us, he managed to glean the details from Aristodemus. In this way, Plato identifies his readers with his characters: we are encouraged to see ourselves, personally as well as intellectually, drawn to the action too.

Other devices Plato uses throw the content of the dialogues onto his readers, forcing them to make it their own. The early dialogues in particular are characterised by ending in agnostic impasses – *aporia*: 'We think we are friends but just what friendship is we have not been able to discover', Socrates says at the end of the *Lysis*, inviting the reader to think more on the issue and on their own experience of friendship. For some readers, the uncertainty that *aporia* implies is unnerving and unwanted, because nothing conclusive is ever reached. But as well as accurately reflecting Socrates' conviction that he knew nothing for sure, and that there is therefore always more to be said – more to be lived – an *aporia* is also a cunning literary device, asking that the dialogues never be treated as philosophical treatises that might be thought to wrap things up. They raise questions that the reader should answer for themselves.

Socrates is also often ironic in the dialogues, particularly when it comes to confessing his ignorance. It's a feature that is much debated among Plato scholars. I think that the irony is not that he secretly thinks he does know about things after all. It was just that inevitably, after a while, he reached a point when the common mistakes that people make in deluding themselves that they know more than they do became familiar to him. And since his goal was to encourage them to understand their ignorance, rather than just tell them about it, he has to go along with them to tease it out. Like an old teacher in front of a new class, he pretends that their queries, difficulties, enthusiasms and conclusions are as fresh to him as they are to them. Sometimes, his bluff is called: 'You have gone too far this time,' Agathon says in the *Symposium* when Socrates repeats again that he is ignorant on such and such a matter. But he insists: he is genuine in his confession. (Irony is also a good strategy for stirring arrogant people up: it irritates them by pricking bubbles.)

More positively, at its best, Socratic philosophy is a form of friendship. Partly because both are nothing if not lived; and partly because the best kinds of friends are those who make the best kind of philosopher. They are people who know each other, can speak freely with each other, are honest and humble towards one another, and can critique and challenge each other. Together, they are better able to embrace human limits. In the dialogues, Socrates has his most rewarding conversations with individuals who can accept friendship of this sort (and conversely, those that cannot are the least productive). To borrow from Emerson, Socratic friends are like those who exclaim, 'Do you see the same truth!' Something is not just told, it is unveiled.

The most obvious underlining of the belief that it is a sense of encounter that Plato is trying to conjure up is that Plato wrote in dialogues in the first place. The *Seventh Letter* suggests that

Plato resisted writing anything at all for a time, since he feared it would detract from what he really thought philosophy was – an exploration done in life. Thankfully for us, he was persuaded apparently because it would enable him to reach a wider audience. The dialogue was his answer to the necessary compromise because if writing is not the real thing, at least dialogues portray people doing the real thing. The characters present intellectual and often abstract arguments that are rebuffed, for sure. And they can be sifted on that level. But we see them running the gamut of human emotion too, for lives lived is ultimately what is at stake.

Seneca wrote the following to a friend:

> The living word and life in common will benefit you more than written discourse. It is to current reality that you must go, first because men believe their eyes more than their ears, and then because the path of precepts is long, but that of examples is short and infallible.

Seneca's is a Platonic sentiment: experience is infallible because it so ably displays human fallibility.

Philosophy school

The dialogues are the most substantial evidence we have that Plato thought Socrates presented philosophy as such a way of life. However, it was not only in writing that Plato himself responded to his encounter with Socrates. The seeds of philosophy, as Plato puts it in the *Phaedrus*, find soil to sink roots, time to grow branches, air to spread leaves and the human warmth necessary to produce fruit – fruit that will last – when nurtured with others. Socrates pursued his philosophy with others on the streets of Athens. A generation on, as the 'Socratic movement' spread, Plato decided to set up an institution. He acquired an old gymnasium and on the site founded his Academy.

Plato knew that an enquiring approach to philosophy did not just necessitate the ability to form intellectual arguments.

The Academy was designed to develop a whole way of life and train people in it. There was no fee, though a private income that brought the blessing of copious leisure was necessary for any serious attendance. 'Students', if that is the right word, probably wore a simple cloak. Many of them subsequently became statesmen, suggesting something of the atmosphere of the place (though of itself that is not so surprising given the aristocratic nature of much ancient philosophy, which meant that many alumni would naturally go on to rule). Others became famous philosophers in their own right, including Aristotle who attended the school for 20 years. One of Aristotle's pupils, Dicearchus, described the Academy as a community in which people were free and equal, and inspired by virtue and research. Many of these values are embodied in the *Republic*, Plato's experimental plan for a utopian city. For example, women could govern as well as men.

Setting up the Academy carried certain risks with it. The idea of a philosophical school might suggest that philosophy was a subject to be taught, that it consisted of a set of doctrines or, worse, necessitated passing examinations: the Academy might become academic. Socrates was peripatetic for these reasons. He did not want to inform others. As an agnostic how could he? He wanted to form them to be open to more of life.

Plato seems to have avoided these pitfalls for the most part, though he clearly moves on from Socrates. For example, one might ask why, alongside the question of how to live, he established disciplines such as geometry, logic and natural science? May this not be evidence that he started to value abstract thought for its own sake? Not quite. The goal of pursuing what we would call scientific knowledge is not that it represents the last word on truth: Plato calls such an idea ridiculous in the *Republic*. Nor, particularly, that scientific knowledge may find use through application. Rather, knowledge of nature is most valuable insofar as it draws connections that then become a basis from which deeper insights may be glimpsed. Science is a prelude to philosophy, and a good, even necessary, one. But

Illus. 7.1: Plato's Academy aimed at personal transformation as well as careful understanding.

its goal is as a form of exercise to ready the mind for intuitions about the way things are, as opposed to what they are made of – the lesser enquiry that science makes by direct observation. If the *Seventh Letter* is by Plato, he explains in his own words why this is the case:

> For this knowledge is not something that can be put into works like other sciences; but after long continued intercourse

if one argument is as good as any other. The best use of dialogue was as an exercise aimed at the transformation of the interlocutors. As Pierre Hadot, the contemporary philosopher who has spearheaded the rediscovery of ancient philosophy as a way of life, explains: 'It was not a matter of combat between two individuals, in which the more skillful person imposed his point of view, but a joint effort on the part of two interlocutors in accord with the rational demands of reasonable discourse.' In other words, the value of expressing yourself clearly was only so as to be able to 'offer' it to another, who had a similarly well-honed argument that, by understanding, you could grasp at what lay beneath the argument too. The point of so inhabiting another view was to identify with something beyond yourself to take you out of yourself. A partial parallel today would be the seminar in which students have to play the role of opponents in a debate. Another is to think of Platonic dialogue as role playing: Plato calls them 'entertainments' in one place, meaning 'serious play acting'.

Hadot argues that it is right to talk of 'spiritual exercises' in the Academy too, since this underlines the centrality of experiencing matters when discussing them, again in line with the goal of a philosophy that is more than rational expression. The idea is that working at this intuitive level – enunciating why such and such does not feel right – was as valid as highlighting logical inconsistencies and flaws. To the same end, students practised other exercises alongside dialogue. One was sexual abstinence, as in 'Platonic relationships', though it would be a mistake to take that as meaning a negation of passion: the aim was to sublimate the energy of erotic love and focus its drive on higher things. Another possible exercise had to do with the analysis of dreams. There is a passage in the *Republic* in which Plato sounds almost Freudian: 'terrible and savage' dreams could provide someone with material for reflection. It would contribute to what Chaucer wrote in *The Monk's Tale*, recalling the Delphic inscription: 'Full wise is he that can himself know.'

Another central exercise was the contemplation of death. Death is of interest because it is the moment when one's life's work comes to an end: the person you have become then will be the person you are in eternity. What someone felt about their death revealed much about their attitude to life and how far they had advanced on the way of life of the philosopher.

In Plato's dialogue the *Gorgias*, Socrates tells a myth about the last judgement that captures the right attitude someone should have to their death. (Similar stories end the *Phaedo* and the *Republic* too, suggesting the importance of this exercise.) It used to be the case in primordial times, the myth goes, that people were judged before they died, by still living judges. Depending on how they had lived their lives they would either go to the Isles of the Blessed or to the prison of Tartarus. However, some cases were being decided badly, an issue that was brought to Zeus' attention by Pluto. Zeus, in his wisdom, noticed that the judges were being misled by the way people dressed for their judgement – donning their finery in order to look fine in soul too. So, Zeus decreed, people would no longer be told when they are to die and they would be judged on that final day naked. With that change, the Great King before the throne of judgement would be judged in the same way as the most humble serf: according to the beauty and perfection, or the distortion and ugliness, of his soul. Socrates tells Callicles, his main interlocutor in the *Gorgias*, that he passionately believes this myth and has taken it to heart:

> I think about how I'll reveal to the judge a soul that's as healthy as it can be. So I disregard the things held in honour by the majority of people, and by practising truth I really try, to the best of my ability, to be and to live as a very good man, and when I die, to die like that.

He calls Callicles to this way of life, because he regards it as worth more than any other. 'Maybe you think this account is told as an old wives' tale, and you feel contempt for it,' he asks. But the spiritual truth is a good one nonetheless. Philosophical success in life is not about having the right arguments, seeming good or even having acted on conscience. It is about being transformed so as to perceive the good, the beautiful and the true. The best judge will see a life naked and in its entirety. The pictures of Socrates serenely drinking the hemlock that artists have produced down the centuries, can be thought of as reaching back to this aspect of life in the Academy. The iconography represents the culmination of its way of life as well as a celebration of Socrates.

Silence may have featured in the academician's portfolio too. Silence was probably a state to which the Pythagoreans aspired – contemplation of the 'music of the spheres' propelling the individual towards a 'harmonious silence'. And Socrates is depicted in silence at various points in the dialogues, if often rather oddly and abruptly – his suddenly standing still, without speaking, for so long that crowds formed around him. More spiritually, he explains in the *Phaedo*, the philosopher's aim is the contemplation of divine things that are beyond opinion, which is to say beyond the grasp of human words. As he is dying he commends his followers to silence, since it is in silence that someone has the best chance of discerning the things that are of heaven.

A question that comes to mind is the extent to which Plato's philosophy school was like a religious institution such as a monastery. The comparison is good, but only in part. Although Plato dedicated a statue of the Muses in the grove that formed part of the site, and his successors added other devotional objects, the Academy did not exist to worship gods like a church, or perpetuate a cult; it aimed at the transformation of the individual and the development of a philosophical life. But the statues did remind individuals that there was more at play in their lives than their own individual wellbeing. So, as a disciplined form of life, a monastery and the Academy were similar. For one thing, given that the school was full of disagreements that may easily have led to permanent factions and splits, there must have been a very powerful sense of common commitment to its ideals to hold people together. To attend the Academy was to be in love with its way of life, in the manner of Socrates who was in love with wisdom: students were fulfilling a vocation. More prosaically, it is perhaps not too fanciful to imagine an unwritten rule of life too, not unlike that of St Benedict, which detailed those things necessary for a communal, purposeful life, such as the partitioning of the day.

The diversification of styles

Plato's philosophy school was hugely successful. It carried his own encounter with Socrates to those who never knew Socrates in person, not by promoting a set of intellectual principles but by inculcating a practice. This was shaped by exercises and disciplined by reason but ultimately the goal was to form individuals who saw the world with a philosopher's eyes – transmitting the charism of Socrates.

It was a pattern others sought to emulate. After Aristotle left the Academy he formed his own, the Lyceum. From what remains of Aristotle's writings one can infer that he thought the ideal for the good life was to become all that you might be. He called it 'great souledness'. For the philosopher, this meant someone who had developed the greatest ability to contemplate, an activity of pure attention which the most excellent would engage in alone: 'He has slow movements, a deep voice and calm speech,' Aristotle amusingly writes. Contemplation was key because, at best, it was non-discursive. To speak philosophically is merely to link words together. Meaning comes from within. In practice, this is something that people can only achieve after much training and effort: the school provided the place where things could be explored and discussed in order to train the attention.

After Plato and Aristotle, there are generally reckoned to be four other schools: the Cynics, the Pyrrhonians, the Stoics and the Epicureans. Although they evolved and emphasised different aspects of their ethos over the hundreds of years for which they existed, one can see them all as attempts to form ways of life that face up to the central Socratic insight that nothing of importance in life can be known with certainty and that a way of life is key to embracing the intuitions that come with that agnostic spirit.

Those that wore the badge of the Cynic were the most extreme. Their approach was to reject those things that people might regard as necessary in life, such as the need to be clean or the need to be courteous. One might say that cynicism was the radical refusal of all certainties, no matter what, because they were all considered delusional – things like cleanliness and courteousness being mere conventions. The Cynics disturbed many people and are infamous for doing everything from masturbating in public to being rude to kings.

Pyrrhonian suspicion of what people think of as necessary in life manifested itself in a different way. Rather than rejection, this school cultivated indifference. Pyrrho, the individual the founders cited as their inspiration, sought to doubt anything that was not immediately and obviously the case in any particular situation – something that is far harder than it may first seem. He believed that to hold to views, opinions or beliefs – which is what one does when one tries to articulate principles, no matter how vague or general – is a recipe for unhappiness: they are bound to prove uncertain.

Stoic agnosticism manifests itself in a different way again. In short, Stoics thought that life becomes tragic because people struggle to shape things that are external to them and over which they have no control and little understanding. To be stoical is, therefore, to actively embrace one's fate. This does not mean one cannot be morally good: moral goodness is doing what is right in line with fate. The role of reason within Stoicism is to work on a rule of life that is harmonious within itself and with the world as it comes to one.

Then there were the Epicureans. The insight they had about uncertainty is that it leads to fear. However, since uncertainty cannot be done away with, the key is to dissipate the fear. Epicurus argued that people are free to face anything that leads to uncertainty in life without fear – the likelihood of bad health, the unavoidability of death, the capriciousness of the gods. Epicurean philosophy is, therefore, less deterministic than Stoicism: one is free to find as much pleasure in bread and water as a feast, Epicurus said. It is also, in a sense, against reason: Epicurus thought that reason tends to encourage grandiose ideas that, because they can never quite rid themselves of uncertainties, causes 'turmoil in the souls of men'. For this reason, Epicureans liked to say that they were not followers of Socrates, though they would never have existed without him.

Christian innovations

The philosophical schools, and the approaches to life they encouraged, lasted well into the Christian period. Plato's Academy was finally closed by the Emperor Justinian in 529 CE. Their influence on early Christianity is therefore pronounced. The so-called Desert Fathers of the first centuries after Christ explicitly discussed ancient philosophy and adopted similar practices of asceticism, contemplation and withdrawal from the city – if purified, as they saw it, from the errors of paganism. There are even letters that purport to have been written between Seneca, a great Stoic, and St Paul, in which they offer one another their mutual admiration. They are completely fanciful but that they were fabricated at all underlines how early Christianity adopted and adapted the Socratic insight in their search for their great unknown, God.

The parallels between Christianity and ancient philosophy can be pushed further, as in some respects they are forms of a not dissimilar spirituality. First, in being uncertain of themselves – the Socratic because they realise they do not know themselves, the Christian because they are born into self-deceiving sin – both are given intimations of what may be called the divine truth that lies beyond them and to which they strive. Second, the exercises by which they move towards this truth of themselves are a work on themselves: followers of Socrates and early Christians were called to ask questions of themselves with a view to a transformation. And third, this spirituality does not conceive of the individual being given truths, as if it were some kind of gnostic reward. Rather, the process itself is its own fulfilment where it becomes a way of life. To borrow a distinction made by Epicurus: in most labours of life, the reward follows when the task is complete; the tougher the task, the more profound the rewards. But with this way of life, 'the learning and the enjoyment are simultaneous'. 'He who loses his life, gains it', is the biblical, more gnomic summary.

One does not need to learn much more of this old philosophical tradition before an obvious question springs to mind. How is it that what is usually taken as philosophy today seems so different? Why does it apparently make so little demand upon the modern philosopher's person (beyond the development of rational techniques, thought and intellectual know-how)? Philosophers may try to live ethically, as in having good reasons for what they do. But rarely is philosophy taken as being a spiritual practice in the sense of the ancients – one that seeks to shape the individual, heart and mind, body and soul. No professor today would say to his or her students it is not my lectures or publications that count, but what I am becoming.

Hadot has asked this question and he puts it down to historical developments that came with the institutionalisation of Christianity. Broadly speaking, it may be summed up. First, over time Christianity tended to treat philosophy more and more as a servant of revealed theology the content of which became settled, lessening the sense of search. The new religion flexed its muscles and built up a body of timeless doctrines with which to govern itself and manage its institutional boundaries. The burden of philosophy's 'job' came to be to elucidate the givens of dogma, sidelining the exploration of uncertainties and apophatic theology; more and more it became the handmaid of dogmatic theology not agnosticism. In the same move, the ancient philosophers' approaches became detached and transformed, re-associated with Christian disciplines whose goal was not so much transformation as salvation. Practice tended to become prohibition. That created the conditions within which philosophy could become an autonomous discipline, a separation of heart and mind that was sealed with the emergence of the modern university. It became what Socrates must have feared, a subject to be taught and examined.

Modern Socratics

Having said that, the separation of philosophy as a conceptual exercise and as a mode of existence was never absolute. And herein lies hope. Throughout the history of ideas in the Christian West, thinkers have regularly lamented the opposition of philosophy as a private art and as a public discourse – suggesting in the process that the two may move closer together once again. Michel de Montaigne achieved a new synthesis in the sixteenth century. He wrote his *Essays* as a therapy to overcome a crushing melancholia. They are philosophical not because he was trained as a philosopher but because they are an analysis of his life – 'assays' of everything from solitude to sleep: 'I am myself the matter of my book', he wrote, forging the way of life of the intellectual writer. He is called the French Socrates and has also been attributed with the revival of an agnostic Pyrrhonism. He had 'Know thyself!' and 'What do I know?' written on the beams of his study-tower and realised that the philosopher's real test was his character not his conclusions.

> The soul which houses philosophy must by her own sanity make for a sound body. Her tranquility and ease must flow from her; she must fashion her outward bearing to her mould, arming it therefore with gracious pride, a spritely active demeanour and a happy welcoming face. The most express sign of wisdom is unruffled joy: like all the realms above the Moon, her state is ever serene.

A more recent example of a philosopher for whom his living became increasingly integrated with his thought was Michel

Illus. 7.2: Michel de Montaigne 'assayed' his life in the privacy of the tower of the Château de Montaigne, Périgord.

Foucault. He too noticed the difference between ancient and modern philosophy, describing it in moral terms. The ancient philosophers elaborated their lives as a creative exercise of their moral will, he said. With Christianity, though, morality came to be conceived of as obedience to a code or rules. The difference is not that the former was libertarian and the latter authoritarian; both could be tough ways of life. The difference is that one led to the cultivation of a way of life, the other to a submission of one's life to an ecclesiastical authority.

The reason this distinction was of interest to Foucault stemmed from his belief that it profoundly shapes the way people live today even in the secular world. He detected this ethic of submission in the everyday, whether that be expressed in adhering to dress codes at work or in the way that ethics as a whole is thought of in terms of rules.

The problem for Foucault, and for us, is that one cannot simply wind back the clock and reinstate the old philosophy. The modern way of life with its pervasive codes of behaviour does not readily allow it. But as a first step, at least, in his last works, Foucault developed a more modest task for contemporary philosophy. It could begin with the effort to think differently – another way of pushing at the boundaries of certainty. Philosophy could study the past not so much to recover what may otherwise be lost, nor to weigh up the ethical dilemmas ancient people faced. Rather, as a new form of philosophical exercise that may suggest new ways of re-imagining the present by engaging with the particularities of now. At a personal level, for Foucault, one manifestation of this was in relation to his homosexuality. Received wisdom in gay culture is that liberation means coming out. However, by contrasting the modern understanding of gayness, which designates a form of human behaviour, with ancient attitudes towards same-sex couples where it was seen as an expression of socialisation and love, Foucault argued that the contemporary label of homosexual could be oppressive regardless of whether someone was open about their sexuality or not. This suggested a further philosophical exercise that sought a way

beyond the prioritisation of sexuality as a determining characteristic of the individual – a 'way out' of sexuality, as he put it, and
into an, as yet, unknown way of being sexual.

Not so academic

Montaigne and Foucault stand out as two examples of modern
philosophers who explicitly engaged with Socrates in his agnosticism and Plato in his emphasis on a way of life. One can point
to others.

Consider Descartes, the man who doubted everything until
he was left only with the thinking 'I'. It might be thought that
nothing could be more removed from life than that, and indeed,
many of his Cartesian followers have practised such hyper-
speculation. And yet, he derived his famous 'Je pense, donc je
suis' in the context of a meditation. It leads the reader through
feelings as well as thoughts. The aim seems to be two-fold. First,
the meditations were not supposed to inculcate radical doubt
for its own sake but to reveal to the philosopher the limits of
human reason. Second, Descartes believed that someone needs
to be in the right position to receive truth, as well as having
the right arguments. Meditation could lead to the construction
of such an attitude. David Hume made not dissimilar suggestions. He discussed a kind of passive cognition that happens to
us. One must make preparations to be open to the more preparations that would connect the philosophy to the life.

Or take a philosopher like Schopenhauer. He is famous for his
pessimism and explicitly said that philosophy cannot change
lives. He thought human beings were the tragic slaves of their
base wills. People may make great efforts to aspire to the higher
things that their 'excess intellect' glimpses above them; but will
'will out'. Love, for example, is always brutalised by the animal
will for coitus. The result, some of his interpreters say, is suffering and labour and radical unhappiness. This though is not
quite fair. Every day Schopenhauer read from the *Upanishads*.
They confirmed for him a rather different ethic: if the world

is determined by will, then the goal of life should be to see through that relentless volition. He interpreted nirvana as the end of wilfulness which, because it is never fully possible in this life, would be like a transition to nothingness. In other words, philosophy for Schopenhauer was like the Buddhist teaching that the value of life lies in not wanting it – and that required the cultivation of an attitude to life, not just thought about it. Even for Schopenhauer, and almost in spite of himself, philosophy elicits a kind of spirituality.

Conversely, consider Karl Popper. The writer Bryan Magee, who often visited Popper in his hermit-like cottage, says that he was not an easy man to know. However, Magee explains: 'A phrase I heard from his lips as often as any other was, "We don't know anything." He looked on this realisation, which he attributed historically to Socrates, as the most important philosophical insight there is, one which ought to inform all our philosophical activity.'

For Popper, certainty is not available to human beings because all human knowledge is capable of being revised. What is taken as knowledge at any particular time must, therefore, be only an approximation to the truth. This is the basis of his theory of falsification in science. However, what can be overlooked is the impact this thesis had upon his life. In his intellectual autobiography, significantly entitled *Unended Quest*, he repeatedly testifies to his contentment. He goes so far as to say that he knows of no happier philosopher. The source of his happiness is intimately connected to the unknowability of the world. At a mundane level, this unknowability means that you are constantly surprised by what you find in the world: 'One of the many great sources of happiness is to get a glimpse, here and there, of a new aspect of the incredible world we live in, and of our incredible role in it,' he writes. More philosophically, he says that it is in his engagement with problems, theories and arguments – the abstractions that people wrestle with as they learn more profoundly about what they do not know – that he has found more happiness than he could ever deserve.

Reclaiming the religious

I've argued that, while the notion of being spiritual but not religious is understandable, it is also not enough. I've also tried to give an account of a Christian agnosticism as one response to the potency found in the essential mystery of life, and the question of God. In this chapter, we have picked up on the tradition in philosophy that leads back to Plato and Socrates. So now, a good question to ask is whether, and if so how, these elements might come together.

It might be tempting to sift some flattering virtues that would be thought distinctive of such an attitude, to draw out similarities and differences between them and, say, the Christian who aspires to love and forgiveness or the humanist who lauds tolerance and justice. The agnostic ethos might be thought to value courage and integrity in its engagement with the unknown. However, there is something misleading in this approach. For one thing, these virtues are far from exclusive to the agnostic. And they also put the cart before the horse. Virtues arise from an ethos as much as an ethos from certain virtues.

But there is a word that captures the agnostic way of seeing for which I am arguing. It is a word that we have already explored at some length, namely the word 'religious'. There is, of course, a risk in using this word. To many to be religious is to be the opposite of agnostic. However, I want to reclaim them both, for to be properly agnostic is, I believe, to be religious – religious in the sense that I used it at the start: the sense and taste for the Infinite, the search for intuitions of being-itself.

Why a religious agnosticism? In another word, Socrates. For him, a sense of the unknown divine was essential for framing his understanding of the human lot. He was a philosopher because he understood human beings are between beasts and angels. He was a philosopher because he dared to contemplate his ignorance. A powerful religious sensibility was part and parcel of this way of life. Socrates was interested in theology – god-talk – not because he thought it would tell him much about deities but because he thought it threw human beings onto a consciousness of what lies beneath and above them. When discussing whether things are good because a god says so, or whether the god says they are good because they are good in themselves, the direction the inquiry takes him is not to question whether the gods are necessary to morality but to show how little humans understand about moral good – and how important the good is, no less.

Socrates was a sceptic of the humble sort. He accepted that just because he could not understand something, did not mean there was not wisdom to be had in ancient traditions, and religious traditions in particular. At their best they, like him, were engaged in the big questions of life. After all, it was an oracle, an utterer of mysteries, that kick-started his philosophical life. Socrates' religiousness also comes across as an expression of the way his philosophy engaged him heart and mind. His rational brilliance was accompanied by an inner daemon that conveyed inarticulate mysteries to him. He was called a philosopher because of his great love, not because of any wisdom he possessed. He was religious because it was wonder that drove him, and led him to toy at the most profound levels of his being with the religious injunction, 'Know thyself!'

With Socrates, we saw how the religious milieu of ancient Athens provided him with an immediate context to develop the agnostic spirit. The question is whether the spiritual and scientific milieu that we find ourselves in today can provide some similar basis from which to develop a contemporary equivalent. I hope so. With science, an agnostic will be led to an attitude of appreciative and critical wonderment – the sense that, at the limits of a scientific understanding, the human imagination is thrown onto other ways of seeking meaning, value and knowledge. And with religion there is a final piece to say now.

John Caputo has written a short book which is very helpful in this respect, called *On Religion*. In it he argues that, on the one hand, many people who might think of themselves as religious because they go to church are, in fact, not religious, because what they seek from church is certainty. Then, on the other hand, there are those who would never darken the doors of a church but are actually profoundly religious, because they actively embrace the mysteries of life. For Caputo what makes someone religious, as opposed to religiose, is summed up in two quintessentially religious moments celebrated in the Christian tradition.

The first is when Mary says to the angel, 'Be it unto me according to thy word'. Her pregnancy is an apparent impossibility, but she says 'yes' nonetheless. The power of the story, Caputo says, following Derrida's idea of 'religion without religion', is in the way it conveys that to be religious is to affirm what is on the edge of experience.

The second religious moment is found in Augustine when he asks what he loves when he loves God. This characterises that part of the religious spirit which is uncertain about what it seeks, because it is unknown, but that still seeks it with a passion. It would not be hard to make a comparison with Socrates, the lover of much pursued wisdom.

Having drawn the distinction, Caputo recognises that the religious owe the religiose a debt, for if the former major on the spiritual, the latter are often the one's who preserve its ecclesiastical manifestations – the containers for the traditions that are so valuable. Perhaps the relationship between a religious sensibility and a churchy sensibility can be thought of as two lines. Sometimes the lines move closely and in parallel. Sometimes they veer wildly apart. When I was a priest and rows flared in the parish about the placing of candlesticks or the wearing of cassocks, the lines were well apart. At an institutional level, the same could be said of churches in their bureaucratic and officious guises: the spiritual is then eclipsed.

Socrates, in a sense, had the advantage of being able to draw directly on the religious milieu of his age in order to inform his philosophical practice, though it proved too much for the authorities in the end. Today, the agnostic must sift the religious practice of believers and the religious discourse of dogmatic theology in search of the apophatic. We seek the moments where God comes to us as a question. However, the effort is invaluable, for one is rewarded with a rich resource for contemplating the indissoluble, endlessly perplexing issues that lie behind the big questions which fire the human and, I would argue, philosophical imagination – those that revolve around the 'why' of existence.

Plato's response to Socrates was to set up a philosophy school. It turned principles into practices, to cultivate a way of life that looked beyond what could be simply settled. Some of those exercises are perfectly doable today. There is no reason why academic philosophy should not be a way to experience thought as well has have it. The right course could even provide space for the contemplation of death. Similarly, silence is to be found in some churches and retreats – where I suspect it is actually not that rare to find yourself sitting next to a wondering scientist.

It is the religious imagination that most successfully brings together the elements necessary for an agnostic ethos: rational rigour – exemplified by Aquinas and the mystical theologians; intellectual commonsense – for the wisdom that alerts one to the wilder fantasies of scientism; heart and mind – for a philosophy that can become a way of life. For me, now, the importance of the religious imagination is that it broadens out what could otherwise be a purely sceptical intellectualism. It adds flesh to the bones, and suggests far more than just an argument. It is manifest in the attitude that sees new discoveries and theories as expressions of what is still not known, rather than as some kind of human triumph. It shows up in the attitude that sees the goal of the quest as a falling into silence – a contemplation full of texture and colour that is born of the struggle to appreciate the extent of the unknown, which may be called God.

How To Be An Agnostic: An A–Z

The darkest place is always underneath the lamp.

Chinese proverb

Hegel once remarked: 'The owl of Minerva spreads its wings only with the falling of the dusk.' Mary Midgley deploys the image in her memoir: 'The thought for which I want to use it is that wisdom, and therefore philosophy, comes into its own when things become dark and difficult rather than when they are clear and straightforward. That – it seems to me – is why it is so important.'

She laments what might be called the gnostic conception of philosophy by telling the story of a man looking for a lost key. Someone walked by and noticed that he was looking only under the lamp-post. 'Is that where it was mislaid?', they ask. 'No', he replies. 'But it is the easy place to look.' The metaphor and the story could stand for the difference we've been teasing out.

A – is for the Agnostic Spirit

A practice of questioning   This can be associated with Socrates, the individual who said, 'One thing I know, that I know I know nothing'. He realised that the key to wisdom is not how much you know, but is understanding the limits of what you know – an understanding that he failed to find in the politicians and poets of his day. If Plato is right, he devised a method of questioning, now called the elenchus, that brought people to a position where they realised the profundity of their not knowing. For some this was too much, and they turned away. For others, though, it revealed a deeper sense of what it is to be human, the troubling puzzle and wonderful mystery of it.

A practice of love This can be associated with Augustine, the individual who asked, 'What do I love when I love my God?' He understood that he loved and longed for something which he would never fully grasp. Love is like that: when people fall in love, and commit to another, they engage in an essentially future-oriented activity – saying from now on, I want to knit my life with yours – though they don't know what that future contains: it's that person they hope always to be discovering, and themselves in that love too. How much more so with God. 'What do I love when I love my God?' Augustine asks: creation, existence, wonderment, silence? 'I asked these questions simply by gazing at these things, and their beauty was all the answer they gave.' No more – but no less either. He did love.

A practice of knowledge This can be associated with Nicholas of Cusa, the Renaissance individual who wrote *On Learned Ignorance*. He realised that the most complex, and therefore probably the most meaningful human questions, are always ultimately beyond our reach. The same principle is well demonstrated by modern physics. Ask a physicist what light is, say, and they will reply they don't know, though they do know a remarkable amount about it – how it looks like a particle if you look at it in one way, and a wave if you do so in another. This practice is important since it stresses that agnosticism is not against progress in knowledge, and it is not wilful obscurantism. Rather, it stems from the very process of learning itself. A way of expressing that in more traditional spiritual terms would be discernment and study.

A practice of negation This can be associated with Meister Eckhart, the individual who went around medieval Europe preaching, 'If thou lovest God as God, as spirit, as Person or as image, that must all go. Love him as he is: a not-God, a non-spirit, a not-Person, a not-image.' In short, whatever you say God is, you must also say God is not, and if you don't you risk nothing less than idolatry. That even goes for the existence of God, since existence is a property of finite things. To say

God is 'immortal' doesn't mean anything positive about God, but just that 'whatever God is, God is not mortal.' Notice the 'whatever'.

A practice of waiting   This can be associated with Pyrrho of Elis, the ancient Greek sceptic, for whom scepticism was not a descent into a relativistic void, but was a way of maintaining the search – 'sceptic' coming from the Greek for enquirer. He suggested that this can be done by suspending your beliefs about the big questions, and waiting on what is revealed to you. Unexpectedly, he also found that the practice brought a profound sense of tranquility too. It's a bit like one understanding of mindfulness meditation, about which Pyrrho may well have known, as the attempt to let new insights in as a result of letting go of old insights, to which we tend to cling.

A practice of wonder   This can be associated with many of the scientists of the modern world, like Robert Hooke, who could look down a microscope, at a common fly, and exclaim, 'The burnished and resplendent fly!' Coleridge's thought is helpful here too: following Aristotle, he noted that philosophy begins in wonder, a wonder that stems from ignorance, and that it ends with wonder too, though now the wonder has become 'the parent of adoration'. It's the joy of not knowing, the thrill of sensing the sublimity of nature. On one account, it reveals the limits of the human capacity to grasp it. On another, it reveals the amazing possibility that we can get a grip on it at all. Within both accounts is the sense that wonder expresses something of the value of nature that is intrinsic to it. The ancient philosopher Longinus expressed this connection well when he wrote:

> For grandeur produces ecstasy rather than persuasion in the hearer; and the combination of wonder and astonishment always proves superior to the merely persuasive and pleasant. This is because persuasion is on the whole something we can control, whereas amazement and wonder exert invincible power and force and get the better of every hearer.

B – is for the Bible

There's a tendency today to insist on the absolute historicity of the life, death and resurrection of Jesus. Unless the New Testament is, at heart, a historical document, the Christian faith is in vain. It's stressed to also show that Christianity is not fundamentally a moral philosophy, it's an actual and already realised change, an inauguration of the new creation which Christians are in the business of continuing to bring about.

But does this not demonstrate so much of what is wrong with the contemporary religious imagination? It is very much in the spirit of the scientific age: to be true, something must be empirically verifiable and historically determinable. Myth and meaning, symbol and archetype, are for merely spiritual types! Those arty sorts read the Bible as if it were Shakespeare, a kind of life-enhancing entertainment; or perhaps like a bit of Plato, some moral square-dancing! No. The truth of the gospel must force itself upon you, as robust as a physical law that can smash an atom: Jesus' rising as macho-belief, for macho-Christians. Only, it leads to all sorts of absurdities. Why four gospels, not one, that differ in so many details? If you go down the historicist's line you spend a lifetime trying to justify the historical inconsistencies and hiatuses. Or why only one Jesus, only one resurrection? That just seems too arbitrary, and a rather clumsy way of communicating with everyone who came, first decades, then centuries after the first Sunday. Or why again, you have to ask, are we still here 2000 years on, when the Jesus of the Bible thought the new creation would come complete in a generation? If you demand historical literalism, you get eschatological farce.

Paradoxically, if you make the Bible a book of evidence, you wring it of its real power, the more subtle quality that has kept it living for generations. If faith stands or falls on its provability, it's likely to fall. And you miss the main point. Of course, faith must relate to what can be ascertained of historical events and facts. But to be faith, it must be more expansive than textual tests or empirical seizure alone allow. Its real value is that it lives in life: hope beyond the evidence.

C – is for Church

When I was ordained, my bishop, David Jenkins, said that the trouble with the church is that you can't live with it and you can't live without it. I live without it more than I did. However, for all the criticisms I have of it, particularly its joining in the battle for certainties, it holds traditions that in my view our world is infinitely poorer without. Where else in our culture can you be ashed, held, and told you are dust and going to die? Where else can you hear otherworldly music enacted in an equally otherworldly context, namely, ancient liturgy? Where else can you sit next to strangers and have remembered before you a story that strains for the divine? Sometimes it is a relief to have the burden of being oneself lifted. Love it and hate it, Church is the place for that.

D – is about Darwinism

Neo-Darwinism is currently the most strident form of scientism. But need one feel in league with the creationists to question it? There are better alternatives.

Consider the philosophical interpretation of Darwinism offered by Karl Popper. For him, Darwinism is not a testable scientific theory but what he called a 'metaphysical research programme' within which many theories may be tested. One should not get carried away with this metaphysical ascription. He did not mean it in a theological sense, but simply to suggest that Darwinism as a whole is not falsifiable and so not of the best kind of theory science can offer.

In fact, in a certain way, Darwinian adaptation is tautologous. If you imagine a fairly stable environment in which a species of fairly similar reproducing creatures live, then the offspring of those creatures that are better adapted to that environment are bound to survive more readily. What Darwinism adds to this picture – and the thing that Popper thought of as its greatest scientific achievement – is that the evolution of species will be gradual; it will occur over long periods of time (though rates of evolutionary change are typically far from clear).

Here are two striking things over which Darwinism struggles. A first is the origin of life. It is possible that at some point in the future scientists who mimic what they take to be a primordial soup in the laboratory will show that certain complex molecules can take on some of the properties necessary for life, such as replication. However, short of an amoeba springing out of the test tube, this won't prove life began this way, for life's origins seem lost behind the veil of deep time.

A second is the variety of life. This might be thought surprising. After all, is it not obvious that natural selection produces an abundance of life, given time? Popper refutes this with a thought experiment. Say life was discovered on Mars, but only in the form of one type of primitive bacterium. Would people say that Darwinism had been refuted? No: they would say that only one bacterium was well enough adapted to survive. So natural selection does not predict the variety of the species we see on earth. Neither does it offer a particularly satisfactory mechanism to explain it. All sorts of others are routinely proposed. Further, there's the issue of how separate species evolve, as opposed to the variations within species. What is not clear is how natural selection might lead to the discontinuities between species – the moment when gene transmission stops – if species themselves are the result of transmitted changes in organisms.

There are other questions. Take, for example, why what might be called higher functions of living animals evolved – like consciousness. Evolutionary psychologists will say that consciousness evolved because it is adaptive; it has causal efficacy in the survival of the species concerned. But what this does not explain is the *experience* of consciousness. Why did evolution allow us not just to detect light that falls across the visible bandwidth, but to see vivid colours, as colours, too?

Where neo-Darwinian thought completely falls apart, in my opinion, is in relation to theories such as memes. According to its advocates, memes are the mental equivalent of genes. Anything that can be thought and is replicated – from a philosophical argument to a cultural icon – would be a meme. What memes are supposed to explain is the transmission of ideas: they compete and only the fittest survive. The advocates of memes usually ascribe religious memes the honour of being the most pernicious, saying that the religious imperative to replicate – to proselytise – reveals its selfish intent.

But it's a poor theory. For one thing, it has a woefully impoverished understanding of ideas and traditions. It is not in the nature of all religions to proselytise, for example. Neither does meme theory have much conception of the environment in which they are supposed to interact. Ideas, for example, spread as a result of the way they interact with people, times and places: one must understand those people, times and places in order to understand why ideas spread. Finally, memes fall foul of a category error. Genetic evolution works well in a biological environment, but to take that theory and apply it to cultural and social environments is as mistaken as thinking that because gravity causes attraction between bodies, so a gravity analogue will explain the reason people are attracted to one another.

Darwin's brilliant idea explains much: from why superbugs resist penicillin to why life takes eons to evolve. However, Darwinism will be superseded, as surely as Newton was by Einstein. This is not to say evolution is wrong; only that it is no more or less than the best theory we have to date.

E – is for Ethos

Melvyn Bragg was interviewed on the BBC's radio programme *Devout Sceptics*. He was asked in what sense he was an agnostic. He said: 'One of the greatest phrases I heard in the last two or three years was Issac Newton's answer to someone who asked him how he discovered the laws of gravity, which changed life profoundly, and he said, "By thinking on it continually." And I keep thinking about that phrase and think that if I keep thinking on things continually … you never know what will happen.'

F – is about Facts

In his essay, 'The Decay of Lying', Oscar Wilde decries what he calls the 'monstrous worship of facts': 'There is something truly monstrous about scientific curiosity because it seems to extend to facts something they do not deserve. Facts must be respected but never worshipped.'

G – is a prayer to God

Dear God,

Of all the many paradoxes about writing about you – given that you're there at all – the oddest must be that you know what I'm going to write before I've penned a word; before I've even thought it. That must be even more dreary for you than knowing you have read it all before.

However, we humans must write and talk. Maybe in your graciousness that's why there are stories of you writing and talking too, at least through intermediaries. Though I have to confess that I wish some of your followers could accept that human words are inevitably a pale reflection of your own words, and that we are forced to use metaphors and the like. You'd think no Christian could make the mistake of treating them as infallible, and would realise they must seek the Word behind the words – or maybe you wouldn't be so foolish as to have such a hope. As the Good Book itself suggests, you are used to casting your pearls before swine.

I'm particularly fond of what happened to Thomas Aquinas – you know, on 6 December 1273 – when he surprised his brethren, though not you, and told his friend Reginald that he would not write any more. What I love about this moment is that it

233

was one of enlightenment, not despair. As a supreme word-smith, he had explored all sorts of insights, about logic and metaphysics and ethics and humanity. However, on that day, he reached a point when he could truly appreciate the most profound truth of all. He realised that words would take him no further forwards. He had to stop writing to continue his life's quest.

I suspect that all religious writings should be read in a similar spirit: they point beyond their own words, to something that may be found in the space between them.

You are unknown. No words can do it. Words must stop.

Amen

H – is for History

Today's appetite for history is striking. In many bookshops the history section is second in size only to fiction. On TV, history programmes command very respectable audience figures, that rise even more if they build in an element of celebrity. History as heritage is a similarly growing industry. So why is history so popular?

It must be partly because history can be communicated so well. As Simon Schama has argued in his book, notably entitled, Dead Certainties, 'the asking of questions and the relating of narratives need not ... be mutually exclusive forms of historical representation'. In other words, it is perfectly respectable to treat history as 'a work of the imagination'. Long gone are the days when it was merely learning dates by rote.

However, underneath this excellent synthesis of style and substance, lies a human need that reaches back to Socrates: the need to know who we are and where we have come from. I have not done any empirical research, but I would not be surprised if the rise of history coincides with the decline of religion. Perhaps religion remains strong in the US because history has far fewer seams to mine and the country understands itself more of as an idea than a tradition.

In other words, history fulfils some of the functions performed by religion. At one level, it provides a narrative within which people can situate themselves: the way history is recalled, researched and related is as much a story of the present as of the past. History also tends to be the story of men and women of consequence, and thus a flattering and fascinating mode of inquiry for those (the majority) of us who are not. But where history's religious shape is seen most clearly is in the way it takes one out of oneself. It achieves this sense of personal perspective by retelling events that are simultaneously familiar and distant. The familiar aspects allow us to empathise with the past, to see ourselves in it. The distant aspects stem from the radical differences of experience and existence that separate times and places. The combination of the two aspects means that we become strangers to ourselves in the process of learning about it.

The romantic poets were articulate advocates of this religious view of history. Take two poems of John Keats. In 'Ode to a Nightingale', the 'full-throated ease' of the bird's song provides an intimation of immortality to the death-dreading young man. But the creature, that was 'not born for death', provides a bridge between the present and the otherwise unbridgeable past. 'The voice I hear this passing night was heard / In ancient days by emperor and clown.' Its song is a form of ecstasy because it takes Keats out of himself in this way. Indeed, it is not just long-dead persons with whom he thereby senses his connection and disconnection. The nightingale enables him to empathise with the biblical character of Ruth and fictional 'sprites' too.

History as a meditation on mortality is the central theme of another of Keats's poems, 'Ode on a Grecian Urn'. Much of the poem describes the deities and mortals, the maidens and satyrs, the priest and lovers pictured on the urn. Keats notices how these figures stand outside of time and how blessed that frozen state is. The lovers who almost kiss will love each other forever because they will always be winning their goal. The trees will never be bare. The pipers never short of song. In the beauty of the urn and the portrayal of this timelessness Keats can equate beauty with truth, truth with beauty. Its eternal history transports him from his own temporality: 'Thou, silent form, dost tease us out of thought/ As doth eternity'.

History on the TV and in books is clearly not always so intensely felt as the romantics would have it. But in its tales of tragedy and triumph, of humdrum and high-powered lives, it conjures up the same ambivalent feelings of familiarity and distance. Inasmuch as it exists on the borders of what is known and unknown, history is an excellent provocation of the mystery of things.

I – is for me (my soul, personhood and resurrection?)

When, in the seventeenth century, Descartes suggested that there might be a distinction between mind and body, part of the reason his presumed dualism appealed, had to do with religious convictions. It is clear that one day all living bodies die. However, if it could be shown that the mind was separate from the body, then that would support the belief that the human individual can survive bodily death. In the Christian dispensation, the soul might rise to immortality. In Eastern systems of religious thought, the spirit might be reincarnated.

Today, the very existence of the soul has become deeply problematic, not least because such dualism is so powerfully resisted. Then there are further questions, such as if the soul did exist, would it be the same or different from mind or consciousness? A short history of the soul is perhaps illuminating, at least in terms of unravelling what is at stake.

The notion that the soul is a crucial part of human nature, perhaps the most important part – the centre of consciousness and mind – emerges from the twilight of prehistory. Ancient Greek Orphic and Pythagorean mystery-teachings held that the soul is immortal. Conversely, in early Judaism, there is no real notion of the immortal soul. Rather, there is *nephesh*, or breath, which infuses and animates a body. In the Jewish schema, life after death was just not that interesting, which is why immortality is not discussed in the Hebrew Bible.

It is only with the birth of ancient Greek philosophy that the search for the soul becomes integral to the Western tradition. Plato explored the thesis that the soul is the immaterial part of a human. It could be thought of as being united with the body, perhaps temporarily. To use more philosophical terms, he argued that the soul may be the form of the human individual. When that form enters into the matter of which the body is made, that matter becomes animated. That same soul will also leave the body too, which provides a definition of death: the matter of the body becomes formless once again and so dissolves. Incidentally, Plato also talks of philosophy as aiming at the perfection of the soul, achieved particularly through knowledge of oneself.

For Aristotle, the soul is the form of the body too, the means by which the body is animated. However, for Aristotle, and contra Plato, the form doesn't enter matter, it already is embodied matter. It has no separate existence. Neither, then, does the soul. This conviction follows from Aristotle's definition of human beings as being social animals: sociability requires bodies since bodies are the means by which we perceive and communicate. Another corollary of this is that only embodied beings have souls. For example, God does not have a soul according to Aristotle, since God does not have a body. Further, Aristotle believed that plants and animals can have souls too, if of a different kind: it is probably only humans who have an 'intellectual soul', witnessed to by their capacity to think abstractly and decide freely.

A third tradition about the soul among the ancient Greeks comes from the atomists. They were materialists, believing that the world was constituted solely of matter in the form of indivisible atoms. So, they had to address the problem of how some matter could be animated, as it is in living organisms. They proposed that there were such things as 'soul atoms' that existed among the 'matter atoms' in living creatures. Death is the dispersal of these soul atoms, a process that actually begins before death, which explains why the older an organism becomes the more decrepit it becomes too.

Christianity, in the theology of Thomas Aquinas, borrows from Aristotle's idea that the body and soul are intimately connected. However, Christianity throws in its particular take on the question of immortality: the issue becomes how Aristotle's affirmation that the soul must be embodied might be reconciled with the Christian conviction in life after bodily death. The resolution of this conundrum is found in the doctrine of the resurrection of the body. For Christians, resurrection is not conceived of as the soul leaving the body behind, but rather as some kind of remaking of the body and soul in eternity.

This again shifts the focus of attention, away from the nature of the soul and to the nature of the resurrected body. It cannot be identical with the physical body, which is clearly subject to death. Neither is the resurrected body a kind of reproduction physical body with immortal properties, perhaps as some contemporary transhumanists may imagine immortality as a 'downloading' of human identity onto a supercomputer-driven humanoid robot. (It's amazing how the story of resurrection refuses to die.) Instead, Christian theology teaches that the resurrected body is a complete transformation of the old physical body, though the nature of that transformation remains something of a mystery. As St Paul put it, 'We shall all be changed, in a moment, in the twinkling of an eye.'

The next big shift comes with Descartes, along with the responses of Spinoza and Locke, the two who proposed that the soul is in at least one sense material. That, in turn, was fiercely contested by Leibniz, who argued for the soul's immateriality, on the grounds that a material soul would deny humankind the possibility of immortality.

A new and important strand in more recent modern philosophy makes another shift in this discourse. It aligns the soul with the person, in the abstract sense of who we are. It makes a further observation, that the person may not be a single thing but multiple and fragmented. This is the theory of William James and Friedrich Nietzsche: for them, we are a constellation of selves, and the sense of consciousness, or being an 'I', is the product of that struggle. Hence the sense of crisis when we ask ourselves who we might be.

Michel Foucault developed the discussion again, reflecting on the impact of the work of Sigmund Freud. Freud taught modern people to think of themselves as 'subjects of inwardness': with the invention of psychoanalysis, we learned ways of becoming introspective in order to search out the truth about ourselves. Our most authentic parts are soul-like and the word 'soul' becomes a synonym for 'authentic', as in soul music.

For Foucault, though, this belief was something of a delusion. Our sense of self is forged through the way that power – manifest in social entities like medical science or political institutions – operates on the body. So the truth about ourselves is not found by turning inward but by considering how our bodies exist in the world. In a striking phrase, Foucault inverted Plato's thought that 'the body is the prison of the soul' and declared instead that 'the soul is the prison of the body'.

This latest strand in humanity's discussion of itself, characterised by an uncertainty about personhood, and the feeling that we are subject to all kinds of external forces that construct us in some way, is a central preoccupation of what is sometimes called postmodernism, and raises the nature of personal identity.

One of the big questions here is how we may understand the sense that our identity is continuous. After all, although much changes in the life of an individual as they traverse their 'seven ages' – from infancy, to schoolchild, to teenager, to employee, to employer, to grandparent, to senility – few would doubt that in some sense they remain the same person. The question is in what sense?

Two main groups of theories try to account for the continuity of personal identity that we experience. The first is the notion that personal identity is intimately connected to the individual's body. Within this understanding, it is in the continuity of being embodied across a lifetime that your personal identity resides. It is a natural assumption to make, though it runs into problems because our bodies change over time. Strictly speaking, as our cells die and are replaced, we actually gain completely new bodies over time. Given that is the case, the philosopher has to give an account of how personal identity survives that physical change.

Attempting to do so leads to the second option, that personal identity is to do with memory or some complex of psychological factors. These, apparently, persist in spite of the physical changes. We can, for example, recount events from our childhood, and they are in some way linked to who we have become. However, the psychological account of identity again falls down because our memories are flawed. Radical psychological changes occur across the course of a life, seemingly disrupting personal continuity. Indeed, you may not even remember your schooldays, and be grateful for the lapse. But that does not imply they have ceased to be a part of you.

So both the physical and psychological accounts of personal continuity run into profound difficulties. And yet, it is still the case that human beings have a clear sense of being single individuals across the course of their lives, for all that they are also continually in the midst of change. So are there any further alternatives that might explain this conundrum?

One takes us back to conceptions of the soul. Borrowing from Aristotle again, it proposes that being the same person over time rests on what is called our 'basic being'. In his book *De Anima*, or 'On the Soul', Aristotle describes our basic being as 'that which lies under' the being of our everyday lives. It is the ground of our being, or the essence of ourselves. It is the substance which undergoes all the changes and yet still maintains a connection with the past. It may be thought of as like energy: energy is conserved, modern physics tells us, for all that it changes from one type to another.

This possibility throws light on the body theory and the psychology theory of personal identity; it could help to highlight what is at stake in their separate strengths and weaknesses. For example, the changing physical body might be thought of as serving the 'basic beingness' of the individual, the continuity of the person resting in that basic being not in the body. Alternatively, the evolving nature of a person's individual psychology might be thought of as the shifting instantiation of the basic being.

When it comes to the weaknesses of the two theories, notably how they cope with change, basic being may help again. For example, it can be thought of as the 'bearer of experience', or as that which makes persons subjects. This would highlight a central weakness of both the body theory and the psychology theory, namely that they do not think of personal identity in terms of human subjectivity, but rather in terms of a sequence of physical or mental events. It is such subjectivity that Socrates was referring to when he says that the reason he is in prison, awaiting death, is because he has and holds to moral principles. The moral principles he has form the personal explanation for his location, and any purely material explanation as to why he's in prison, such as that his sinews led him there, seems woefully inadequate.

In other words, rather like trying to understand the nature of consciousness, the nature of personal identity, or the soul, will be incomplete unless it incorporates the element of human subjectivity. We experience things, we don't just undergo events.

J – is about Jesus

Christianity is compelling to many Christians for Jesus-shaped reasons. That sounds silly to say. But it's this problematic notion that God comes to us as a person. The Christian doctrine of the incarnation says more than that God comes to us through people, with which presumably many religions agree. It says that God *is* a person, and you've got to have faith in this divine man in order to receive the salvation Christianity affords. Which is why to question the nature of the incarnation is high on the list of heresies.

But there's a risk here. I wonder if it creates a kind of idol out of the personal. I have this feeling that it was an over-reaction of early Christians to interpret the 'Jesus event' as so strongly incarnational, and to end up worshipping the Christ. You need more than just the ethical teachings of Jesus, I can see that. Jesus reveals something that is true about the human condition: if you don't love you die; if you do love they kill you, was Herbert McCabe's way of summing it up. But isn't to identify divinity with a particular person a kind of category mistake? I can see the force of the Buddhist saying that if you meet Buddha on the road, kill him.

Then, there is the related problem of the historical Jesus. I recall the scholar E.P. Saunders summing up Jesus of Nazareth's eschatological convictions in his New Testament lectures – such as that the world was shortly to come to an end – and I wonder how such ideas can really sit with the confession a Christian has to make that this same 'mistaken' Jesus is Lord.

Shouldn't we in some sense be getting over Jesus, not getting too stuck on him, to put it rather crudely? For the fixation on Jesus as an historical figure is self-limiting. The problem with being so tied to the life of the person called Jesus is that his significance is so tied to events between the dates of his birth and death too. It's called the scandal of particularity. Christianity is anchored in, but also anchored to, a particular place, time and individual. But we already live 2000 years later. It is quite possible that humans will exist for some millennia yet. How plausible will referring back to the man seem to our relatives 10,000 years on?

K – is for Kant

Immanuel Kant argued that all scientific and moral judgements are imposed by the mind on the world; that is the only way we can apprehend things. Not that things do not exist. It is just that we cannot know what they are as things in themselves. So there is the world of phenomena, the apparent world, and the world of noumena – the unknown 'thing in itself'. Kant called this transcendental idealism, meaning that the noumenal world can be inferred from reason but is itself another order of being. By subtle and circuitous routes in his *Critiques* he sought to describe exactly what can be said by reason and what cannot. Ultimately, he saw the identification of the noumenal world as evidence for the existence of God – because it is unknown.

L – is for love

In the *Symposium*, Plato records two myths that tell of the origins of love. They present diametrically opposed conceptions of desire.

The first is put into the mouth of Aristophanes. At first, he says, people were whole. They looked like wheels – rounded and complete. But, being mortals, they were hugely ambitious. They planned an attempt on the gods, an invasion of heaven. Needless to say, they did not succeed and Zeus punished them by cutting them in two, so that they would lose their strength. As he cut them, Apollo turned their heads around so that they could see the wound.

Next though, looking at what he had done, Zeus took pity upon the lost, dismembered halflings. So, he moved their genitals around too, placing them beneath their heads, in order to provide a way for them to reconnect with their lost halves and see the joy in the other half's face as it happened. This is the origin of love: to find the lost half of our original whole, to make one out of two, and heal the pain of loneliness and alienation. The power of love is nothing less than the desire to be made complete. The ecstasy of love-making is the annihilation of the separate self in the other.

This myth captures the irresistible nature of love very well. It conveys the extraordinary lengths people will go to for love, the blindness that lovers have to their own faults and the world around them, and the agony that they go through should they be separated once more.

However, it also perpetuates the idea that love can be completed. It feeds into the romantic myth that there is someone out there for you, who, once found, will perfect your life. What can be overlooked is its dark undercurrents. Should two people find their lost halves in each other, the myth says that their embrace is total. Aristophanes imagines Hephaestus passing by two such lovers and asking them what they want. Being the craftsman god, they ask him to weld them together. Once so fused, the lovers are unable to move. It is as if they are dead.

Socrates relates the second myth which was given to him by Diotima, the priestess. It is the tale of the birth of Eros, following the sexual congress of Penia and Poros, poverty and resourceful cunning. This myth portrays love as a desire for what one lacks too but, unlike Aristophanes' myth, that lack can never be wholly satisfied by finding a lover. Neither does it seek only lovers, for it strives ultimately for wisdom.

Moreover, Eros himself is not a god, but moves in between the realm of the gods and human beings. In other words, that human beings love is simultaneously the sign that they aspire to divine things, though they can never reach them. After all, gods do not love, for they lack nothing. Whatever the joys of such an existence might be, they are not the joys of what human love can achieve, like children (a pregnancy of the body, Diotima says) and philosophy (a pregnancy of the soul).

Socrates' encounter with Diotima does not stop there. She tells him that if the origins of Eros is the lower mystery of love, the higher mystery is the upper path along which love can lead someone. This is the famous ascent of the *Symposium*. What it describes is the way that love's continuous desire for what is true leads the individual from loving others to loving beautiful things, to eventually loving what is beautiful itself. Like the light that leaps from a diamond, hiding the gem itself, this is a theophany, a sense of the divine, a glimpse of something too beautiful to grasp in its entirety. The test is the beautiful things the vision inspires in people's lives – the love the individual shows.

Diotima's ascent inspired a whole tradition within philosophy. In Platonism, the mystery that Diotima described to Socrates becomes an ontology. For example, in Plotinus, the goal of loving is a transcendent unity, and human beings can reach out to it because this One itself gives forth divine emanations. One of the most powerful adaptations of Diotima's mystery is found in Augustine with his comment that our hearts are restless until they find rest in God. God is, here, being identified with the climax of Diotima's ascent. If one recalls the unknowability of God that is a central theme in Augustine, then part of what he is saying is that love itself is a mystery: like Socrates who never ceased loving, because wisdom always ultimately eluded him, Augustine remained a lover of God, who was the goal of the pilgrimage of his whole life.

Someone might complain that this presents a perpetually frustrated picture of love. They would prefer Aristophanes' view in which love can come to an end, even if in a form of death. However, the more profound interpretation that Augustine places on love is that to love is to be thrown onto the nature of existence itself. Put more colloquially, it is why lovers say, 'I am glad you are alive': in loving they realise that they are alive themselves. The mystery of love is not to be found in its satisfaction, but simply in the attempt to love – to live ever more fully.

M – is for Mountains

In 2002, Tate Britain displayed a number of landscape artists, well known in the US though hardly ever seen on the other side of the Atlantic, in an exhibition entitled 'American Sublime'. With their massive mountains, rolling plains, towering clouds and vivid light, these artists of the so-called Hudson River School played with nature and scale in a way that both frightens and inspires. The pictures evoke the sense which, as Edmund Burke wrote, is 'when we have an idea of pain and danger, without being actually in such circumstances. Whatever excites this delight, I call sublime.'

The connection between wonderment and the sublime is to do with the overpowering sense that is inspired in such landscape, suggesting that there are values intrinsic in nature that human beings should respect as well as study. This can be forgotten. Scholars suggest that, in its American guise, sublime landscape connects directly with the religious origins of the country. The West, for example, was called God's country. Paintings can suggest that the New World is an emanation of the divine. Holiness and spirituality are then readily coupled to national pride and destiny. Thus, as professor of art history Roger Hull writes:

> American nature was emblematic of America's size, strength, cultural and economic potential, and materialistic potential. American nature was unlike any other in the world, and certainly different (and by implication 'better') than the old, used, domesticated nature of England and Europe. William Cullen Bryant urged his friend Thomas Cole, the American landscape painter who had been born in England, to soak up in his imagination 'that wilder image' of American scenery before he took a trip to England and the continent. Bryant's advice was a warning to Cole to remember the virility of American nature and not be seduced by the gentler forms of nature he would encounter on his trip.

This sensibility is therefore very different from that of the agnostic. For people like Bryant, at least, landscape is expressive of what human beings are capable of, not of their limits.

The opposing view is found in the writings of nineteenth-century agnostic and mountaineer, Leslie Stephen. His book *The Playground of Europe*, in which he describes the peaks of the Alps, is still in print. He argued that, before the industrial era, most peoples had just feared mountains. Now, though, in what was called the golden age of mountaineering, they loved them because, though climbable, they challenge. For climbing a mountain is not the same as conquering it (as in the thought that men and women can conquer nature). Rather, mountains

Illus. 8.1: Leslie Stephen's agnosticism found expression in his love of the Alps.

return the climber to a place of solitude that modern life has otherwise banished.

> The qualities which strike every sensitive observer are impressed upon the mountaineer with tenfold force and intensity. If he is accessible to poetical influences as his neighbours – and I don't know why he should be less so – he has opened new avenues of access between the scenery and his mind. He has learnt a language which is but partially revealed to ordinary men.

Stephen emphasises the importance of experiencing the mountain, not just seeing it from afar, even less reading about it – echoing, perhaps, the Socratic insight that philosophy must be lived and not merely spoken.

> I might go on indefinitely recalling the strangely impressive scenes that frequently startle the traveller in the waste

upper world; but language is feeble indeed to convey even a glimmering of what is to be seen to those who have not seen it for themselves, whilst to them it can be little more than a peg upon which to hand their own recollections. These glories, in which the mountain Spirit reveals himself to his true worshippers, are only to be gained by the appropriate service of climbing – at some risk, though a very trifling risk, if he is approached with due form and ceremony – into the further recesses of his shrines.

As Anthony Kenny points out in his essay on Stephen in *The Unknown God*, Stephen was at odds with John Ruskin here. Ruskin was another mountain enthusiast but one who thought that the appeal of mountains was like that of cathedrals: they were reflections of superior human sensibilities, not themselves superior to thought. In mountains, Ruskin was reminded of what humanity is capable. Stephen disagreed. In his essay, *An Agnostic's Apology*, his final complaint was against the arrogance of the theist and atheist in the way they ride roughshod over ultimate mystery.

[Agnostics] will be content to admit openly, what you whisper under your breath or hide in technical jargon, that the ancient secret is secret still, that man knows nothing of the Infinite and Absolute; and that, knowing nothing, he had better not be dogmatic about his ignorance.

Mountains evoked in him the same humility: 'Their voice is mystic and has found discordant interpreters: but to me at least it speaks in tones at once more tender and more awe-inspiring than that of any mortal teacher.' His is the agnostic attitude. After all, only faith can move mountains.

N – is about Nothing

We've been asking this question, why is there something not nothing? There are some physicists who resist the mysterious nature of this thought by denying it is a real question. Victor Stenger argues that something is the natural state of things, and the nothing out of which it supposedly came, is a distraction. 'There is something rather than nothing because something is more stable.' But Stenger needs to take nothing more seriously, for nothing would exclude both stability and instability against which something might be.

Not dissimilarly, it's suggested that the vacuum of space actually consists of a quantum foam, out of which universes may emerge spontaneously, unpredictably. Or that the universe is the self-creation of M-theory. Something like that may or may not happen – it's way off being shown empirically – but even if the evidence mounted, you'd then need to ask why quantum foam or M-theory, not nothing? The same would apply to the various candidates for our universe being part of a multiverse too: the question applies equally to whatever exists.

A different class of solutions attempt to finesse the issue by pointing out that time may be infinite, with no beginning or end. Our universe would then be just one of an infinite many, just one bubble before the next collapse and bubble. But everlasting time doesn't resolve the question either, as the universe still requires something called time to be everlasting in.

Incidentally, God is not a scientific answer to this natural mystery, as an intelligent design advocate might tell you. It means something else to invoke God having pondered the why something: as Wittgenstein pointed out, 'not how the world, but that it is, is the mystery.' God is a way of keeping the question open, and not simply trying to close it down out of atheistic discomfort.

O – is Oedipal

Freud thought religion infantile. In *The Future of an Illusion*, he argued that it would become clearer and clearer to humanity that religion was an obsessional neurosis which, like children negotiating the reality of their fathers, arises out of the Oedipus complex.

'If this view is right, it is to be supposed that a turning-away from religion is bound to occur with the fatal inevitability of a process of growth and that we find ourselves at this very juncture in the middle of that phrase of development', he wrote. It is not clear over what time-scale Freud saw this fatal inevitability emerging but 80 years on there is little sign of the turning-away.

It is commonplace to note that Freud's desire to do away with religion has an Oedipal structure itself: Judaism was the religion of his fathers. Jonathan Lear, in his philosophical introduction *Freud*, makes a more novel observation. He compares Freud's conception of religion with that of Kierkegaard, who thought Christianity, in practice, a monstrous illusion too. However, for Kierkegaard, the ramifications could not have been more different. Kierkegaard interpreted the illusion of religion as a sign that the Christians of his time were not being authentically religious at all. The way they practised their religion was 'a misleading fantasy of religious commitment', as Lear puts it. For Kierkegaard, the future of the illusion was not a turning-away from religion but a struggle with faith proper.

What this suggests about Freud is that he saw religion through the lens of a larger conception of scientific progress, part of which included shaking off the vestiges of what he took to be infantile beliefs. Reason and experience – what he interestingly called 'our God Logos' – will show that religion is not compatible with the evidence. It is a thought, dare one say, an illusion, that has common currency to this day (though, in another twist, the atheists, who follow the same *logos*-god as Freud, now commonly decry Freudianism for its lack of scientific veracity – another Oedipal moment perhaps, if Freud is thought of as one of the fathers).

Today, Christianity seems to operate with an illusion – the illusion of its incompatibility with science. It feels or is forced to compete for the same ground – the ground marked out by the scientific criteria of fact, proof and relevancy. Kierkegaard's call would be to recover a conception of religion that is truer to itself. For him, that call was to radical faith, interpreted as

Illus. 8.2: Sigmund Freud's 'royal road' to the unknown unconscious borrows from the Christian tradition of radical uncertainty.

beyond reason. Here, I have argued it is to the radical unknowability of God that needs to be recalled, to the extent represented by a passionate agnosticism. Rather than debunking reason, this is an approach that focuses on reason's limits.

P/Q – is about Probabilities

Richard Dawkins, in *The God Delusion*, has popularised the idea that you can weigh up the probability of God's existence. God is a scientific hypothesis, like any other, he begins, and so the likelihood of that hypothesis can be assessed using standard Bayesian techniques. Unsurprisingly, he concludes God is massively unlikely. John Henry Newman, the Victorian theologian who was recently made blessed, did something not dissimilar over a century ago and, unsurprisingly, with opposite results and great sophistication.

He drew a distinction between certainty and certitude, realising that we hold all sorts of things to be true in life with pretty flimsy evidence, given the weight of significance we then associate with the presumed fact. One example is that your parents are your parents, which is why it is so shattering to be told your parents are not your parents – something that happens with fair regularity.

So, he agrees: the way we form our beliefs is probabilistic, though – and here's Newman's sophistication – we do so not just by making cool mathematical calculations, but by bringing our whole person and experience to bear upon the issue. We use our heart as well as our head, our imagination as well as our deliberation. To use just your head is only to give what he calls 'notional assent' to something. To use both, though, is to arrive at 'real assent' which is a concurrence and convergence that can be said powerfully to ring true; put all these strands together and it is possible to form a 'cable' of belief: any particular strand of itself may be flimsy, but wound together, the cable is strong. Belief in God is 'an action more subtle and more comprehensive than the mere appreciation of syllogistic logic', or Bayesian probabilities, we may add.

Reason is a crucial component in this process, because without learning, virtues like integrity and rational discernment, we might come to hold all manner of beliefs. When it comes to questions like God, we must also accept the limitations of human understanding. However, so fully equipped, there is every reason for hoping to have certitude about matters great and small, as indeed we do in so many parts of life. Including, Newman believes, the question of God. 'The pure and indivisible Light is seen only by the blessed inhabitants of heaven; here we have but such faint reflections of it as its diffraction supplies; but they are sufficient for faith and devotion.'

However, Newman also realised, I think, there is a limit to the certitude that can be arrived at by such methods, that limit depending upon the matter in question. In particular, you may have certitude about God's existence, when all things in life are considered. But what that doesn't give you is faith in, say, Christianity and not Islam. The specifics of different theistic religions, which are so important, seem equally probable from this probabilistic point of view, which is to say that each has a coherent, persuasive story to tell, to account for the fullness of your experience. (Perhaps, if the question of parentage can be made analogous to that faith, this is like acknowledging that while it's not unimaginably improbable that you're wrong about your parents, it is that you're wrong about having parents at all.)

Probability alone cannot tell you which theism to follow because the likelihood of any particular revelation seems so similar. 'If the abstract probability of a Revelation be the measure of genuineness in a given case, why not in the case of Mahomet as well as of the Apostles?' he asks. Quite so, acknowledging the limits of probabilistic assessments when it comes to faith.

Newman overcame these limits by his trust in the Catholic Church: he reasoned that each of the many members of the church contributes their real assent to the faith held within the traditions of the church, and that accumulation of witnesses was convincing to him. There, though, I must part company with him.

What I take from him, nonetheless, is that it's possible to arrive at a certitude about God by a holistic probabilistic approach such as his – though, for me, God comes as a question – but that certitude about Christianity or Islam, or Anglicanism or Catholicism, requires something else. I generally opt for Anglicanism when I go to church for different reasons: it is a serious tradition, and the tradition I know best, so if I want to be serious about the spiritual life, which I do, then I do well to be serious about this one. I guess that many of the thinking and ecumenically minded believers I know think something similar: they place their trust in the tradition they know the best – trusting that it's truth is rich enough – while also acknowledging that they can learn much from the truths of other traditions.

R – is for Reading and Writing

Plato was wary of writing. He suspected that, in the way it objectified philosophy, it could become an excuse not to live it. He thought that, in the way it tidied philosophy up, it could become a means of concealing meaning that can only be experienced. So convinced was he of this risk that in the *Republic*, he bans poets from his model city-state. It seems an extreme position to adopt. But poets were authority figures. The body of work from Hesiod to Homer people remembered and recited, and in Plato's time had started to write down, was the dogmatic canon of the day. The danger is that poets would appeal to the dogmatic instincts of citizens in providing a ready-made source of knock-out proof-texts for the positions they opposed.

These days the best novels are often quasi-religious texts. Jeanette Winterson, an author who has been accused of deliberately confusing literature and religion, wrote in an article for the London *Times* (available on her website): 'If you believe, as I do, that life has an inside as well as an outside, you will accept that the inner life needs nourishment too. If the inner life is not supported and sustained, then there is nothing between us and the daily repetition of what Wordsworth called "getting and spending."' She is conscious of the differences between religion and art, 'having spent most of my early life in a gospel tent with a pair of evangelical parents', as she puts it. However, art is religious in a deeper sense: 'It asks us to see differently, think differently, challenging ourselves, and the way we live.' In other words, writers and artists should aim not to tie things up, but to open things out. It is an agnostic imperative that is pursued.

How have writers overcome the dangers Plato highlights that would close literature down? Shakespeare is a pivotal figure in this. Stephen Greenblatt, in his book *Will in the World*, puts his finger on a key moment. He explains how, in *Hamlet*, the playwright discovered a new device for portraying interiority on the stage. It not only elicited a passionate response in audiences. With it, he could sustain, throughout the course of a whole play, the sense in which we are unknown to ourselves.

Greenblatt calls this device opacity. It is not a deliberate obfuscation, for that would only create a frustratingly baffling piece of work. Rather, it is a persistent refusal of the rationales, motivations and ethical justifications that the playwright typically built into the morality tales of his day, and which real people have deployed to understand their own lives before and since. Shakespeare, I would say, has before him the Socratic conviction of knowing mostly of his ignorance. His genius is to know how to turn that ignorance over and over again in the characters, images, echoes and plots of his plays. The reason why this opacity works so astonishingly well on stage is that it reflects our own inability to know ourselves. Greenblatt adds the speculation that Shakespeare's discovery of this device was intimately connected to the agnostic character of his own life – 'his skepticism, his pain, his sense of broken rituals, his refusal of easy consolations'.

King Lear is the most striking example of opacity. As soon as the story begins it does not make sense. Lear asks his daughters how much they love him, so that he can divide his kingdom accordingly. Not only is the kingdom already divided but the question itself is meaningless. Lear's own unfathomable needs are exposed. When Cordelia replies, 'Nothing', it fills him with dread, a fear that grows to the tragic climax of the play. Why does he go mad? Perhaps because he is giving up the crown. Perhaps because he is old. We never know for sure because there is no sure reason to be had.

The refusal to settle things is common in many great works of literature. The result is, of course, not always tragic. Proust's

In Search of Lost Time, never quite gets to the bottom of it all. But we learn an enormous amount about paying attention to life in the process.

S – is for Silence

Now, there's silence and silence, of course. There's the silencing of the oppressed. There's the silence of pure ignorance. There's the silence that causes people to speak. The Romantics, when silenced by the sublime, had that experience. It precipitated an avalanche of words, poems and stories.

But there's also the silence of finitude before infinity. Sara Maitland, in *A Book of Silence*, likens this to the silence of the desert, the place the hermits went to pursue learned ignorance. Desert silence precipitates a kenotic response, an emptying of the self; a sense of transparency and dissolving before the infinity of sand, sun and air. It brings a kind of purity of heart and mind that is open to the divine.

Thomas Carlyle put it well: 'Silence is deep as Eternity; speech is shallow as time.' Maybe that's why God seems silent, why the agnostic can't be sure God exists. In that absence, God's trying to tell us something.

T – is about Therapy

Foucault noticed that it was early Christianity which first instigated a practice of self-examination that required the individual to examine their inner life and reveal it to another – that practice being the confession of the penitent to a wiser confessor. What is doubly interesting about confession is that it presupposes that the penitent might easily deceive themselves. They might confess one sin that was actually symptomatic of another; so penitents must not just confess but actively search their souls. It was in this capacity that the wise confessor was so important. Their role was to exercise discernment, thereby steering the penitent in the direction that would reveal the greatest truths about themselves. The goal was change. In bringing failures to light, confession was connected to the proleptic promise of baptism; penitents were 'putting on salvation'.

Sadly, Foucault thought, this exercise of personal transformation was itself transformed as the church became a dogmatic institution. With the need to manage the souls of millions, confession became a sort of check-list exercise. In confession, the penitent did not search their souls but ticked off the sins they had committed in order to be restored to the church. The role of the confessor was not so much to nurture change as exercise what Foucault called 'pastoral power'.

Psychoanalysts exercise a secular version of confession. Whether it be in the making of connections between the free associations of the client or offering insights that the client would never have been conscious of themselves, the pattern is the same. The truth is found within and it is discovered by speaking it out. Eventually, the analysand will reach a point at which all their confusions, neuroses, rationalisations and delusions will have been exposed to the light of day. Their analysis will be complete.

I remember a psychoanalyst once telling me that she was nearing the end of her therapy. I was fascinated by the idea. What would that be like – perhaps enlightened, or wholly conscious, or supremely in control, or in a state of maximal closure? When I asked, she laughed and replied nothing like that at all. All that the completion of her analysis signified was that she and her therapist had done all the work together that they possibly could. When I jested that it seemed to me that there must be more work for her to do, she pointed out that I did not know her before she started the therapy.

The point is that therapy does not aim at the resolution of all problems, complete knowledge of oneself, or even the increase in happiness, though it might well help someone to manage a debilitating neurosis. Therapy brings one to the limits of what can be known and understood about oneself. In this sense, the end of one's analysis is the start of a life aware of one's ignorance. The direction that any one individual chooses to take after that will vary. For Nietzsche, having undergone a therapy of writing in his so-called middle-period books, the next step was to develop the will to live in spite of what he had concluded about the nature of existence. He created the heroic character of Zarathustra to explore what that might mean. For the Christian, as John Cottingham explains in *The Spiritual Dimension*: 'Dependency, vulnerability, the insistence that strength is made perfect in weakness, are the hallmarks of the Judaeo-Christian spiritual tradition (and perhaps the key Islamic notion of submission says something not too dissimilar).'

Jonathan Lear believes that Freud can be read as providing an answer to the Socratic question of how one should live and the intuition that it begins with knowing oneself. The problem, as Socrates himself knew, is that people readily deceive themselves. Like prisoners in a cave confusing shadows with reality, they would prefer to think that they know the meaning of things and that they understand their own nature. Admitting ignorance, they suppose, would be to condemn humankind to its self-delusion, lost like the blind leading the blind. Freud's way out of this fix was to devise a way of talking that borrowed from the early Christian tradition of radical uncertainty about oneself. Socrates founded his philosophy on a practice that is recognisably similar. He developed the habit of persistently asking questions of himself and others that revolved around a central conviction: 'I am very conscious that I am not wise at all.'

U – is for the Unorthodox

Some of the greatest religious spirits have been heretics – not least, the founders of the great religions.

W – is for Why?

Meaning is nothing if not subjective. This is the fundamental reason that the scientific worldview, for all it unpicks, does not do, or deliver, meaning of itself. It sits on the wrong side of the subject/object, fact/value, material/spiritual divide. The Faustian pact with which our world flirts is trusting the results of science and its method above all others for fixing truths. The paradox is that this culture of certainty produces anxiety because, at the end of the day, to be certain is to be in denial about what it is to be human. We aren't sure of much. Thus we live more healthily but not more happily; we live more magnificently but not more meaningfully; we live with more knowledge but not more wisdom.

Secular philosophies suggest that meaning can be found within this frame nonetheless. One possibility is to argue that the big questions of life are overblown or mistaken. The moral imperative of how one should live should be rephrased to the more manageable one of how one might become more cultivated, more ethical or simply less demanding of life. The task of knowing thyself is mitigated by the commonsensical comment that most of the time, in most situations, one probably knows oneself enough to get on with matters in hand. When climactic moments come, like death, one should just accept them, not question them.

Faith offers another possibility as a source of meaning. The thought here is that, if meaning is subjective then, for it to rest assured, there must be an absolute source of subjectivity for it to rest assured on, namely, the personal God. Some believe that this 'meaning of meaning' is manifest in the Bible or the church. Other more subtle believers would say that it emerges like shapes in the dark: that it seems shadowy is merely a reflection of our inability to see clearly, not of its objective reality.

Agnosticism offers another possibility: meaning as mystery. At one level, this is almost to assert a cliché. It is not unless one is prepared to 'step out into the unknown' that one's life expands, deepens and grows. Similarly, it might be thought close to tautologous: '[The] ultimate springs and principles are totally shut up from human curiosity and enquiry,' was Hume's phrase, implying that meaning, inasmuch as it depends only these ultimate things, will remain mysterious too.

That said, Hume believed that the mystery of things meant the best strategy was to stop chasing after that which is beyond us. 'A correct judgement,' he wrote, 'avoiding all distant and high enquiries, confines itself to common life, and to such subjects as fall under daily practice and experience, leaving the more sublime topics to the embellishment of poets and orators, or to the arts or priests and politicians.' He advised sticking to the humdrum of which we can be sure and, while ignoring the 'sublime' reflections of priests and politicians may on occasion feel quite sensible, he's also advising you give up on poetry and the arts too. That is to cut out a large part of life.

So there's a different kind of agnosticism I'm advocating: the mystery is not simply an impasse. It is a quest. Meaning is not found by dwelling in the regions that one believes one understands, and erecting walls around them, material or metaphysical, in order to pretend they are all that is. Paradoxically perhaps, the desire for meaning is satisfied by dwelling on the thresholds of ignorance.

Not that any old mystification will do. The tradition that began with Socrates offers a way that is practical as well as contemplative. Here was a man who though claiming to know nothing could never have been accused of having a black hole at the heart of his life. No one was wiser than he, not because he was wise, but because he loved more powerfully and penetratingly what most only long for to a degree. He stirred those around him into life by irony, argument and example, and mostly by the encounter with his passionate spirituality.

X/Y/Z – is for You

'Know thyself!' – the Delphic inscription, with which we began. For as Jung noted, it's only when you're not afraid to grope in the dark that you've a chance at insight, love, hope – even faith.

Further Reading and References

Introduction

An earlier version of the dialogue between Stephen Hawking and his father was published on the *Guardian's* Cif Belief website (www. guardian.co.uk/belief). The idea comes from a discussion of Herbert McCabe, in his book *God Matters* published by Continuum (1987). There are fragments of a few other Cif Belief articles I've written in other places too.

Bonaventure's examination of light is found in his *Commentary on the Sentences of Peter Lombard*, Book II, Distinction 13.

Friedrich Schleiermacher discusses his religious sensibility in *On Religion: Speeches to Its Cultured Despisers*. Paul Tillich presents his ontology in Volume I, Part II of his *Systematic Theology*. Accessible sermons are also available in collections.

Nietzsche's announcement of the death of God comes in *The Gay Science*, Book 3, 125, translated by Walter Kaufman and published by Vintage Books (1974).

Karen Armstrong discusses the birth of American fundamentalism and figures like A.C. Dixon in *The Battle for God: Fundamentalism in Judaism, Christianity and Islam*, published by Harper Collins (2000), see pages 178–9.

T.H. Huxley's essay 'Agnosticism' can be found in the misleadingly entitled *Atheism: a Reader*, edited by S.T. Joshi, published by Prometheus Books (2000), see page 33 for the quote.

God's Funeral, by A.N. Wilson, published by Abacus (1999), sets Victorian agnosticism in a wider historical context.

Scholarly studies on Victorian agnosticism include: *The Unbelievers: English Agnostic Thought*, by A.O.J. Cockshutt (Collins: 1964) – a good survey of players. *The Origins of Agnosticism: Victorian Unbelief and the Limits of Knowledge*, by Bernard Lightman (Johns Hopkins University Press, 1987) – good on agnosticism's relationship to the philosophy of Kant and why Victorian agnosticism as a movement died.

Søren Kierekegaard's *Fear and Trembling* is a Penguin Classic, translated by Alastair Hannay (1985): see page 62 for the quote.

Simone Weil's remarks are in *Letter to A Priest*, published in several anthologies, and by Penguin (2003).

True Religion, by Graham Ward, published by Blackwell (2003), examines why the emergence of the scientific worldview is not the end of religion but the remaking of it.

All the quotes from Plato are taken from *Plato Complete Works*, edited by John M. Cooper, published by Hackett Publishing Company (1997). The quote from the *Phaedrus* is at 278d.

1. Socrates' Quest: The Agnostic Spirit

Greek Religion, by Walter Burkert, translated by John Raffan, published by Blackwell (1985), is the standard text on the eponymous subject.

The Religion of Socrates, by Mark L. McPherran, published by Penn State University Press (1996), is the most thorough examination of the historical Socrates' attitude and feelings about religion and belief that I have seen.

The Road to Delphi: The Life and Afterlife of Oracles, by Michael Wood, published by Picador (2003), is a fascinating and evocative study of the role of ancient oracles.

Protagoras' writings only survive as a few fragments, including the two quoted here.

The quote from Plato's *Laws* is at 948c. The quote from Plato's *Timeaus* is at 29a–c.

Xenophon's Socratic 'proof' for the existence of gods is in his *Memoirs of Socrates* 1.4. The account of Socrates' response to the oracle begins at *Apology* 20e.

Plutarch's account of Socrates' peripatetic method is in *Whether a Man Should Engage in Politics when He Is Old*, 26, 796d.

The 'four-part cure' is cited in *The Epicurus Reading: Selected Writings and Testimonia*, translated and edited by Bran Inwood, L.P. Gerson and D.S. Hutchinson, published by Hackett Publishing Company (1994).

The discussion about gods and goodness (or piety) is in Plato's *Euthyphro* 9c following.

Diotima's contribution in Plato's *Symposium* begins at 201d. Alcibiades appears at 212d.

The interview with Bertrand Russell is reprinted in *Russell on Religion: Selections from the Writings of Bertrand Russell*, published by Routledge (1999), Chapter 4, 'What Is an Agnostic?'

2. Cosmic Religion: How Science Does God

Newton: The Making of Genius, by Patricia Fara is published by Picador (2003).

Leibniz makes this attack on Newton in a letter to Caroline of Ansbach.

The quote from Milton's *Paradise Regained* is in Book IV, 1.330.

A few paragraphs from the section headed 'Alchemy's inheritors' was previously in an article for Big Questions Online (www.bigquestionsonline. com), a publication of the John Templeton Foundation.

Steven Weinberg makes his comments about meaning in the Epilogue of his book *The First Three Minutes*, published by Basic Books (1993); and his comments about a theory of everything in Chapter X of *Dreams of a Final Theory: The Scientist's Search for the Ultimate Laws of Nature*, published by Vintage (1994). I also spoke with Weinberg to clarify his views in 2008.

The views of Martin Rees I gathered in an interview conducted in 2008.

The views of Roger Penrose I gathered in an interview also conducted in 2008. He writes about his Platonism in *The Emperor's New Mind*, published by Oxford University Press (1999), as well as in other publications since.

The quote from Michel Heller's *The Comprehensible Universe*, published by Springer (2008), is found in the Afterthoughts section, 'The Mind of God and the Mind of Man'.

Paul Davies' *The Goldilocks Enigma: Why is the Universe Just Right for Life?* is published by Allen Lane (2006). The long quote comes from Chapter 8, the section headed 'The laws of physics might be just local by-laws'.

I interviewed Trinh Xuan Thuan in 2008, and his views are discussed at length in *The Quantum and the Lotus*, a dialogue between him and Matthieu Ricard, published by Three Rivers Press (2001). The long quote of Ricard is in Chapter 9, Chaos and Harmony.

The Tao of Physics: An Exploration of the Parallels between Modern Physics and Eastern Mysticism by Fritjof Capra is published in a 35th anniversary edition by Shambhala (2010). The first long quote is in the preface to the first edition. The second quote referencing Heisenberg and the third quote discussing replacement are in the last chapter 'The Future of the New Physics'.

The Universe Story: From the Promordial Flaring Forth to the Ecozoic Era – A Celebration of the Unfolding of the Cosmos by Brian Swimme and Thomas Berry is published by HarperOne (1994). He made his pithy comments, quoted here, in an interview with Robert Wright for meaningoflife.tv.

I discussed these matters with Gordon Lynch. One book where he examines the nature of 'progressive spirituality' is *New Spirituality: An Introduction to Belief Beyond Religion* published by I.B. Tauris (2007).

John Polkinghorne has written about his views in numerous books. I interviewed him in 2008.

The Beginning of All Things: Science and Religion by Hans Küng is published by William B Eerdmans Publishing Co. (2008).

David Attenborough made his comments to the press when *Life in the Undergrowth* was launched.

Thomas Traherne's thoughts on flies and celestial strangers are in the excellent anthology *Thomas Traherne Poetry and Prose*, selected and introduced by Denise Inge, published by SPCK (2002), pages 111–14.

Simon Conway Morris has explored his ideas in *Life's Solution: Inevitable Humans in a Lonely Universe* published by Cambridge University Press (2008). I also interviewed him in 2008.

Reinventing the Sacred by Stuart Kauffman is published by Basic (2010).

The Philosophy of Science: A Very Short Introduction, by Samir Okasha, published by Oxford University Press (2002), does what it says on the cover.

Thomas Kuhn's revolutionary ideas are in his 1963 book *The Structure of Scientific Revolutions* (University of Chicago Press).

Karl Popper's revolutionary ideas are in his 1959 book *The Logic of Scientific Discovery* (Hutchinson).

A very useful summary of issues in the philosophy of science comes from a discussion Brian Magee had with Hilary Putnam, reproduced in *Talking Philosophy*, published by Oxford University Press (1978), Chapter 12, from which the Putnam quotes are taken.

Walter Isaacson's biography of Einstein is *Einstein: His Life and Universe*, published by Pocket Books (2008). It includes a chapter discussing his religious beliefs, Chapter 17 'Einstein's God'. His relevant writings and thoughts are also gathered at www.einsteinandreligion.com, including these quotes.

3. How To Be Human: Science and Ethics

All that remains of the writings of the pre-Socratic philosophers are in *Early Greek Philosophy*, published by Penguin Classics (2001), with introductory material by Jonathan Barnes. Empedocles' 'Twofold Tale' is on pages 120–2.

Plato has Socrates tell of his change from natural science to philosophy beginning at *Phaedo* 96a.

Michael Atiyah deployed his metaphor of the Faustian pact in a lecture given in 2000 entitled 'Mathematics in the Twentieth Century'. It has been reproduced in *Mathematical Association of America Monthly*, August–September 2001.

Happiness:Lessons from a New Science, by Richard Layard, is published by Allen Lane (2005).

Mill's comments are in his autobiography published as *Autobiography* by Penguin Classics (2006). His thoughts on happiness come in Chapter V 'A Crisis in My Mental History. One Stage Onward'.

I've written about happiness more fully in my book *Wellbeing* published by Acumen (2008).

I interviewed Chris Frith in 2010.

The *Nature* article is by John Bolhius and Clive Wynne in *Nature* 458, 832–3; 2009.

Dishonest to God by Mary Warnock is published by Continuum (2010).

An example of the distinction between *zoē* and *bios* is deployed by Aristotle in his *Politics*, see 1252b30.

For more on virtue ethics see my *Ethics for the Curious* published by Hodder Education (2010).

Simone Weil's idea of gravity and grace is in *Gravity and Grace* published by Routledge (2002).

Rowan Williams made his comments during a speech in Leicester Cathedral, entitled Faith in the Public Square, in 2009.

The quote from Aristotle's *Nicomachean Ethics* is at 1177b33.

The Essential Mary Midgley, edited by David Midgley, is published by Routledge (2005) and provides an excellent survey of her work. See 'Salvation and the Academics', pages 228–38, for her reflections on DNA.

Dominique Janicaud's *On the Human Condition* is published by Routledge (2002), see pages 54–8.

Michel Foucault's comments, along with many others on religion, are usefully gathered in *Religion and Culture*, edited by Jeremy Carrette and published by Routledge (1999).

4. Socrates or Buddha? On Being Spiritual But Not Religious

The Making and Breaking of Affectional Bonds by John Bowlby published by Routledge (1989) is one place where he discusses his attachment theory, particularly the last chapter which has the eponymous title.

Jung's essay 'The Spiritual Problem of Modern Man' is published in *Modern Man In Search of A Soul*, published by Routledge & Kegan Paul (1933).

Marx's comments about religion as opium were first published in *Contribution to Critique of Hegel's Philosophy of Right* (1843).

Thomas Aquinas considers the problem of the 'waters above the heavens' in his *Summa Theologica*, Book I, question 68.

Thomas Jefferson's thoughts on the corruptions of Christianity are in his letter to Dr Benjamin Rush, from Washington, on 21 April 1803.

Auguste Comte's philosophy is explained in his *General View of Positivism*, translated by J.H. Bridges and published by Robert Speller and Sons (1957). The quote is taken from Chapter 1.

For more on Heidegger's views on art and unveiling see the essay 'The Origin of the Work of Art' in *Basic Writings*, edited by David Farrell Krell, published by Routledge (1993).

Wittgenstein's philosophy of propositions forms the basis of his *Tractatus Logico-Philosophicus* published by Routledge Classics (2001).

Mark Rothko's comments are reported in a commentary on the Rothko room at Tate Modern in London, and originate in a statement he made at a MOMA symposium 'How to Combine Architecture, Painting and Sculpture' in 1951.

The Big Bangs: The Story of Five Discoveries that Changed Musical History by Howard Goodall is published by Vintage (2001).

The line from Wallace Stevens comes from the poem 'The Man With The Blue Guitar'. His *Collected Poems* are published by Faber and Faber (2006).

Peter Singer explores the notion of transcendent causes in *How are we to live?* published by Oxford University Press (1997), with the discussion of transcendent causes coming on page 253ff.

The Faith to Doubt: Glimpses of Buddhist Uncertainty by Stephen Batchelor is published by Parallax Press (1990).

Augustine's comments are in his *Confessions*, Chapter 10 – the translation by R.S. Pine-Coffin is published by Penguin (1961) – and I'm indebted in the discussion of this dynamic of his spirituality to Denys Turner and his book *The Darkness of God* published by Cambridge University Press (1995).

The quote from Anthony Price is from his *Love and Friendship in Plato and Aristotle* published by Clarendon Press (1997), on page 42.

5. Bad Faith: Religion as Certainty

Atheism: A Very Short Introduction, by Julian Baggini, is published by Oxford University Press (2003): see page 106 for the quote. In *What's It All About? Philosophy and the Meaning of Life*, published by Granta (2004), he offers an atheist's take on the 'big questions'.

Denys Turner's lecture 'How to Be an Atheist' is in his collected talks *Faith Seeking*, published by SCM Press (2002).

Philosophy: The Latest Answers to the Oldest Questions, by Nicholas Fearn, is published by Atlantic Books (2005).

Herbert McCabe is quoted in *The Thought of Thomas Aquinas*, by Brian Davies, published by Clarendon Paperbacks (1993), page 111.

Karen Armstrong discusses her ideas on *logos* and myth in *The Battle for God* (see above). A concise version is in *A Short History of Myth*, published by Canongate (2005): see page 122 for quote.

Serious Concerns, by Wendy Cope, is published by Faber and Faber (1992).

Disciplining the Divine: The Failure of the Social Model of the Trinity, by Paul Fletcher, is published by Ashgate (2009).

No God But God: The Origins, Evolution and Future of Islam, by Reza Alsan, is published William Heinemann (2005), see page 263 for quote.

6. Christian Agnosticism: Learned Ignorance

The story about Thomas Aquinas is in Brian Davies' *The Thought of Thomas Aquinas* (see above).

Wittgenstein made his comments about the aroma of coffee in his *Philosophical Investigations* (610), and on the unutterable in a letter to a friend, Paul Engelmann, in 1917. They are discussed in *Theology after Wittgenstein* by Fergus Kerr published by Basil Blackwell (1986) in Chapter 7 'Wittgenstein's Theological Investigations'.

Gregory of Nyssa writes about Moses in his *The Life of Moses*.

De docta ignorantia, by Nicholas of Cusa, is available online. This quote comes in Chapter 1, 'How it is that knowing is not-knowing'.

The quote from Meister Eckhart is from his sermon XCIX, available in various collected works.

Dialogues Concerning Natural Religion by David Hume is published by Oxford Paperbacks (2008)

The Unknown God: Agnostic Essays, by Anthony Kenny, is published by Continuum (2004), with his reflections on Arthur Hugh Clough's poem in Chapter 1, 'The Ineffable Godhead': see page 20 for the quote. Chapter 8 compares Clough and Arnold.

Dennis Potter made his remark about religion as wound in a final interview he gave to Melvyn Bragg broadcast by Channel 4 on 5 April 1994.

T.H. Huxley's reflections were in a review of *Agnosticism* published in the Times Literary Supplement of Friday, 27 February 1903.

7. Following Socrates: A Way of Life

The discussion of Plato's Academy in Chapter 4 of *Plato: An Introduction*, by Paul Friedländer, published by Princeton University Press (1973) and translated by Hans Meyerhoff is fairly old now but is hard to beat.

The Seneca quote is from *Moral Epistles* 6, 6.

The Plato quote from the *Seventh Letter* is at 341c.

Pierre Hadot's idea of philosophy as a way of life is developed in several books. An accessible text is *What Is Ancient Philosophy?*, published by Harvard University Press (2002). The quote I use can be found on page 62 of this book.

Philosophy as a Way of Life: Spiritual Exercises from Socrates to Foucault, edited with an introduction by Arnold I. Davidson and translated by Michael Chase, published by Blackwell (1995), develops the idea further.

The Art of Living: Socratic Reflections from Plato to Foucault, by Alexander Nehamas, published by University of California Press (1998), is also fascinating.

Plato's myth in the *Gorgias* begins at 523a.

Aristotle's characterisation of the wise man is in his *Nicomachean Ethics* 1125a12.

The quote from Montaigne is in his essay 'On educating children' (I: 26). *The Complete Essays*, translated by M.A. Screech, is published by Penguin Classics. The quote is on page 180.

A summary of Michel Foucault's idea of thinking differently is in the introduction to the second volume of his *History of Sexuality, The Use of Pleasure*. The seminar he gave on 6 January 1982, transcribed in *The Hermeneutics of the Subject: Lectures at the Collège de France 1981–1982*, published by Palgrave Macmillan (2005), focuses on the relationship between Christian and ancient philosophical moral practice. Some of the interviews in *Foucault: Live Collected Interviews, 1961–1984*, edited by Sylvère Lotringer (Semiotext[e], 1996), are also illuminating.

Essays and Aphorisms, by Arthur Schopenhauer, with an introduction by R.J. Hollingdale, published by Penguin Classics (1970), is a good introduction to his thought and way of life. Schopenhauer's equivocation about whether philosophy can change a life is discussed in Schopenhauer, by Julian Young, published by Routledge (2005), on pages 158–64.

Bryan Magee writes about knowing Karl Popper in his *Confessions of a Philosopher: A Journey through Western Philosophy*, published by Phoenix (1997). Popper on Socrates is discussed on page 561.

Unended Quest, by Karl Popper, is published by Routledge (1992), with the quote about happiness on page 145.

On Religion, by John Caputo, is published by Routledge (2001).

8. How To Be An Agnostic: An A–Z

The Owl of Minerva: A Memoir, by Mary Midgley, is published by Routledge (2005). The quote is on page x.

The Longinus quote is from, 'On Sublimity', in *Classical Literary Criticism*, published by Oxford University Press (1989), page 143.

A summary of Karl Popper on Darwinism is in *Unended Quest*, Chapter 37 (see above). Melvyn Bragg's quote is in *Devout Sceptics* (see above).

The Devout Sceptics interviews by Bel Mooney are collected in a Hodder and Stoughton book with the same title (2003): see page 57 for Paul Davies' quote.

Oscar Wilde's essay on facts can be found in his collected works.

An earlier version of the prayer to God was published on the *Guardian*'s Cif Belief website (www.guardian.co.uk/belief).

Roger Hull makes his comments on the American Sublime in the catalogue to the exhibition.

Leslie Stephen's 'An Agnostic's Apology' is in *Atheism: A Reader*, edited by S.T. Joshi, published by Prometheus Books (2000).

Victor Stenger explores something and nothing in *God the Failed Hypothesis: How Science Shows That God Does Not Exist*, published by Prometheus Books (2008).

Freud, by Jonathan Leer, is published by Routledge (2005).

The God Delusion by Richard Dawkins is published by Bantam Press (2006).

Newman's discussion comes from his *Essay in Aid of a Grammar of Assent* and I'm indebted to the discussions of it by Anthony Kenny in a TLS article of July 28, 2010, and in *Newman's Unquiet Grave* by John Cornwell, published by Continuum (2010).

Jeanette Winterson's website is www.jeanettewinterson.com.

Will in the World, by Stephen Greenblatt, is published by Pimlico (2004).

A Book of Silence by Sara Maitland is published by Granta (2009).

Thomas Carlyle's quote on silence is in his essay 'Sir Walter Scott', in *Critical and Miscellaneous Essays*.

The Spiritual Dimension: Religion, Philosophy and Human Value, by John Cottingham, is published by Cambridge University Press (2005).

The Hume comment on avoiding high enquires is from his *Enquiry Concerning Human Understanding* Section XII, Part III.

Index

Page numbers in *italics* denotes an illustration